Approaches to Teaching the *Thousand and One Nights*

Approaches to Teaching the *Thousand and One Nights*

Edited by

Paulo Lemos Horta

Modern Language Association of America
New York   2023

© 2023 by The Modern Language Association of America
85 Broad Street, New York, New York 10004
www.mla.org

All rights reserved. MLA and the MODERN LANGUAGE ASSOCIATION are trademarks owned by the Modern Language Association of America. To request permission to reprint material from MLA book publications, please inquire at permissions@mla.org.

To order MLA publications, visit mla.org/books. For wholesale and international orders, see mla.org/Bookstore-Orders.

The MLA office is located on the island known as Mannahatta (Manhattan) in Lenapehoking, the homeland of the Lenape people. The MLA pays respect to the original stewards of this land and to the diverse and vibrant Native communities that continue to thrive in New York City.

Approaches to Teaching World Literature 173
ISSN 1059-1133

Library of Congress Cataloging-in-Publication Data

Names: Horta, Paulo Lemos, editor.
Title: Approaches to teaching the Thousand and one nights / edited by Paulo Lemos Horta.
Description: New York : Modern Language Association of America, 2023. | Series: Approaches to teaching world literature, 1059-1133 ; 173 | Includes bibliographical references.
Identifiers: LCCN 2023008800 (print) | LCCN 2023008801 (ebook) | ISBN 9781603295963 (hardcover) | ISBN 9781603295970 (paperback) | ISBN 9781603295987 (EPUB)
Subjects: LCSH: Arabian nights—Study and teaching (Higher) | BISAC: LANGUAGE ARTS & DISCIPLINES / Study & Teaching | LITERARY CRITICISM / Medieval | LCGFT: Literary criticism. | Essays.
Classification: LCC PJ7737 .A67 2023 (print) | LCC PJ7737 (ebook) | DDC 398.22—dc23/eng/20230621
LC record available at https://lccn.loc.gov/2023008800
LC ebook record available at https://lccn.loc.gov/2023008801

CONTENTS

Preface	vii
PART ONE: MATERIALS	
Contexts	3
Texts	9
Film and Popular Culture	17
The Instructor's Library	21
PART TWO: APPROACHES	
Introduction *Paulo Lemos Horta*	27
Contexts of Origin	
The *Thousand and One Nights* as Arabic Literature *Bruce Fudge*	32

The *Thousand and One Nights* and Rethinking
   Arabic Literature
   Wen-chin Ouyang
	40

The Textual Tradition of the *Thousand and One Nights*:
   Teaching the Collection's Complexity
   Ulrich Marzolph
	48

The *Thousand and One Nights* as Urban Literature *Nadine Roth*	57

The *Nights* as Crime Fiction: Teaching "The Tale
   of the Murdered Girl"
   Roger Allen
	66

The Tales as World Literature	
"Ali Baba" and "Aladdin" as Modern World Literature *Paulo Lemos Horta*	75
Travels with the Tales of Sindbad *Maurice Pomerantz*	84

Controversies

Shahrazad's Gender Lessons *Suzanne Gauch*	90
Reading Race and Racism in the *Thousand and One Nights* *Rachel Schine*	97
Race, Gender, and Slavery in the *Arabian Nights* *Parisa Vaziri*	106
The *Thousand and One Nights* in World Film History *Samhita Sunya*	112

Intertexts

Teaching the *Arabian Nights* through Graphic Novels *Shawkat M. Toorawa*	119
The *Thousand and One Nights* in American Film and Fiction *Margaret Litvin*	132
The *Thousand and One Nights* and Mediterranean Framed Narrative Traditions *Karla Mallette*	140
Intertextual Labyrinths: Borges and the *Nights* *Dominique Jullien*	146

Contexts of Circulation

The *Thousand and One Nights* as Nigerian Literature *Abdalla Uba Adamu*	153
Orality and Performance of the *Thousand and One Nights* *Susan Slyomovics*	161
The "Thousand and Second Night" Motif *Evanghelia Stead*	173

Notes on Contributors — 181

Works Cited — 185

PREFACE

Long a staple in the American academy in great books courses covering Europe and beyond, the *Thousand and One Nights* is taught with frequency in a variety of linguistic and disciplinary contexts, principally English, French, Spanish, medieval, comparative, and world literature, as well as imperial and postcolonial literature. In Middle and Near Eastern studies courses in the United States and Europe, it is taught in Islamic studies and Arab women's writing courses; in English it appears in courses from Chaucer to Imagining the Orient; in Spanish, in surveys of medieval literature, folktales, and histories of science and technology; in comparative literature, from introductory world literature surveys through graduate seminars on imperialism and translation. This volume makes the further case for inclusion of the *Nights* in courses on identity and critical race theory.

Despite the wide range of levels and courses in which the *Thousand and One Nights* is taught, professors using the story collection across the spectrum of disciplines and languages share similar needs. Many instructors would find useful more background information regarding the story collection itself and the historical context from which it originated, particularly relating to the Arab and Muslim world. They would also benefit from information regarding the intricate webs of transmission and translation that trace the history of the *Nights*. Many could use a stronger base of knowledge of the contexts of the *Nights* to achieve their stated purposes of diversifying curricula—for instance, to challenge their students' stereotypes of the Islamic world, to showcase a strong female storyteller, and to explore issues of empire and race.

The structure of this volume reflects this broader need to contextualize the *Thousand and One Nights* for students both as a historical artifact and as a work of literature. Reflecting this need, the "Materials" section provides teachers with a sense of the basic facts known about the *Thousand and One Nights* and how these differ from popular and lay knowledge. It surveys distinct editions of the story collection and the history and aftermath of its translation into French and other European languages. This section singles out the key resources needed to teach the *Thousand and One Nights*. Particular attention is paid to the question of which texts to use in the classroom, from the first bootleg translations from French through the latest versions by contemporary editors and translators.

The task of matching materials, perspectives, and methods with particular pedagogical contexts is the challenge explored in the second section, "Approaches."

The first subsection, "Contexts of Origin," focuses on the origins of the *Thousand and One Nights*, first as a story collection composed in Middle Arabic and subsequently as a work of world literature transformed in translation. This section provides instructors with necessary background information on the original Arabic core of the *Thousand and One Nights* and serves as a useful guide in considering which tales to teach in different contexts. College students are most likely to encounter the story collection as a representative work of medieval Arabic literature, the status accorded to it in anthologies of world literature in the North American marketplace.

Readers familiar with the marvels and deserts of the *Aladdin* films will discover that the stories in the original cycle mark those wonders as the product of a distinctly urban civilization. The city stories in the *Thousand and One Nights* point the way to contemporary genres of fiction that combine both realism and fantasy. Crime fiction is often an urban genre, and enthusiasts for Scandi noir and literary historians of Victorian England and Sherlock Holmes may be surprised to learn that crime fiction may have originated with "The Story of the Three Apples" in the *Thousand and One Nights*.

Until recently, anthologies and contemporary translations primarily referred to the Arabic tales of the *Thousand and One Nights*, disregarding the tales later added in European translations. This is the *Thousand and One Nights* of most American core, great books, civilizations, and humanities courses as well as of surveys of world literatures and Arabic literature. As such, it is at once the most omnipresent and least understood incarnation of the *Nights* in the American academy.

The volume then considers how to teach the famous tales added in French, including "Aladdin and the Wonderful Lamp," "The Story of Ali Baba and the Forty Thieves," "The Enchanted Horse," "Prince Ahmad and the Fairy Banu," and "The Night Adventures of Harun al-Rashid." The recent publication in Arabic, French, German, and English of *The Book of Travels*, by the Syrian Maronite storyteller Hanna Diyab, who contributed these tales to the story collection, has inspired a new wave of criticism, including my own *Marvellous Thieves: Secret Authors of the* Arabian Nights and my edition of *The Annotated* Arabian Nights (Seale). These tales are more widely read than taught, but the discovery of the agency of Diyab as their storyteller and creator has begun to change that, recuperating their ties to the original *Thousand and One Nights* and its sibling story collections the *Hundred and One Nights* (Fudge) and *Tales of the Marvellous and News of the Strange* (Lyons). Questions of translation and comparison help foreground the preoccupation of this section, which focuses on the teaching of the *Nights* tales as world literature. "Aladdin" and "Sindbad" are perhaps the most famous stories in the collection in not only the European but also the world imaginary, but their trajectories speak to two very different notions and histories of world literature, the first modern and the product of European knowledge of the Levant, and the second premodern and concerned with how the tales already circulated across borders in Arabic.

The third subsection, "Controversies," confronts head-on the major challenges to teaching the story collection in the contemporary classroom. The exaggerated racism of translations produced by the Victorian explorer Richard Francis Burton comes as little surprise and can be remedied by using modern versions. But how should instructors handle the racist elements present in and projected onto editions of the original tales themselves, infamously in the frame tale of Shahriyar and Shahrazad? Racism and clumsy cultural misrepresentations are also a hallmark of Hollywood films based on stories from this collection, from the *Thief of Bagdad* (1924) to the animated *Aladdin* (1992). Can Shahrazad and her tales survive this legacy of Orientalism? The answer may necessitate paying more attention to a broader array of literary and cinematic representations of the *Thousand and One Nights*, including in modern India, Iran, and Japan.

This challenge highlights the importance of method that is foregrounded in the fourth subsection, which highlights intertexts in teaching the *Thousand and One Nights* under the rubric of visual studies, medieval studies, and comparative literature. Beyond anthologies of world literature, students are most likely to encounter the *Nights* through analogues, sequels, or retellings. What does it mean to conceive of the *Thousand and One Nights* in terms of visual culture and as medieval and comparative literature, paying attention to the device of the embedded tale and the interplay among tales from the story collection as they are transformed and transmuted? Why should one teach the tales of the *Thousand and One Nights* alongside their analogues in the European story collections of Boccaccio or Chaucer? The influence of the story collection on Latin American literature is perhaps best evidenced by Jorge Luis Borges's use of the tales in his short fictions; in contemporary American letters, works such as G. Willow Wilson's *Alif the Unseen* continue to invoke the *Nights*. At the same time, as Neil Gaiman's work demonstrates, the reception of the tales has led to a robust new genre of graphic novel retellings and adaptations in a multiplicity of languages. How should our teaching of these rewritings be informed?

No single collection can do justice to the varied contexts in which the *Thousand and One Nights* are taught in the North American academy, but a final section, "Contexts of Circulation," at least gestures toward the geographic breadth of courses that include the tales, from Nigeria and Egypt to sequels in a variety of contexts.

What these contributions share is a certain urgency in making available materials and methods for teaching this popular story collection with reference to new pedagogical preoccupations in the areas of not only genre and influence but also gender and race. The *Thousand and One Nights* suffers in a sense from its own popularity. If it is, as is often noted, the most widely circulated and influential collection of stories next to the Bible, the omnipresence in popular culture of a few stories such as "Aladdin" and "Ali Baba" has prevented a more precise understanding of the original cycle of stories in their historical context, as well as the ways in which the original and the added stories are transformed in new cultural contexts. The influence of these stories shows no sign of waning, as indicated by the blockbuster Disney live-action remake of its animated classic *Aladdin* in 2019, with the most ethnically diverse cast ever to lead a film to a billion dollars in the global box office. Neither are the many misrepresentations and misuses of the tales in contemporary political contexts likely to disappear. In this knowledge, we must continue to find new and better ways to teach these tales.

Note on Names and Titles

With regard to names, this volume follows the practice of the recent English translations of the *Nights* by Malcolm C. Lyons and Yasmine Seale and uses the character names most familiar from these texts, such as Shahrazad and Shahriyar (skipping the macron that would signal a long vowel, Shahrazād). Titles are also standardized with reference first to these English editions; for example, "The Story of the Merchant and the Jinni," "The Porter and the Three Women of Baghdad," and "Aladdin and the Wonderful Lamp."

A List of Tales Featured in the Essays

The tales listed in the left-hand column are discussed in detail in the essays listed by contributor in the right-hand column.

TALE	ESSAY
Aladdin and the Wonderful Lamp (Seale 417–89)	Horta, Litvin
The Story of Ali Baba and the Forty Thieves (Seale 265–88)	Horta, Sunya
The Tale of Anas al-Wujud (Lyons 2: 148–77)	Slyomovics
The City of Brass (Lyons 2: 518–46)	Fudge, Roth
The Story of Dalila the Crafty (Seale 169–99)	Roth
The Tale of the Enchanted Prince (Seale 67–76)	Vaziri
The Tale of the Hunchback (Lyons 1: 173–243)	Mallette, Sunya
The Inspector's Story (Lyons 1: 189–97)	Fudge, Vaziri
The Tale of Ma'ruf the Cobbler (Lyons 3: 690–730)	Roth
The Merchant and the Jinni (Seale 21–36)	Mallette
The Story of the Porter and the Three Women of Baghdad (Seale 77–158)	Gauch, Mallette
The Tale of the Second Dervish (Seale 106–26)	Litvin
The Story of King Shahriyar and His Vizier's Daughter, Sharazad (Seale 3–19)	Gauch, Schine, Stead, Toorawa, Vaziri
The Story of King Sindbad and His Falcon (Seale 50–51)	Adamu
The Story of Sindbad the Sailor (Seale 201–62)	Jullien, Pomerantz
The Thousand-and-Second Tale of Scheherazade (Poe; Seale 650–64)	Stead, Sunya
The Story of the Three Apples (Seale 159–68)	Allen
The Story of Nur al-Din and Shams al-Din [The Story of the Two Viziers] (Lyons 129–72)	Vaziri

Part One

MATERIALS

Contexts

The *Thousand and One Nights* has displayed a protean ability to travel between languages and cultures across time, shape-shifting in response to new influences along the way. The Persian frame tale, in which Shahrazad recounts ever more astonishing tales to her husband, Shahriyar, in a bid to survive another day, was likely translated into Arabic sometime in the second half of the eighth century, serving as the stimulus for the addition of further stories and arguably ushering in a new literary genre in Arabic (Chraïbi, *Arabic Manuscripts*). The resulting story collection in Arabic was not a singular work but an array of texts coexisting with many analogues and constantly engaging with other literary genres. In eighteenth-century France, the acquisition of an incomplete manuscript of 282 tales by the translator Antoine Galland prompted the addition of further, sometimes unrelated, stories, and the phenomenal success of this version established the genre of the Oriental tale. The manuscript Galland translated was the product of a long period of development in which the *Thousand and One Nights* adapted elements incorporated from oral tradition to the conventions of more canonical literature. Traveling over the course of centuries in fits and starts, and taking on new forms and cultural influences, the *Thousand and One Nights* is the archetypal work of world literature, as figured in the essays of Jorge Luis Borges and current theoretical models of world literature.

The *Nights* did not itself attain the status of a privileged literary text in Arabic. As the Moroccan author Abdelfattah Kilito has observed, it lacked an identifiable author, a fixed text, an appropriate high literary style, and the necessary complement of an interpretive commentary (*Arabs* 116–25). It constitutes a work of "middle Arabic literature," in the preferred terminology of Aboubakr Chraïbi (*Arabic Manuscripts* 62–64). The absence of an authoritative or complete manuscript in Arabic was seen by European translators as an opportunity for their own editorial and authorial interventions. In their versions of the story collection, modern translators from Richard Francis Burton to Joseph-Charles Mardrus prove Emily Apter's dictum that translators are forgers for purporting a faithfulness they cannot achieve (159). Before them, in *Les* Mille et une nuits: *Contes arabes traduits en français* (*The* Thousand and One Nights: *Arabic Tales Translated into French*), Galland valued elegance over fidelity and freely added to the collection the tales related to him by a Syrian Maronite traveler named Hanna Diyab in 1709, including "Aladdin and the Wonderful Lamp," "The Story of Ali Baba and the Forty Thieves," and "Prince Ahmad and the Fairy Banu." These added tales were long considered "orphans," but the discovery of the manuscript of Diyab's *Book of Travels* confirms that he relayed the stories to Galland and should be considered their coauthor.

Canons of the *Nights* will vary in the North American academy in accordance with the pedagogical goals of each instructor of French, English, Arabic, or world literature. The original tales of the core cycle best exemplify the features of middle Arabic literature and are widely used in the university classroom through textbooks and anthologies of world literature. Yet these are not the tales that have circulated most widely outside the Arab world as world literature. The most popular tales from the *Nights* in European and world letters, "Aladdin," "Ali Baba," and "Prince Ahmad," were added in French by Diyab and Galland. It is no accident that these three tales loom large in the early history of cinema in both Europe and India, or that one of the first feature-length animated films was Lotte Reiniger's *Die Abenteuer des Prinzen Achmed* (*The Adventures of Prince Achmed*).

The challenge of teaching the *Nights* in the American university classroom is well captured by Robert Irwin in the preface to his intellectual biography of Ibn Khaldun. The world of Ibn Khaldun shares more with that of the *Nights* than with our own, but many teachers and scholars want to make him timely. We assimilate Ibn Khaldun to our own polemics and debates and cast him as precursor to modern authors on evolution and economics. While Ibn Khaldun's writings have been interpreted this way, they also offer resistance to that position and an exciting glimpse into a world and ways of thinking foreign to modern readers today. Immersion in the world of the *Nights* or Ibn Khaldun affords "access to a premodern and radically different approach to understanding societies and their histories," one in which supernatural beings like jinn determine the course of history and modern ideological divides do not apply. The reader emerging from "all this strangeness" may "contemplate one's own intellectual and social world with a fresher and perhaps more critical eye," understanding that "contrasts matter more than the comparisons" (Irwin, *Ibn Khaldun* xiii).

Without a guide, trying to navigate the vast universe of the *Nights* by way of the trends of the North American academy can lead to greater disorientation. The contrast between the material and the purpose to which it is put in teaching is sharpened when students encounter the *Nights* in core or survey courses where it is included as part of a focus on representation and critiques of the hierarchies of empire and patriarchy. American students in particular may arrive at the text with a vague knowledge of "Aladdin" or "Sindbad the Sailor" (gleaned from Guy Ritchie's 2019 film or animé) and expectations of a young adult tale of adventure written in line with the entertainment industry's increasing embrace of inclusivity in representing race, gender, and sexual orientation. The experience of reading the *Nights* does not so much subvert or neatly reverse these expectations of a text that fits into a more inclusive curriculum, but, as Irwin warns with respect to Ibn Khaldun, it sucks the reader into a vortex of altogether distinct imperatives, as narratives with their own powerful undercurrents may clash against the particular points a teacher wants to make.

It is fitting that authors from Naguib Mahfouz to Ted Chiang deploy the device of time travel to enter the stories within stories of the *Nights*, for these authors appear particularly attuned to the appeal and the fascination of a realm separated from readers by the barrier of time. In many ways these works of sci-fi or fantasy that understand the historical remoteness and strangeness of the *Nights* serve as more useful paratexts for us as teachers than secondary literature that insists we can gloss over all differences and make the tales serve our purposes as pedagogues too easily.

Consider the engagement with cultural difference in the *Nights* frame tale, with which teachers often anchor their consideration of the *Nights* in the classroom. Summoned by his older brother Shahriyar for a visit, the young king Shahzaman returns unannounced to his palace to find his wife in the arms of "a kitchen boy." The world goes dark before his eyes and he puts them both to the sword. Or so reads the oldest known Arabic manuscript of this tale, dating to the fifteenth century. In the nineteenth century, William Hay Macnaghten edited an Arabic text that reflected one crucial change in this tableau: young Shahzaman finds his wife entangled in the limbs of a "black slave."

Macnaghten was hardly a neutral observer. He edited the *Nights* from the colonial Indian government's retreat high in the mountains of Simla as he prepared the first British invasion of Afghanistan in 1838. He and his team did not possess a good Arabic library or the proper resources for editing the text (as would be noted by Henry Torrens, a junior officer in Macnaghten's employ and the first to render this new Arabic edition of the *Nights* in English) and found it impossible to compete with Edward Lane, who was readying a rival translation of the *Nights* in Cairo in the same years, in the fields of textual history and notes. Soon Macnaghten, Torrens, and the munshis who had done much of the work of glossing and interpretation for them would turn their attention full time to intelligence and their linguistic skills to interrogation and data gathering. It is not impossible that the manuscript upon which the Macnaghten edition was based contained the term "black slave," but the manusucript has not survived. What we know in the light of Torrens's observation of their lack of access to relevant materials is that it was not made as the result of some comprehensive philological exercise or in consideration of a rich store of rival manuscripts of the *Nights* whose preponderance of evidence might have justified abandoning the wording in Galland's fifteenth-century manuscript.

The addition should be understood in terms of its time and place and, ideally, left there. But Macnaghten's wording lives on. You will find Shahzaman's queen in the arms of a "black slave" if you open the most comprehensive contemporary version of the *Nights* available in English, Malcolm Lyons's version based on the Macnaghten text, widely distributed by Penguin Random House. And so it is he, rather than a "kitchen boy" of indeterminate complexion, that is put to the sword within the first twenty lines of the book. Owing to a very late emendation to a thousand-year-old frame tale, dating no earlier than the eighteenth or nineteenth century, Lyons's readers encounter on the first page a tableau where Shahzaman's queen has taken a "black slave" as lover and he is summarily executed alongside her.

Returning to Shahriyar's palace, Shahzaman soon witnesses a more public and spectacular betrayal. He sees the queen followed by a retinue of twenty, alike from a distance, who disrobe to reveal themselves as ten women and ten men and embark on an orgy. While the oldest known fifteenth-century manuscript of the *Nights* specifies that the men are enslaved and of a dark complexion, it does not specify corresponding characteristics in the women. Silence on this question allows some commentators to assume that the women are South Asian and others that they are Persian and coded as "white" (see respectively the essays in this volume by Vaziri and Schine). Contextually, it might also make sense if their complexion were similar to the men's, as after their revels they again become a group of "twenty concubines to anyone who saw them" (Mahdi, Thousand 1: 59), which could help explain the subterfuge. Eighteenth-century manuscripts make the queen's concubines "white," as Muhsin Mahdi noticed when editing his fifteenth-century manuscript. But then he did something curious. Though his editorial practice was governed by the zealous conviction that only the fifteenth-century manuscript was authoritative and that all that was added later (such as the ending to "Qamar al-Zaman") should be excised, he interpolated the change made in the eighteenth-century manuscripts into his own. The concubines that arrived and left as an indistinct group were now, unmistakably, "ten white and ten black," in Husain Haddawy's translation from Mahdi's edited text (Haddawy 7; Mahdi, Thousand 1: 59; Antrim 22). A little further on, in the second tale with which Shahrazad regales Shahriyar, the translator adds a note describing another set of "white" enslaved people in a tale likely set in thirteenth- or fourteenth-century Persia as "Caucasian" (Haddawy 47). Is this early note also intended to clarify the "whiteness" of the Queen's concubines in the frame?

Projecting "Caucasian" identity into the past may not aid comprehension. When I have taught the frame in Haddawy's version or a draft by Yasmine Seale—translations that render the concubines as "white" and "black," students have been confused. Who are these enslaved "white" women? Have they been trafficked? Isn't the plot of the frame borrowed from India, via Persia? What would "white" and "Caucasian" mean in those contexts? Translators often make the implicit explicit, and seek to help the reader by providing some context in the gloss, but in doing so they risk fixing associations that may be less rigid in the original, as in the case of the frame, where the oldest manuscript does not spell out racial distinctions among the enslaved in the queen's retinue.

When not long afterward in the frame tale the two brother kings witness the emergence of a "demon," in Haddawy's gloss, that term imperfectly captures the sense of jinn in the *Nights*, who are, as in the Quran, creatures of free will. Good jinn feature in *Nights* tales such as "Maʿruf the Cobbler," and in Diyab's later tale of "Aladdin and the Wonderful Lamp," but "demon" does not signal that possibility in English. Not all the Arabic texts specify the complexion of the jinni that keeps a stolen bride at the bottom of a lake—for instance, the Macnaghten does not. But Mahdi does, and Haddawy specifies that the brother kings are seduced by the stolen bride of the "black demon" (12).

In this context, Mahdi's interpolation (from later manuscripts he deems less authoritative) to specify that the women in the queen's retinue are "white" tilts the axis of the whole story. It performs a similar function to the change from "kitchen boy" to "black slave" in the Macnaghten text. Prior to these alterations that date to the eighteenth and nineteenth centuries, the frame presented an escalation of betrayals, as might be expected introducing a story collection where tales and embedded tales progress through escalating marvels and ever greater astonishment. A minor king is betrayed by his queen with a servant; a greater king is betrayed in public by his queen with an enslaved man, against the backdrop of ten concubines also taking lovers; a powerful jinni is betrayed by his stolen bride with a total, counting the two brother kings, of a hundred men. But the changes wrought by Macnaghten and Mahdi signal less an escalation than a repetition. With these late additions, the women Shahzaman witnesses having sex at the start of the tale—his queen, his brother's, and the concubines—are all white women who take Black lovers.

But must we preserve in amber these changes made to a manuscript three or four hundred years later? The changes do bring the tale closer in time and in recognizable social types to modern imperialism, slavery, and racism, with their attendant institutions and prejudices. Projecting modern conceptions of race onto all the betrayals does make the tale more pertinent to our own concerns and the terms of our social and political discourses. One way to pay attention to the imperial and the colonial is to freeze-frame a collection that has evolved over a millennium at moments defined by the greatest imprint of Western imperialism. Reading this way emphasizes the fact that the *Nights* has something vital and urgent to teach us about modern imperialism and its aftermath and dovetails with debates over the creation of modern categories of gender and race. Protagonists in the history of the *Nights*' first translation into English were also protagonists in the key debates in colonial India over language and education (they sided against Thomas Macaulay, who made the case for an English-language bureaucracy and system of education, and in favor of vernaculars). The architect of the first British invasion of Afghanistan was the editor of the most comprehensive Arabic edition, and his political secretary was the first to translate the *Nights* from Arabic into English (see Horta, *Marvellous Thieves* 88–131). It is a textbook demonstration of the nexus of power and knowledge, a direct line between imperial conquest, colonialism, and literary production. We need teaching that is attentive to these contexts.

A further path for a decolonial pedagogy for teaching the *Nights* is to decolonize the editing and translation history of the *Nights*, accentuating other Arabic variants of the *Nights* collection and tales and agencies other than the imperial, such as Diyab's. This is what I sought to do in editing *The Annotated* Arabian Nights for W. W. Norton. I quote at length from analogous tales from the *Nights*' sister collections *Tales of the Marvellous and News of the Strange* (Lyons) and *A Hundred and One Nights* (Fudge), and I bring Diyab's contribution to the collection into focus by including not only his tales in Galland's versions but his own versions of the tales as jotted down by the French translator. We need critiques of Lane and Burton and the imperialist school of editing and translation and the texts we have inherited from them, but we also need to direct students to Arab agency in the form of these other collections and to storytellers like Diyab. Perhaps most of all we have been in need of new translations, as even the best contemporary translations by Haddawy and Lyons are based on editions that interpolate their own racial categories into their texts.

My most important intervention in teaching the *Nights* was to commission a new translation for Norton. The process of workshopping Seale's draft translation in the summer of Black Lives Matter in 2020 in my class on the *Nights* at New York University provided important insights. Originally it followed Haddawy's practice in using "demon" for "jinni" and in describing the enslaved people in the queen's retinue as "ten white and ten black." Following student feedback, and in the light of the editorial history of the *Nights* outlined here, I was able to substitute "jinni" for "demon." Knowledge of Macnaughten's editorial intervention initiated a search for other language to describe the complexion of members of the queen's retinue in the frame. Editing the new translation of the tale to counter the additions regarding race of past editors and translators, I found that in the next iteration of the course students were able to engage better with the tales and with issues of race and racism in the medieval Arab world.

The essays gathered in this volume suggest that teachers not skip over these episodes of racism but work to historicize, contextualize, interpret, and generate a greater consciousness of the problem of anti-Black racism in the *Nights* as in the societies that created and translated the stories (see the essays by Schine, Vaziri, and Sunya). The Black presence in the *Nights* reflects the reality and diversity of the cities that generated the tales, however subject to social hierarchies, restrictions, and prejudices. It is also necessary to consider the role of choice of tales with regard to representativeness and representation in a volume dedicated to pedagogy in a variety of levels and contexts. Is it sufficient to teach the *Nights* by way of the frame tale in a single session of an introductory world literature survey?

If the instructor must lead with the frame tale, teaching it in a comparative perspective may prove more analytically fruitful and inclusive. The *Thousand and One Nights* frame, taught alongside the variant frame of the *Hundred and One Nights*, reveals more about the underlying psychological rivalry between its protagonists and provides a different point of entry into the mindset of Shahrazad and her sister in the variant frame story. The men are motivated by a beauty contest between them, by a narcissism that perhaps lies behind the psychotic response to betrayal. The younger sister, Dunyazad, plays a larger role in the *Hundred and One Nights*, as it is she who marries the monarch (in other versions of the frame Dunyazad is a housekeeper or maid). Dunyazad also has greater agency in feminist and postcolonial retellings that might productively be paired with the frame in the classroom, such as Nélida Piñon's *Voices of the Desert* and Assia Djebar's *Sister to Scheherazade*.

In the classroom the instructor may do well to follow the lead of contemporary dramaturges such as Tim Supple in selecting tales other than the frame as a point of entry into the story collection and its rich store of genres, characters, and agencies. "The Porter and the Three Women of Baghdad" satisfies many of the requisites in representing the *Thousand and One Nights* as a whole: it is a quintessentially urban tale that reflects the mercantile culture of Baghdad and

Damascus that generated the tales (see the essay by Roth in this volume); it forms part of an Arabic core common to most extant manuscripts; and, taking the form of a storytelling competition between men and women, it captures both recurring tensions in the frame and other tales and exposes readers to a wider range of the types of stories present in the collection. The mystery of three women living alone without a male guardian, investigated by no less than the caliph Harun al-Rashid and his vizier Jaafar as merchants in disguise, affords the instructor the chance to provide students with historical and social context to understand the many subversive turns in the tale. Both the outer frame of the three women of Baghdad and the mysteries of the dervishes to be revealed in their own tales are narratively compelling and show to best advantage the formal possibilities of the tale-within-a-tale for suspense and tales of recognition. If the dénouement in which the caliph marries off the women of the house with little regard to their wishes is unlikely to satisfy twenty-first-century expectations of justice in the North American classroom, this can prove a fruitful point of departure for discussion.

"Sindbad" provides a window into the heterogeneity of responses that cultural difference provoked in Arab merchants and the tales they told and listened to. It provides a fascinating insight into the cosmopolitan prejudices that Arab travelers carried and acquired in Southeast Asia. Other tales, like "The City of Brass," "The Three Apples," and "Dalila the Crafty," bring students closer to the history of genres like science fiction, crime, and trickster tales that they consume outside the classroom in series and podcasts today (Fudge, "Signs"; Allen) and can be used in class both to burrow into the historical and social context of the original tales and to look forward to their resonance with these familiar genres. Finally, tales added in the early 1700s from Diyab often prove popular with students, as they have with readers from their first inclusion in the story collection by Galland. Relative to medieval tales they appear closer in narrative convention, psychological drive, and complexity, and they have more often been adapted across the world in film, television, and video games. They often pertain more clearly to the genres of the fairy tale, fantasy, and horror ("The Jealous Sisters," "Sidi Numan"), with which the story collection has come to be associated in popular culture. Diyab's tales play well in the classroom.

Texts

The Arabic Tales

The core Arabic tales are available in contemporary editions and translations by Mahdi and Haddawy, Lyons, and Horta and Seale. These versions allow the teacher to situate this core cycle of tales in its original cultural milieus and disentangle the story collection's imprint in Middle Eastern literatures from the legacy of the tales and commentaries added in French and English translations, which tilt toward the supernatural. The picture that emerges from this kernel is of urban and urbane story cycles and competitions between women and men, far removed from the exoticism associated with the famous film versions of *Nights* tales, as Supple observed in collaborating with Hanan al-Shaykh on his own retelling.

This core includes widely influential and frequently taught tales, including the frame tale of the two brother kings that introduces Shahrazad, "The Merchant and the Jinni," "The Fisherman and the Jinni," "The Three Apples," and "The Porter and the Three Women of Baghdad." Tales of jinn and magic occur, but they are often embedded within domestic conflicts and storytelling competitions between women and men (as in the frame tale and "The Porter and the Three Women of Baghdad"). For the teacher of literatures in European languages, an added advantage of focusing on an Arabic core is the opportunity to recognize the revolutionary influence of the reception of these tales in traditions of realism from Charles Dickens through Gabriel García Márquez. Such is the presence of merchants as protagonists in the Arabic tales that Chraïbi has dubbed the *Nights* "the mirror for merchants" ("Situation" 6), and this focus on the middle and lower stations in life was a key contribution of the *Nights* tales in nineteenth-century European literatures, as Irwin has observed ("The *Arabian Nights* and the Origins of the Western Novel" 146). García Márquez's love for the story collection is well known, but it would be a mistake to view his debt to the stories strictly through the prism of magic. The market scene in *Love in the Time of Cholera*, for instance, alludes to and plays upon the market scene with its erotic connotations at the start of "The Porter and the Three Women of Baghdad."

In the past three decades students have often been introduced to the tales in the "wonderfully readable translation" by Haddawy, published in course-friendly editions (Fudge, "More Translators" 137). The Iraqi American translator taught English literature in Nevada and was attentive to the cadences of American English, producing a version that reflects his love of Ernest Hemingway, with short, clipped sentences that belie the unpunctuated character of the original manuscripts of the stories. Haddawy's version is reliable and accessible. A limitation of Haddawy's version is that it was anchored in the Arabic text produced by Mahdi in the first volume of *The* Thousand and One Nights (Alf layla wa-layla): From the Earliest Known Sources. Mahdi's project—to produce a definitive urtext of the Arabic core based on a single manuscript—has been subsequently superseded by archival discoveries that suggest a much wider universe of relevant Arabic and Turkish manuscripts of the story collection and its tales. In his zeal to recover an urtext from beneath the intervention of European Orientalists, Mahdi eliminated not only the tales added in French, thanks to the respective interventions of Diyab and Galland, but also much of the corpus of the original tales reflected in other Arabic manuscripts and printed texts.

In the classroom, the reduction of the canon of *Nights* tales to the forty tales and 282 nights of storytelling rendered by Haddawy from Mahdi's text has unintended consequences, notably in the form of a reduction of the range of female characters represented. Most widely available editions of the *Nights* tend to omit the story collection's strongest female characters (other than Shahrazad herself), and this is the case with Haddawy's version, from which favorites like Dalila are missing. In the absence of exposure to the female tricksters and enslaved women who outwit criminals and the wisest scholars of Baghdad alike, students encounter a curtailed sense of the types of agency wielded by women in the story collection.

A main virtue of the *Nights* in Lyons's translation is its comprehensiveness, unlikely to be matched or surpassed in English in the near future. Since Malcolm Lyons bases his 2008 translation on the more comprehensive Calcutta II text, by Macnaghten, Dalila and Zumurrud do feature in his version. The edition features perennial favorites of contemporary fantasy authors, such as "Hasan of Basra" and "The Queen of the Serpents," as well as several canonical tales integral to the history of world letters and missing in other modern editions that otherwise tout themselves as complete, among them "Qamar al-Zaman," "The Hunchback," "The City of Brass," and "Ma'ruf the Cobbler."

This three-volume, thousand-plus-page edition also benefits from Irwin's lively introduction. As in his other writing on history and the *Nights*, Irwin has an unparalleled eye for the heterogeneous matter of the collection and how its content and lessons exceed our contemporary preoccupations. Lyons's text has been lauded for conveying the peculiar turns of phrase and slang and a sense of the long, unbroken text of the original, reflected in Lyons's expansive paragraphs. At least one Arabist, Bruce Fudge, cautions that these very qualities can interfere with the comprehension of the stories, as climaxes and character entries and exits lie buried mid-paragraph ("More Translators" 143). Further, Fudge notes, whereas a contemporary French translation by Jamel Eddine Bencheikh and André Miquel of the same text clearly separates dialogue from narration, Lyons challenges readers by declining to break up the text.

My selection of Arabic tales in *The Annotated* Arabian Nights is designed to satisfy most pedagogical uses and contexts in the teaching of the *Nights*, matching the selection included in anthologies of world literature. Dalila takes center stage in the bold and lyrical new version I commissioned by Seale, the first woman to translate the story collection into English. *The Annotated* Arabian Nights features "Dalila" and "Sindbad" in addition to the aforementioned core Arabic tales—the frame, "The Merchant and the Jinni," "The Fisherman and the Jinni," "The Three Apples," and "The Three Women of Baghdad." Seale brings a poet's instinct to these tales, capturing a sense of the original's rhyming prose. This is evident in the frame tale of the two brother kings: "The elder, Shahriyar, was strong on a horse and bold with a blade, never beaten and never burned, quick to revenge and slow to forgive" (5). The pedagogical cast of this edition is reflected in the critical apparatus—introduction, introductory essays to each tale, and marginal notes and images illustrating variant versions and influence. It is the only edition to include the visual material referenced by contributors to this volume on teaching: woodcut prints from manuscripts and books; illustrations by Edmund Dulac, Walter Crane, and many others; set designs and costumes for the Ballets Russes productions of *Scheherazade*, and still images from influential films such as Raoul Walsh's *Thief of Bagdad* and Reiniger's *The Adventures of Prince Achmed*. Teachers devoting an entire course to the *Nights* might do well to supplement this edition of the core Arabic tales with a selection of a wider range of stories from Lyons. To this end a tale index in this volume gives the relevant page numbers in the Seale and Lyons translations for the tales they are principally concerned with teaching.

Historical Translations of the Arabic Tales

Famous European translators of the *Nights* sometimes loom as large as the tales themselves, and there are a range of classroom contexts in which it may make sense to refer to a historical translation of the *Nights*: courses on imperialism, Orientalism, and postcolonialism as well as surveys of eighteenth- and nineteenth-century European literatures. In singling out the centrality of Galland, Edward William Lane, and Burton to the genealogy of Orientalism, Edward Said's polemic revived interest in these figures and afforded them opportunities for critical reconsideration. The controversial nature of their entanglement with institutions of imperial power and education have made French and English translations of the *Nights* useful texts in the classroom.

The *Arabian Nights* of the European imaginary is fundamentally that of Galland's French translation, published 1704–17. Galland remained paramount even as new translations were produced and circulated, often as additions to libraries where readers were acquainted with the story collection in Galland's version. (For example, if the illustrations and commentaries of Lane's 1840 edition command attention in contemporary reviews while the translation they accompany does not, it is in part because of an assumption that Galland is still read and supplemented with William Harvey's illustrations or Lane's notes on magic.) Galland's text was immediately bootlegged in England in the famed Grub Street edition, and individual stories like "Aladdin" widely circulated in inexpensive chapbooks. Burton's exorbitantly priced text (which eventually would figure in the imagination of James Joyce, Salman Rushdie, and Orhan Pamuk), in comparison, was privately circulated for a thousand subscribers; even reprints, such as that printed by Oscar Wilde's publisher Leonard Smithers, were aimed at wealthy collectors. In a class on Orientalism, teachers would do well to refer to Galland (in the original or in Jean-Paul Sermain's excellent modern three-volume edition) or Robert Mack's reprint of the Grub Street translation.

The first effort to translate the Arabic core into English, which produced the most readable Victorian version for students, was undertaken by Henry Whitelock Torrens in Calcutta in the 1830s. Torrens was a British colonial bureaucrat and man of letters, a novelist and a journalist who championed a free press in

India as a check on colonial authority and who opposed and satirized Macaulay's "Minute on Indian Education" of 1835. Believing, in accord with German Romanticism, that the poetry of a people best captured their distinctive spirit, he experimented with the occasional rhyming prose, alliteration, and anachronism and was more successful than other Victorians in conveying the poetry of the *Nights*. In his day, he regretted not having access to the libraries of Cairo, which might have afforded him the possibility of appending an extensive commentary to this translation. Torrens's liberalism and lack of an ethnographic goal mean that his readers are spared the sort of misogynistic and racist observations that pepper the commentaries of the better-known, if less literary, Victorian versions by Lane and Burton.

Lane's philological work and *Arabic-English Lexicon* are still well regarded to this day, and his *Nights* commentary benefits from a sympathy for Islam and the popular superstitions of Cairo, the translator's home for twelve years in the 1820s, 1830s, and 1840s. His notes on the jinn and magic influenced authors from George Eliot to Borges. The text of his translation, which never attracted the same admiration among his contemporaries as did his commentary or Harvey's illustrations, has not aged as well. Reviewers noted that, however well his King James diction suited the miracles of the *Nights*, it failed the comic tales (Horta, *Marvellous Thieves* 162). Fearing Torrens as "a formidable rival" (qtd. in Horta, *Marvellous Thieves*, 159), Lane conceded to him the literary realm and sought to make his page count by recycling material from his ethnography of Cairo in his commentary. Sadly, on the subject of the lives of Muslim women in Cairo, of which he had little direct experience, he relied on the lore spouted by informants. Thus Lane's *Nights* omits many of the stronger female characters from his Bulaq text and reproduces his informants' observations on the alleged promiscuity of Cairene women as facts.

In the classroom Torrens and Lane provide different windows into the interrelation of translation and imperialism. Torrens as a young political and intelligence officer was a protagonist in debates on language policy in India. He answered Macaulay's "Minute on Indian Education" with his own satirical salvo, intended as a riposte that mocked the assumption of the superiority of English literature. Torrens's translation of the *Nights* into English was itself part of a compromise struck by these defenders of so-called Oriental languages against the Anglicist camp that would not sanction the funding of the publication of Macnaghten's Arabic text of the *Nights* without an accompanying translation into English. Lane's only comments on European imperial intervention in Egypt were critical. He resented the period of French occupation of Egypt that preceded his stay for layering a European modernity over what he perceived to be continuous traditions that could be traced back to the medieval world of the *Nights*. And yet, after Lane's death, his *Nights* would be reissued in London in 1883 with a jingoistic preface proclaiming its usefulness as a handbook for colonial administration in occupied Egypt. At odds with Lane's own sensibility, this use of Lane's work demonstrates Edward Said's contention that the power-knowledge nexus of Orientalism need not depend on the individual cooperation of each scholar. In the Middle East, British imperial policy had a way of recycling the work of past scholars, whatever their politics, for its own ends.

Breaking with ethnography, the main case for the literary appreciation of the *Nights* was made by the Pre-Raphaelite poet John Payne, a member of Dante Gabriel Rossetti's circle. While his 1884 version would seem to be forgotten, it influenced Burton's version in his day, and some elements reach through to Seale's in our own. Payne had long sought to match Rossetti's *Sonnets for Pictures* with his own verse's ear for songs, and a concern with music and rhythm governed his lyrical approach to translating the *Nights*. He conceived of the story collection as a Wagnerian opera of the decline of a civilization that had reached its apogee under Harun al-Rashid—in his emphasis, its most frequent character. He restored the frame of Shahrazad and its recurrence in the main text of the translation, neglected by previous English translators of the *Nights*. Characters mattered to him as in a musical drama, each recurring like Shahrazad with her leitmotif. He claimed to be in thrall to the unbroken rhythms of the original, uninterrupted by punctuation and paragraph breaks. He even ventured to render the prose in English without punctuation, which forced the musical translator to find other ways to communicate breaks and pauses of breath. If his final published version opts for punctuation, it is nonetheless governed by a poet's ear for meter and beat, for rhythm and leitmotif. Apart from the imprint on other versions, Payne's text (complete with commentary) had its greatest impact in mid- to late-twentieth-century America, in a mass-market paperback edition prefaced by Joseph Campbell. It was this edition that would influence George Lucas and his own space opera of the Wagnerian decline of an empire, the *Star Wars* films.

The ephemeral quality of even the most famous translations of the *Nights* and the uses to which they put the past is well illustrated by the fate of Burton's, published in 1885, the year of the criminalization of homosexuality in the United Kingdom. Burton opposed this legislation and argued against it in the lengthy "Terminal Essay" on the subject he appended to the tenth volume of his *Nights* in 1885 (10: 63–260). The focus on homosexuality in the *Nights* and across vast swathes of the world was intended to draw a sympathetic light to that sexual orientation also in Berlin, Paris, and London, as his handwritten revisions to the essay show (*Marvellous Thieves*, 293–95). This stance helped draw interest in Burton among Pre-Raphaelites and decadents, like his close friend Algernon Swinburne, and correspondence with German scholars who likewise resisted the calls for the criminalization of homosexuality well into the turn of the century. Yet Burton was also an apologist for other social practices espoused by Arab and Muslim societies with which he identified as traveler and pilgrim, notably slavery (Horta, "Cosmopolitan Prejudice"). And with the same selective eye with which he saw the *Nights* as evidence of a wider Arab and Muslim tolerance for homosexuality, he deployed the story collection at the service of his anti-Black racism. His example should serve as a caution that no matter how progressive a cause may lead translators to be invested in the universe of the *Nights*, it may also blind them to other competing claims and identities.

Lawrence Venuti's study of translation champions Burton's foreignizing method as disruptive of regimes of fluency (265–73), and Edward Said and Kwame Anthony Appiah include Burton as an anchoring case study in their respective studies of Orientalism and cosmopolitanism. In the classroom the teacher might employ Torrens, who pioneered the traits associated with Burton's translation that Venuti admires—archaism, rhyming prose, sentences that often preserve the word order of Arabic—to more successful ends. The teacher may want to weigh the benefits of including case studies of Burton as a translator, Orientalist, and cosmopolitan against the costs of exposing students to a racism and defense of slavery that were already out of step with the norms of his time in 1885. Burton's *Nights* survived for its long-unparalleled comprehensiveness. The appearance of Lyons, translating all the same corpus of tales from Arabic from Calcutta II, and of Seale, translating the complete set of tales added in French, now negates the need to access stories through Burton's translation.

"Aladdin" and Other Tales Added in French

"Aladdin" and other stories added by Galland to the *Thousand and One Nights* based on the storytelling of Diyab in 1709 have proved the most popular and have come to define the story collection in world letters. This phenomenon is greatly responsible for the association of the *Nights* tales in the European imaginary with the romance, gothic, and fantasy genres, though, as Irwin observes, tales of mercantile mores and adventures left as deep an impression in the development of European realism ("The *Arabian Nights* and the Origins of the Western Novel").

Tales added in French pose a particular problem in the classroom, as the *Thousand and One Nights* is often included in survey courses in a variety of disciplines that seek to position the story collection as representative of medieval Arabic culture. What role, if any, should these added tales play?

The achievement of scholars of Arabic literature, notably Mahdi in the 1980s, to establish a firm text of the core Arabic tales of the *Thousand and One Nights* had the intentional corollary effect of discouraging the study or teaching of the tales added in French. The revival of interest in new translations from the Mahdi-edited Arabic text was accompanied by a decline in interest in refreshing tales added in French, among them "The Enchanted Horse" and "Prince Ahmad," in new translations. Haddawy himself followed Mahdi in dismissing in the strongest terms these tales added by Galland as frauds imposed on an unsuspecting public that were best erased from literary history. With little then known about the Syrian storyteller who gave the tales to Galland, scholars doubted Diyab's creative agency, and it was possible to dismiss the tales added in French as documents of cultural appropriation to be excised from the canon of the story collection. Haddawy was eventually persuaded by his publisher to render for a separate volume of popular tales "Aladdin" and "Ali Baba" but not "Prince Ahmad," "The Enchanted Horse," or "The Night Adventures of Harun al-Rashid." "Aladdin" lived on in retellings, but teachers should be aware that even the best adaptations (such as Philip Pullman's *Aladdin and the Enchanted Lamp*) take great liberties with the text, adding and omitting entire episodes and characters.

The removal of the tales added by Galland from the corpus of the *Nights* meant that many of the most influential tales in world literature and cinema—such as "Prince Ahmad"—have long been available in English only in historical translations from the eighteenth and nineteenth centuries that confront students with archaisms and, in the case of Burton, an affected medievalism. "Prince Ahmad" and "The Enchanted Horse" are available in versions by Burton and Mardrus in an Everyman's Library edition that samples historical translations of the *Nights* (see Ouyang, *Arabian Nights*), where the interest lies—as in Borges's famous essay on the *Nights* translators ("Translators")—in how they depart from modern scholarly translation practice.

The recent discovery of Diyab's account of his voyage from Aleppo to Paris, *The Book of Travels*, which reveals the supplier of "Aladdin" and other famous tales to Galland as a storyteller and creator in his own right, has revived interest in the Syrian French tales among scholars and publishers. Now that the extent of Diyab's storytelling talent has been confirmed—his travelogue even employs *Nights* techniques such as the embedding of tales within tales for suspense—there is a new urgency to provide anglophone readers with a sense of the literary achievement of Galland's French rendering of the tales recounted to him by Diyab. No longer should the teacher follow Mahdi and Haddawy in dismissing "Aladdin" and other tales as mere acts of Parisian cultural appropriation. There is even the likelihood that some of the cultural assimilation of French mores in these tales, long credited to Galland, may be shaped by Diyab's own experiences during his sojourn in Paris, during which he was presented in the palaces of Versailles. The wording of the fabulous descriptions of princesses and palaces, with regard to the enumeration of jewels, for instance, more closely resembles Diyab's account of Versailles in his travelogue than anything Galland wrote about his youthful travels in the Ottoman world.

The scholarly reappraisal of Diyab as a creative agent in his own right following the discovery of his *Book of Travels* has meant that English-speaking readers are finally well served by a translation of these famous tales added in French beyond "Aladdin," previously available only in Victorian translations or anglophone retellings. *The Annotated* Arabian Nights (Seale) makes available tales that can be taught in a wide range of classroom contexts—not only the fairy tales "Prince Ahmad and the Fairy Banu" and "The Enchanted Horse" but also the more urban tales of crime and justice, such as "Ali Baba" and "The Night Adventures of Harun al-Rashid." These genres and stories can be related to analogues in sibling story collections such as *A Hundred and One Nights* (Fudge) and *Tales of the Marvellous and News of the Strange* (Lyons) as well as the urban reality of eighteenth-century Aleppo at the intersection of trade and intellectual currents between Asia, the Middle East, and Europe. Now that we know that the tales added in French are not merely the product of Galland's invention, they interest us not only as documents of imperialism and Orientalism but also, like Diyab's *Book of Travels*, as Arab impressions of Paris and Versailles, which they may reflect and represent. A whole new set of questions and contexts suggest themselves for the teaching of tales in which Diyab may have imprinted his own sense of modernity and engagement with cultural difference in ways that resonate with current debates on cosmopolitanism.

Film and Popular Culture

The advent of the precursors and early forms of cinema at the close of the nineteenth century coincided with the height of the influence and popularity of the *Thousand and One Nights*, already omnipresent in stage plays, pantomimes, panoramas, and other forms of public spectacle across Europe, the United States, and other sites of the *Nights* spheres of influence, from Beirut to Tokyo. Many of the early silent film versions of the *Arabian Nights*, "Aladdin," and "Ali Baba" are filmed records of these earlier forms of entertainments rather than original creations for the screen. Released in the United States, Ernst Lubitsch's 1920 *Sumurun* loosely improvised on "Nur al-Din" and, featuring a comic figure that draws on the popular "Tale of the Hunchback," conveys the sense of an entire *Arabian Nights* clowning tradition by adapting a popular pantomime by Friedrich Freksa. The Polish star Pola Negri's seductive dancing, a nod to Marjana, earned the film a restricted rating. *Chu Chin Chow*, an adaptation of "Ali Baba" and one of the most popular musical comedies on the English stage during the Great War, was adapted for the screen in 1925 and 1934. Some of its improvisations on the plot and on the character of Marjana as a spy can be detected in Bollywood musical versions of Ali Baba such as *Alibaba aur chalis chor*, from 1954.

Early filmmakers soon found that the *Nights* tales lent themselves particularly well to showing off the new technologies of cinema, and original adaptations of the *Nights* for the screen proved revolutionary in their use of effects during the silent era, from Europe and North America to India. A notable example of these earliest breakthroughs in special effects is Georges Méliès's *Le palais des* Mille et une nuits (released in English as *The Palace of the* Arabian Nights). In a variation of the basic plot of "Aladdin," a poor prince woos a beautiful princess with the aid of a sorcerer, Khalafar, played by Méliès himself. The film inaugurated some of the specific iconography of *Arabian Nights* and fantasy films, notably through the sensation caused by the sight of the heroes fighting an army of skeletons.

Two German films, Paul Leni's *Das Wachsfigurenkabinett* (*Waxworks*) and Fritz Lang's *Der müde Tod* (*Destiny*), both from 1921, prominently featured the

Arabian Nights in groundbreaking fantasy, horror, and expressionist visions. Leni's film drew on the motif of the caliph Harun al-Rashid in disguise that had proved so captivating and politically charged on the page and stage in Europe in the eighteenth and nineteenth centuries. Here the caliph, played by Emil Jennings, uses his disguise to engage in a romantic misadventure. The first tale in Lang's triptych film presented a so-called Frank scaling a palace of the faithful to further a forbidden cross-cultural romance with an Arab princess, borrowing a motif from crusader romances that also features in the *Thousand and One Nights* itself in the form of the tale of "King ʿUmar al-Nuʿmān and His Family." A long cinematic history precedes the controversy over Guy Ritchie's introduction of a wooing European prince in his live-action remake of *Aladdin*, released in 2019, and Disney's development of a series around the haughty character Prince Anders.

Raoul Walsh's 1924 *The Thief of Bagdad* is credited with developing the vocabulary of the Hollywood adventure fantasy set in the Middle East, inclusive of Disney's animated *Aladdin* of 1992 and Steven Spielberg's 1981 *Raiders of the Lost Ark*, and indeed both films flaunt the influence openly, borrowing tigers and crowded bazaar scenes of outsized baskets from the Douglas Fairbanks starrer. Walsh's film, a pastiche of "Prince Ahmad" and "Aladdin" with dashes of the characters of Ali Baba and his brother, already borrowed heavily from German *Arabian Nights* fantasies, notably the flying carpet scene from Lang's *Destiny* (Fairbanks famously bought the American rights to *Destiny* so the film would not steal the thunder from his own film's climax). It would be more accurate to observe that Fairbanks's film, like the 1940 Alexander Korda reboot *The Thief of Bagdad*, crystallized an *Arabian Nights* fantasy genre already very much in vogue, as also proved the case upon the release of Walsh's film in India.

Beyond the silent film era, Hollywood films based on the tales of the *Thousand and One Nights* were central to the development of special effects, nowhere more markedly than in Ray Harryhausen's *Sinbad* trilogy: *The Seventh Voyage of Sinbad* (1958), *The Golden Voyage of Sinbad* (1973), and *Sinbad and the Eye of the Tiger* (1977). If 1977 would seem to be the year science fiction definitively displaced the *Arabian Nights* fantasy as the cutting-edge genre for experiments in special effects with the release of *Star Wars*, George Lucas's debt to Harryhausen with regard to stop-motion animation of monsters has also long been acknowledged. Lucas borrowed perhaps more than is commonly recognized: in his films the Sith Lords who draw their strength from the dark side of the Force age, wrinkle, and scar when they use their powers in precisely the same manner as do the dark sorcerers when they use their magic in Harryhausen's *Sinbad* trilogy.

In the classroom, a good way to pique students' curiosity toward Harryhausen's mid-twentieth-century *Sinbad* trilogy is to play this game of debt and attribution with regard to other filmmakers who acknowledge a profound debt to him: James Cameron, Peter Jackson, and Guillermo del Toro. Sinbad's famous duel with a skeleton at the climax of *The Seventh Voyage of Sinbad* is the thread that links Méliès's first special effects extravaganza to more familiar set pieces such as the army of the dead in Jackson's *Lord of the Rings: The Return of the King*. The debts transcend images and motifs directly borrowed from *Arabian Nights* films and material. Del Toro nods to Harryhausen in giving the titular army in *Hellboy 2: The Golden Army* the jerky, stop-motion quality of the skeletons and creatures of the *Sinbad* trilogy. In this manner, Harryhausen's pioneering stop-motion animation remains part of contemporary film vocabulary for directors who seek to convey a dreamlike, unnatural quality when CGI technology would allow for a more fluid and naturalistic motion.

The singular influence of Harryhausen's *Sinbad* trilogy, from the dark robes and magic of the Sith Lords of Lucasfilm's Skywalker saga through the special effects of Jackson and del Toro, speaks to the ability of a filmmaking tradition to create its own parallel *Arabian Nights* lore complete with its distinctive images and motifs often independent of the original stories. DreamWorks Animation's underrated *Sinbad: Legends of the Seven Seas* of 2003, a film buried by a studio uncertain how to market an *Arabian Nights* film in the midst of the Second Gulf War, is also rich with references to Harryhausen's *Sinbad* trilogy, borrowing heroines, costumes, and background clutter from its universe. Edward Said, himself quite fond of the Hollywood *Arabian Nights* blockbusters of the midcentury and his childhood, emphasized in his cultural criticism the discrepancy between Western discourses of the so-called Orient and Middle Eastern realities. American cinematic discourses and tropes pertaining to the *Thousand and One Nights*, with their self-referential quality, take this disconnect to an extreme.

Teachers would do well to look beyond Hollywood to other cinematic traditions' use of the *Arabian Nights*. Romantic tales of beautiful youths and forbidden love provided Pier Paolo Pasolini with the outline for the 1974 *Il fiore delle Mille e una notte* (*The Flower of the* Thousand and One Nights; released as *Arabian Nights*), the *Arabian Nights* installment of his trilogy of life made up also of *The Decameron* and *The Canterbury Tales*. Pasolini's concern with shooting on location, naturalistic acting, and general neorealism serves as a useful corrective to the Hollywood association of the story collection with fantasy and a reminder that across the globe many television networks associate the *Nights* with late-night soap operas, Ramadan miniseries, and frank portrayals of adult themes and realities and not merely fairy tales of untold riches.

It is also useful to disentangle the legacy of *Nights* in animation arising from the *Aladdin* and *Sinbad* films produced by Jeffrey Katzenberg for Disney and DreamWorks and the attendant broader American equation of the *Nights* with marvels and the exotic from uses of the work in more mundane contexts, from Popeye to Scooby-Doo. Lotte Reiniger's stunning silhouette film from 1926, *The Adventures of Prince Achmed* (fig. 1), serves as a reminder not only that Disney did not invent feature-length animation but also that the form was not always viewed strictly through the prism of entertainment for young children. In the classroom students are surprised by a scene in which Achmed views the

Figure 1. Film still from *Die Abenteuer des Prinzen Achmed* (*The Adventures of Prince Achmed*), directed by Lotte Reiniger, 1926.

princess bathing naked and another where he is warmly received with many kisses and much flirtation by young women in a harem. Another film made with paper cutouts, Karel Zeman's 1974 Czech classic *Pohádky* Tisíce a jedné noci (*Tales of the* Thousand and One Nights), may startle viewers with its critique of mercantile greed and capitalism. In fact, the representation of Sindbad as a merchant motivated by a recurrent appetite for new fortunes is more faithful to the character in the Arabic and French cycles of tales than the swashbuckling muscular sailor and seafarer of the 1947 technicolor film starring Douglas Fairbanks, Jr., and the Harryhausen trilogy.

The cinematic history of the *Thousand and One Nights* is in fact so rich and varied that it can be reduced neither to the exotic fare of the genre associated with Universal Pictures' 1942 adventure film *Arabian Nights*, starring Maria Montez and Sabu, nor to animation, special effects, and fantasy. A more comprehensive guide would require its own volume, and I have contented myself here with merely sketching some of the principal genres reflecting the reception of famous tales and films, including the fairy tale and fantasy imprint of "Prince Ahmad" in *The Thief of Bagdad*, the clowning that governed much early silent cinema versions, the music hall comedy of British "Ali Baba" stage plays and films that resonate with the many Bollywood musical versions of the same tale, and the realism that likely speaks to the greater part of the reception of the story collection in moving images in television series, like the Hallmark Entertainment *Arabian Nights*, that tease out Shahrazad's own tale and those she tells in the form of soap opera and romance. For further resources I direct the teacher to Irwin's entry on film in Ulrich Marzolph and Richard van Leeuwen's Arabian Nights *Encyclopedia*, and to Samhita Sunya's essay in this volume on teaching the *Nights* with reference to Japanese, Indian, and Iranian film.

The Instructor's Library

Reference Works

The *Thousand and One Nights* is well served by both a companion and an encyclopedia. Perhaps the single most useful reference work for the teacher of the *Nights* is Irwin's *The* Arabian Nights*: A Companion*, also available in German, Italian, Danish, Japanese, and Persian. Both a scholar of medieval Arabic history and a novelist, Irwin brings both qualities to bear in his text, which has the advantage of being assignable to and welcomed by both undergraduate and graduate students. Irwin wittily surveys the story collection's unheralded status in Arabic letters and its literary refractions of the street and sex life of medieval Cairo, Baghdad, and Damascus and guides the reader through formal readings of the tales and the vast history of their reception in European literature. He incisively cuts through the history of European translations, rightly dismissing Burton. Irwin's subsequent articles on the politics and racism of the *Nights*, among other topics, form a kind of sequel to the companion and prove timely for consideration of the story collection in today's classroom.

Irwin also contributed an entry on film versions of the *Nights* to the other vital reference work for teachers and students, Marzolph and van Leeuwen's two-volume Arabian Nights *Encyclopedia*, which every course covering the *Nights* should have on reserve. Organized both thematically and by story, the encyclopedia references each tale included in the more comprehensive Macnaghten text that served as the basis for the versions by Torrens, Payne, Burton, and Lyons. Van Leeuwen, the Dutch translator of the *Nights* and scholar of many facets of the collection, including its reception in European literatures, and Marzolph, a comparatist scholar of folklore in Persian, Arabic, and European literatures and, alongside Aboubakr Chraïbi, the doyen of current *Nights* scholarship, combine to cover a vast field in entries that serve as perfect and concise introductions to their subjects. Teachers should also make recourse to Chraïbi's reference works *Les* Mille et une nuits*: Histoire du texte et classification des contes*, *Classer les récits: Théories et pratiques*, and *Arabic Manuscripts of the* Thousand and One Nights.

In English, other comprehensive encyclopedic surveys include those in Marzolph and van Leeuwen's Arabian Nights *Encyclopedia*; in *The Oxford Companion to Fairy Tales*, edited by Jack Zipes; and in *Folktales and Fairy Tales*, edited by Anne Duggan and Don Haase. A fuller range of scholarship on the *Nights* is listed by Marzolph in his Arabian Nights *Bibliography*.

Literary Criticism

On the original core cycle of tales in Arabic, one may recommend to teachers and students Daniel Beaumont's *Slave of Desire: Sex, Love and Death in the* Thousand and One Nights, a sharply crafted psychoanalytic study of what makes the core cycle of tales still relevant and controversial to this day. For key reference points on the aesthetics and storytelling of the story collection, see Sandra Nadaff's *Arabesque: Narrative Structure and the Aesthetics of Repetition in the* Thousand and One Nights, Mia Gerhardt's *The Art of Story-telling: A Literary Study of the* Thousand and One Nights, and David Pinault's *Story-telling Techniques in the* Arabian Nights. Fudge is lucid in his exploration of the relation between the *Thousand and One Nights* and the *Hundred and One Nights*, which he translated; of underworlds in the *Nights* ("Underworlds"); and of the modern translations of the collection into English and French ("More Translators"). Other major points of reference for scholarship on the original core Arabic cycle of tales include Dwight Reynolds (on the history of the text ["*Thousand*"]), Andras Hamori (on historical context [*On the Art*]), Bencheikh (on transgression), Mahdi (on the Galland manuscript [*Thousand* (2013)]), Miquel (on Sindbad), Joseph Sadan (on Judaism and anti-Semitism), Muhsin al-Musawi (*Islamic Context*), Kamran Rastegar (on Orientalism and the Enlightenment), Ibrahim Akel (on the Arabic manuscripts ["Liste"]), Claude Brémond (for a structuralist approach [Bencheikh et al.]), Hasan M. el-Shamy (for motifs ["Motif Index" and *Motif Index*]), and Ferial J. Ghazoul (who argues for the coherence of the original cycle of tales in *The* Arabian Nights*: A Structural Analysis*).

The production and reception of the *Nights* in French and English literature has invited a vast scholarship. Among the most recent and accessible works are Marina Warner's *Stranger Magic: Charmed States and the* Arabian Nights and my own *Marvellous Thieves: Secret Authors of the* Arabian Nights. Warner chronicles the presence of the *Nights* in the subterranean currents of the Enlightenment, including the disciplines of anthropology and psychology. I demonstrate that the famous European *Nights* translators took credit for the composition of stories and commentaries greatly shaped by unsung collaborators and informants, notably Diyab. On Galland, the teacher may read the work of Mohamed Abdel-Halim (for a biography), Frédéric Bauden and Richard Waller (for a critical edition of his Parisian diary [Galland, *Journal*]), and Raymond Schwab (for a more literary appraisal), and on the French reception of the *Nights* Dominique Jullien (on Proust [*Amoureux*]), Sylvette Larzul (on the

Diyab tales), Sermain (for an edition of Galland), Ruth Bottigheimer (on parallels with the European tradition of the fairy tale), and Madeleine Dobie (for a postcolonial reading). Mack, van Leeuwen, Peter Caracciolo, and al-Musawi (*The Arabian Nights in Contemporary World Cultures*) are indispensable to the understanding of the influence of the *Nights* in eighteenth-, nineteenth- and twentieth-century letters.

Fittingly for a book that was printed with the figure of a maze in Burton's translation and has been compared by Borges to a maze ("Metaphors" 37), there is an interminable labyrinth of essay collections on the *Nights* in print. Many are excellent, but not all are easy to navigate for the nonspecialist teacher or the student. Among the most useful and handy are Marzolph's *The* Arabian Nights *Reader* and *The* Arabian Nights *in Transnational Perspective*, Ouyang and Geert Jan van Gelder's *New Perspectives on* Arabian Nights, Philip Kennedy and Warner's *Scheherazade's Children: Global Encounters with the* Arabian Nights, and Akel and William Granara's *The* Thousand and One Nights*: Sources and Transformations in Literature, Art, and Science*. A more comprehensive list of materials useful to teachers can be found in the bibliography drawn from the contributions to this volume.

Part Two

APPROACHES

Introduction

Paulo Lemos Horta

In recent decades, accelerating following the events of 9/11, the *Thousand and One Nights* has become a more frequent presence in world literature courses and other syllabi in the American academy. The impulse to turn to the *Nights* in the aftermath of a trauma that seemed to encapsulate the dangers of cross-cultural miscomprehension is understandable, though in some instances and respects, perhaps naive. Husain Haddawy, the Iraqi American translator, captures this gesture well in the epigraph to his translation of the *Nights*, dedicating his translation to those who have the grace of turning hate to love (*Arabian Nights*). Egyptian and Lebanese retellings of the *Nights* against the backdrop of the Arab Spring and the Syrian refugee crisis (Horta, "Beyond the Palace") only reaffirm the centrality of the story collection in the modern literary imaginary of the Middle East.

In the American classroom, however, the enormous diversity contained within the *Nights* sometimes works against the purpose for which the tales are most often employed: to represent Arab and Muslim cultures with sympathy. Shahrazad has become one of the most powerful feminist symbols of storytelling and resistance to political tyranny, greatly through the influence of rewritings by women authors within and outside the Middle East. Yet what the twenty-first-century reader registers as the misogyny of the original frame tale to the *Nights* may barely countenance such a strong and modern feminist reading. A course syllabus that samples only the frame narrative gives short shrift to Shahrazad's sisters, the many strong female characters who outwit their opponents in tales that help buttress the collection's feminist credentials: among them Badr, Dalila, Zumurrud, and the enslaved girl Tawaddud, who bests the foremost scholars of Baghdad.

Indeed, tales less frequently taught may surprise students with their tolerance of same-sex intimacy and sex in specific cultural milieus or their critiques of mercantile capitalism and dreams of socialist utopia. Seldom has such a widely taught text been so relatively little understood with regard to its original context of composition, compilation, and dissemination. The speed with which the *Nights* has become a staple of the American undergraduate experience has sometimes outpaced an understanding of what the story collection is and how it might best be taught to advantage in different contexts.

The first challenge for teachers of the *Nights* is determining whether to sample only from the original core of Arabic tales, and their specifically Arab and Muslim contexts, or also to include the more widely circulated tales added in French that were so instrumental in the European reception of the story collection. A crucial consideration is the choice of translation, whether the instructor seeks the most literal version or the most beautiful, whether the chief aim is authenticity or readability. Putting together the Everyman's Library edition of the *Nights* in 2014, Wen-chin Ouyang and I selected tales from different translations, both popular and scholarly (see Ouyang, *Arabian Nights*), and my own inclination is still to recommend different editions of the stories for distinct purposes rather than to privilege a single text as the definitive version. This is one of the lessons of Jorge Luis Borges's essay "The Translators of the *Thousand and One Nights*," which often figures in course syllabi as one of the most influential reflections on the enterprise of translation. Of course, I had not imagined the possibility that I would be able to commission a new translation to better serve students myself, as I have been able to do with *The Annotated Arabian Nights* (Seale).

In practice, all instructors of world history, film, and comparative religion and literature may be interested in certain common issues such as the animating conflicts between men and women and between Islam and other faiths within the story collection. All teachers of the *Nights* will benefit from the experience of other instructors regarding which tales might best inform lectures and animate class discussion from the vantage point of the analytical frameworks of feminism, Orientalism, postcolonialism, translation theory, and cinema studies, among others. A good pedagogical practice must perform all the above functions, for the scholar of Arabic or English and the generalist alike.

Scholars regard the tales of the *Nights* in their original contexts as windows into the lives of ordinary people at the time of their collation in Baghdad, Cairo, and Damascus in the fourteenth and fifteenth centuries. In this manner the story collection has served a similar function as Carlo Ginzburg's classic work of cultural history *The Cheese and the Worms: The Cosmos of a Sixteenth-Century Miller*. This is the emphasis of the most influential and widely taught secondary source on the *Nights*, Robert Irwin's *The Arabian Nights: A Companion*, originally published in 1994. Irwin writes of the work as street entertainment, of the relatively low status of its tellers, plying their trade in cafés, and of its typical dramatis personae as the outcasts of society. In this light, the tales illuminate the life of common folk, revealing, for instance, insights into common perceptions of sexual behavior. In more recent work, however, Irwin has sought to correct the bias of his *Companion*, recognizing, for example, the contrast in the story collection between the visions of the common people's politics and the more prevalent conservative affirmations of the power of figures of authority such as Caliph Harun al-Rashid.

The impulse to read the story collection as a window into the mores of a people was already pronounced in nineteenth-century translations by Edward William Lane and Richard Francis Burton, though it is important not to read too much into their influence on a wider European readership. After all, the most universally circulated versions of translations by Antoine Galland, Lane, and other European translators of the *Nights* omitted their original prefaces and gutted their notes and commentary, and it is not at all self-evident that early readers of the tales, whether under the rubric of the *Thousand and One Nights* or bound together with unrelated European tales, regarded them as realistic portraits of the Middle East. Chapbooks publishing individual tales such as "Aladdin and the Wonderful Lamp" were not shy in relocating the action to Paris, London, New York, or Copenhagen, further lessening the likelihood of readers' mistaking the tales for ethnographic documents.

Marvels and the supernatural have long preoccupied scholars in their interpretations of the reception and influence of the *Nights* in European letters. Scholars pay particular attention to the use of the plots and styles of the story collection in the genres of Romantic poetry, the Gothic, the fairy tale, science fiction, and fantasy. The broad perception of an association in the European imaginary between the *Nights* and the exotic has invited studies of Orientalism with reference to various media: book illustration, painting, set decoration, and dramatic, musical, and cinematic adaptations.

The exotic has also governed the attention of scholars in translation studies, with disproportionate attention paid to Burton's 1885 version, in his own time perhaps the least widely read of eighteenth- and nineteenth-century versions of the *Nights*, yet the most influential on avant-garde authors such as James Joyce in the early twenty-first century. Revising his classic study, *The Translator's Invisibility*, Lawrence Venuti proclaims Burton's *Nights* to be exemplary of the politics of foreignizing translation in his conclusion, entitled "A Call to Arms" (265–77). Postcolonial critics, notably Tarek Shamma, beg to differ, noting the dovetailing of Burton's foreignizing strategy of translation with stereotypical and racist attitudes of imperialist and Orientalist discourse. Shamma's intervention encapsulates the desire of postcolonial critics to answer the influence of Orientalist translations with the anticolonial retellings of Tayeb Saleh and Salman Rushdie, among others.

New scholarship has upended received expectations about the status of the *Nights* as alleged popular literature in Arabic letters, and as so-called marvelous fictions within European literatures. Aboubakr Chraïbi's research project pertaining to the Arabic and Turkish manuscripts of the *Nights*, published in 2016, has revolutionized the field (*Arabic Manuscripts*). In the mid-1980s Muhsin Mahdi could still speak of a corpus of less than a dozen known manuscripts of the story collection and privilege the most authentic of these (Thousand), providing the basis for Haddawy's English translation. Chraïbi and his research team have uncovered a dramatically expanded universe of partial and complete manuscripts of tales from the *Nights*, well over a hundred, though the existence of earlier manuscripts than Galland's remains to be documented (some manuscripts are still in private collections). Among the first casualties of his findings was the lingering assumption of the status of the story collection as low, popular, even trashy literature. Chraïbi prefers the term *middle Arabic literature* to classify the register of the tales (*Arabic Manuscripts* 62–64). In fact, manuscripts of the *Nights* have been found in the most prominent libraries associated with higher and canonical literatures, such as the Süleymaniye Mosque in Istanbul and Christian monasteries across the Middle East (belles lettres was not anathema to these institutions). As scholars begin to decipher the marginalia of scholars, monks, and imams, a radically expanded understanding of the literary and historical function of the work will be available.

Robert Irwin's writing on the debt of realist fiction to the *Nights*, in turn, has exploded the assumption that the *Nights* was incorporated into European letters merely as escapism and exoticism. Even the supernaturalism of the *Nights*, Marina Warner argues, spoke to the undercurrents of modernity within Enlightenment Europe, notably the disciplines of psychology and anthropology. Edward Said's project of bringing the literary traditions of Europe and the Middle East into dialogue animates Warner's work, even as Warner demonstrates the possibility of more nuanced readings of the presence of the *Nights* in European letters, including the imperial and postcolonial. Whereas Warner is principally concerned with tales of magic, Irwin shows that the realism of eighteenth- and nineteenth-century European prose was no less indebted to the *Nights'* tales of cities peopled with merchants, porters, and cobblers.

In the light of this scholarship, a much more nuanced understanding of the role of imperialism and Orientalism in disseminating the tales of the *Nights* in a much wider range of literary texts has become available. Comparative and postcolonial approaches also offer a broader panorama of voices for scholars and teachers to sample, where Salman Rushdie and Orhan Pamuk are juxtaposed with other retellers of the *Nights* from the Maghreb and the Persian Gulf.

Much richer and more precise contextual understandings of the *Nights* in Arabic and European letters afford the teacher the opportunity to ask more specific questions in the classroom. With regard to the role of women in the *Nights*, one might ask, Whose misogyny, whose feminism? In tales throughout the story collection, women are depicted, often simultaneously, as evil and deceitful and as wise and brave. Much attention has been lavished on tales in which women's agency rests in their use of sorcery and magic, but in the frame tale and many embedded tales, women persevere through their superior wit, cunning, and knowledge. As discoveries continue to be made in the manuscript history of the *Nights*, scholars can begin to ask how stories of strong, clever women served particular audiences, and stories of deceitful, malicious women served others. Or were portraits of women as clever or deceitful intended or received as two sides of the same coin? Furthermore, the new availability of other story collections that contain some of the same tales provides the scholar with an unprecedented opportunity for comparison. For instance, in the tales of the *Hundred and One Nights* (translated by Bruce Fudge), Shahrazad's sister Dunyazad plays a critical redemptive role. The Lebanese novelist Hanan al-Shaykh's addition to the vast corpus of feminist retellings of the *Thousand and One Nights* affords the pedagogue a comparative vantage point from which to gather a rich variety of contemporary feminist perspectives on the story collection, within and outside the Middle East.

This treasure trove of new riches allows the teacher to deal with the particular challenge of teaching such popular tales—namely, the students' familiarity, and in some cases overfamiliarity, with the material. Students' encyclopedic knowledge of particular canons of *Nights*-related lore will never cease to amaze me. I will never rival my students' knowledge of the City of Brass expansion to Dungeons and Dragons, the myriad Bollywood versions of "Ali Baba and the Forty Thieves," the anime and manga series based on the voyages of Sindbad, the episodes of the Egyptian soap opera based on "Dalila the Crafty," or for that matter the Turkish soap operas set in the universe of the *Nights*. The student who signs up for a unit or course on the *Nights* may well be an autodidact with strong opinions on the relative merits of the DreamWorks *Sinbad* and the Disney *Aladdins* or on Burton vis-à-vis other translators of the story collection. Since few corners of the globe appear to lack their own cultural takes on stories from the collection, teachers should be ready to be surpassed in their knowledge of Russian operas, central European retellings, and Ethiopian lore regarding the tales and jinn of the *Nights*. The trick is to provide resources, critical methods, and analytical tools for case studies of material with which students may already be familiar.

This task has been rendered easier by new scholarship that again affiliates the so-called orphan tales more firmly within traditions of storytelling in and beyond the Middle East in its commerce with other regions. Hanna Diyab, the fabled storyteller remembered by Galland in his Parisian diary of 1709, has now been confirmed as a creative agent and author in his own right, bridging the universe of the cafés and storytelling of his native Aleppo with his own experience of Paris and Versailles. The stories added to the canon of the *Nights* by the Syrian storyteller and the French translator, such as "Ali Baba" and "Aladdin," are restored to the status of tales with a proven Arab provenance, even if they were added in French. There is an emerging critical consensus that "Aladdin," "Ali Baba," and other tales added through his intervention should be known as "Diyab's tales."

It is thus much easier to bridge students' knowledge and interest in the most famous tales added in French with a broader canon of stories inclusive of the original cycle of core tales in Arabic, as well as famous additions from the Arabic like the story cycle of Sindbad. New scholarship on both the previously neglected manuscripts of the Arabic stories and Diyab's role in ushering the French tales into publication in Paris in 1709 dovetail in suggesting the inadvisability of insisting on notions of authenticity when determining the limits or contours of the collection of tales known as the *Thousand and One Nights*.

In turn, students' familiarity with manifestations of the *Nights* in popular culture and their critical grasp of patterns of misrepresentation of the Middle East in the mass media allow the teacher to address questions of Orientalism with some complexity. Given high awareness of the stakes of debates pertaining to migrants and refugees from the Middle East in Europe and the United States, students are receptive to the varied concerns of scholars writing from and about the Middle East. If the political context for such study is sometimes somber, the tools at the teacher's disposal have never been richer.

CONTEXTS OF ORIGIN

The *Thousand and One Nights* as Arabic Literature
Bruce Fudge

The Moroccan critic Abdelfattah Kilito has attempted, on several occasions, to describe the unstated criteria by which a work may be included in the canon of "classical Arabic literature." In his estimation, these qualities are the following: it must have an identifiable author; it must be written down, preferably at the urging of some distinguished patron; it should contain citations of or references to earlier works, such that its literary genealogy is evident; its language should be difficult; it should require commentary and be inaccessible to those without the proper education (e.g., *Arabes* 131–33). The *Thousand and One Nights* (*Alf laylah wa-laylah*) did not meet these requirements and was excluded from the shelves of respectable Arab letters, a trend largely continued by Western scholars. When the *Nights* appear on an Arabic literature syllabus, they are usually tacked on at the end, outside the general chronology or conventional classifications. This is not exclusively a Western phenomenon, however. Kilito himself notes that in reading the *Nights* he felt he was stepping outside of the Arabic tradition:

> D'ailleurs, les *Nuits* font-elles partie de cette littérature? Il me semble qu'elle peut s'en passer, et en réalité elle s'en est bien passée. Elle serait exactement la même si cette œuvre n'existait pas, alors que son paysage serait, à l'évidence, complètement différent sans les *mu'allaqât*, ces fameuses odes "suspendues," ou sans les *maqâmât*. Dans les histoires plus ou moins récentes de la littérature arabe, le livre des *Nuits* ne figure dans aucune des rubriques communément retenues; il ne s'est pas rattaché, par exemple,

> à une chronologie (même si l'on sait que l'une de ses premières versions est contemporaine de Hamadhânî et de Tanûkhî); il n'apparaît pas, dans le chapitre consacré à la prose, à côté de *Kalîla et Dimna* ou de *L'Epître du pardon*. Ce n'est généralement qu'en fin de parcours qu'il est cité, et comme par acquit de conscience, dans le voisinage du Roman de Dhât al-Himma et du Roman de Sayf ibn Dhî Yazan, à côté d'autres œuvres au statut indéterminé.   (*Arabes* 130–31)
>
> For that matter, is the *Nights* really part of that literature? It certainly seems to have done well outside of it. Arabic literature would not look any different if the *Nights* had never existed, but the absence of, say, the *Muʿallaqāt*, the celebrated "hanging odes," or the *maqāmāt* would completely alter the literary landscape. In recent histories of Arabic literature, the *Nights* does not figure under any of the conventional rubrics: it does not form part of the chronology (even if we know that one of the first version was contemporary with Hamadhānī and Tanūkhī); it never appears alongside *Kalīlah and Dimnah* or the *Epistle of Forgiveness* in the chapter on prose. It is generally cited at the end, as if out of a sense of duty, in the company of *Dhāt al-himmah* and *Sayf ibn Dhī Yazan* and other works of indeterminate status and identity.   (my trans.)[1]

So what of the Arabic origins of the *Nights*? Shahrazad's storytelling may appear here as an anomaly, a sui generis compilation that stands apart from all other premodern Arabic poetry and prose. That is simply not the case, however. Whatever the myriad influences on the collection, the *Nights* is very much a product of its own Arab Islamic milieu, and an understanding of the relations between work and milieu will produce, one dares to hope, better readers of the *Nights* and a broader vision of the history of Arabic literature.

There are many ways to see the importance of the Arabic context and origins of the *Thousand and One Nights*. This essay looks at three: the history of the collection, the origins of individual stories, and literary forms and structures.

History of the Texts

The history of the text of the *Thousand and One Nights* usually entails the question, "Which *Nights*?" For the existing manuscripts, editions, and translations, the reader may consult Ulrich Marzolph's contribution to this volume. I discuss an earlier period, when the *Nights* in some form existed, but from which no versions have survived.

The oldest known manuscript is that used by Antoine Galland for his French translation of 1704 to 1717. It dates probably from the fifteenth century. We nonetheless know that a work with the same or a similar title and frame story existed over half a millennium before. There are at least three witnesses to the presence of Shahrazad in Arabic before 1000, and all are easily accessible in translation.

The first is a very small manuscript fragment dating to the ninth century, studied in detail by Nabia Abbott. Her essay serves as an excellent example to students of the painstaking work involved in reconstructing the history of texts. Two tenth-century authors left us descriptions of a work translated from the Persian known as *Hezār afsāneh* (*A Thousand Tales*). The first is al-Masʿūdī in his compendium *Murūj al-dhahab* (*Meadows of Gold*); the second is the Baghdad bookseller Ibn al-Nadīm's inventory, the *Fihrist*. Conveniently, Abbott translates both passages in her essay on the manuscript fragment (150–51). Ibn al-Nadīm's account is somewhat more detailed, but both give a skeletal version of what is unmistakably the frame story of Shahrazad telling tales to save her life.

Students tend to focus immediately on the plot description, but Ibn al-Nadīm and al-Masʿūdī are less concerned with the story itself than with the context. The story of Shahrazad is listed as one of several sources translated into Arabic from other languages, and these passages are perfect illustrations of the Abbasid culture of translation and cultural borrowing and adaptation (see Gutas). This movement is primarily associated with translations of philosophical and scientific works from Syriac or Greek, but there were other languages and genres involved as well, and the *Thousand and One Nights* owes its existence to this process. Any survey of Arabic literature or Islamic history will treat the translation movement, but the *Nights* is seldom if ever mentioned.

Students may also notice from these excerpts the context of the works among which the *Thousand and One Nights* is listed. There is a didactic or moralistic aspect to the other collections; they were not pure entertainment. In order to emphasize this aspect, one should perhaps tweak Abbott's translation. Describing how Alexander the Great was the first to have stories recounted to him at night, Ibn al-Nadīm is careful to specify that Alexander did so not for pleasure "but only as a means of keeping vigilant and on his guard" (Abbott 150). The sense is more likely that he sought to protect and improve himself by means of the examples given in the tales. That is, there was some moral or otherwise beneficial purpose to these stories, something to be gained or learned from listening to them. To acknowledge this context helps to understand the ambiguous status of the *Nights*: entertaining stories are a serious business.

Another point is that if the collection came to Baghdad via Iran, it could not have contained the tales we know so well, featuring the caliph Harun al-Rashid and various Islamic metropolises. So, from the very start, we can see that the collection must have undergone various modifications and transformations, although the Shahrazad story, still not without changes, remained a relatively stable frame for the inclusion of various tales.

Having established the existence (and unstable identity) of the collection, we might then ask, Who read it and what did they think of it? Here we see that a few bad reviews are no reason to despair. If medieval Arab Islamic scholars had any kind words for the *Nights*, they did not write them down. Opinions are uniformly negative, beginning with Ibn al-Nadīm, whose summary concluded with these words: "I have seen it in its entirety several times. It is in reality a coarse book of silly tales" (*Al-Fihrist* [Tajaddod] 363; my trans.).[2] In the following centuries, some scholars followed Ibn al-Nadīm in a critique of the collection's literary merits, whereas others condemned the wasteful practice of frivolous reading. (Note that the most common modern complaint, of obscene or pornographic elements, is absent.) Examples of such judgments are collected in Aboubakr Chraïbi (Mille et une nuits 3–49) and Dwight Reynolds ("Popular Prose" 252–54, 266). Most evidently, these critical passages seem to confirm an image of a group of conservative scholars attempting to control both literary and moral standards.

But a careful reading will show there is more going on here. Students should notice that, despite the negative judgments, the authors cited all seem to be familiar with the *Nights* and its contents (although there is the possibility they are simply repeating received opinion). Whatever the highbrow judgment, clearly the collection was well known and widely circulated. Second, they refer unambiguously to the *Nights* as a written text. There is no question of an oral tradition here. Despite the ubiquitous image of Middle Eastern families reciting stories from generation to generation, the tales of the *Nights* were written down; they were distinct from oral storytelling or folktales. This fact is important for understanding both the nature of the narratives and their transmission. (This is not to deny the potential overlapping or migration of tales between the oral and the written: see Sadan; Marzolph, "The *Arabian Nights* in Comparative Folk Narrative Research.") The final thing for students to notice is that the *Nights* is seldom mentioned alone. Most often the collection is mentioned alongside other frivolous or inferior works, and sometimes criticism of this kind of narrative does not mention the *Nights* specifically. The stories do not exist in isolation. They were in fact part of a much larger pool of stories.

Sources and Variants: Where Do These Stories Originate?

If the stories did not circulate orally as folktales, then where did they come from? Some, such as the tales of the Seven Viziers or the Ebony Horse (as well as the frame story), have origins farther to the east, but there are a fantastic number of parallels in Arabic writings as well, very often unexplored.

Libraries throughout the Middle East and Europe contain many anonymous, untitled manuscripts of similar (sometimes identical) entertaining tales. The *Thousand and One Nights* is distinguished not only by its extraordinarily compelling frame story (and some brilliantly crafted initial story cycles) but also by having a title. Of all these manuscript collections of popular storytelling, it seems that only two others are sufficiently well known to have titles and be published and recently made available in English. These are the *Hundred and One Nights*, also featuring Shahrazad, though in a frame that likely predates that of the

Thousand and One Nights (see Fudge, *Hundred*). The other is a work based on a unique Istanbul manuscript edited and published by Hans Wehr in 1956 and translated into English by Malcolm C. Lyons as *Tales of the Marvellous and News of the Strange*.[3] There are countless more stories collected and bound together in various versions and permutations, but it is difficult to discuss collections that do not have names. (Perhaps to Kilito's list of classical criteria one should add the following: must have or acquire a title.)

The point is that the *Thousand and One Nights* is just one (admittedly very impressive) story collection among many others of the same type and much of its content appears in other manuscript collections. Most if not all the stories exist or existed in various versions. A tale may be told differently in one edition of the *Nights* than in another. In some cases, though, we can even see the same tale in an entirely different genre of writing.

A good example, excellent for teaching purposes, is "The Inspector's Story," which forms part of the Hunchback cycle, one of the first in the traditional *Nights* arrangement. This delightful story has an analogue in a tenth-century anthology, *Al-Faraj baʿd al-shiddah* (*Deliverance after Distress*) of al-Tanūkhī. Muhsin Mahdi compares the two stories and provides a great deal of historical detail ("From History"). He is especially concerned with a distinction between "history" (al-Tanūkhī) and "fiction" (*Nights*). Students can benefit from his historical and philological knowledge while questioning his literary analysis. But the comparison shows how closely a *Nights* tale can resemble more conventional Arabic letters: these two are clearly the same tale and there is nothing marginal about the sources of *Nights* here.

Another profitable avenue for discovering how a *Nights* tale might incorporate sources from other genres is a reading of "The City of Brass," a remarkable tale of travel, adventure, and renunciation set in the North Africa of the Umayyad period, as men go in search of jinn that the prophet Solomon had long ago locked in brass bottles. The story draws on various elements of histories (both of the pre-Islamic prophets and of Umayyad times), Qurʾanic verses and commentary, pre-Islamic poetry, and various fanciful travel accounts and imaginative geography. Again, one of the most striking tales in the *Nights* is assembled almost entirely from other, apparently more respectable, Arab Islamic sources. (On the tale and its various geographic, exegetical, and historical sources, see Fudge, "Signs of Scripture"; Hamori, *On the Art*.)

Laying sources aside, there is also the question of variant versions of the tales themselves. "The City of Brass," for instance, exists in various versions both within and without different *Nights* editions. It is instructive to note how flexible these narratives can be. Possible reading assignments could be

> "The Story of Sindbad and the Seven Viziers" in both the *Thousand and One Nights* and the *Hundred and One Nights*;
>
> "The Ebony Horse" in both the *Thousand and One Nights* and the *Hundred and One Nights*;

"The Story of the Barber's Brothers" from the *Thousand and One Nights* and "The Story of the Six Men" from *Tales of the Marvellous and News of the Strange*; and

"The City of Brass" with any of the similar, treasure-hunting, world-renouncing tales such as "The Camphor Island" or "The Vizier and His Son" of the *Hundred and One Nights* or "The Four Hidden Treasures" from *Tales of the Marvellous*.

The list could go on. All of the above are available in English translation. A manageable exercise using Arabic sources is the juxtaposition of three short narratives featuring a Muslim warrior fighting the Franks who gets lost in the wild and is taken in by a beautiful Byzantine woman. The episode appears in the tale "Umar bin Nuʻmān" (nights 46 through 48 of the *Thousand and One Nights*) and has its analogues in a fourteenth-century historical chronicle (Ibn Kathīr 181–83) and in the expansive popular *sīrah* (often translated "epic") *Sīrat al-Amīrah Dhāt al-himmah* (396). The same episode is treated differently according to the genre in which it appears. As a bonus, Ibn Kathīr's account contains one of the condemnations of entertaining tales mentioned above, although the *Nights* are here spared.

The purpose of such comparative readings is to demonstrate the fluidity, the malleability of the narrative components, as well as to grasp how they are assembled from other elements of the culture. This is not merely a matter of knowing the historical context of the tales; it has implications for how we read and interpret them as well. We see the prominence of motifs as the essential components of storytelling, and the existence of myriad variants may give us pause before we proceed to a thematic analysis.

Formal Qualities

In *The* Arabian Nights*: A Companion*, Robert Irwin notes that the *Nights* and comparable Arabic fictions are governed by "rules" and "invisible constraints." The reader may initially wonder at the marvels of Shahrazad's world, but "after a while, [one] starts to notice things—such as how many of the heroes of the *Nights* are born to elderly couples who pray for a child.... In time, each story comes to resemble another story, and the reader begins to recognize the patterns and permutations" (214). I would take this further. One would ideally read not just more *Nights* tales (though that is always a good thing) but also more versions of the same stories and their analogues in other genres. Reading tales in isolation does not give us a sense of how they were put together; reading them all together gives us an idea of how they would have been received, how they would have appealed to their premodern readers.

So if one does read more and more of this kind of tale, whether in the *Thousand and One Nights* or analogous collections, what features or qualities does one find?

The most obvious is repetition. Various motifs, events, stock figures, and story lines recur, but the repetition occurs also at the level of language. Words, phrases, descriptions, and epithets, almost always simple and easy to understand, are recycled over and again. Very little is withheld from the reader and, for the most part, plots are familiar and straightforward. Clearly, scribes were not aiming to keep the reader or listener in suspense, at least not by means of the plot. What they did value was a sense of the strange or exotic. The emphasis on wonder is important here, although it may take various forms (Chraïbi, *Arabic Manuscripts* 42–62; Mottahedeh). "The City of Brass" and the Hunchback cycle serve well for an examination of wonder.

Wonder and repetition may seem like curious bedfellows, but in fact it is precisely the capacity to create astonishing situations with a limited stock of motifs that constitutes the genius of the *Nights* at their best.[4] We might say, with H. A. R. Gibb, that this type of literature is "standardized and almost stereotyped in its main lines," that the author or storyteller "was obliged to keep within the range of themes which his audience understood," and that "to strike out on fresh paths . . . would have outstripped their confirmation" (18, 19). In a similar vein, Andras Hamori writes that the repetitive use of a limited number of motifs and patterns is coupled with a "sedimentation of convention" and "reticent patterns of composition" that characterize the genre as a whole (Hamori, *On the Art* vii).

These are perceptive characterizations of *Nights*-style narratives. If the reader does not recall Gibb and Hamori making them, that is because they did not. The citations are, in fact, descriptions of classical Arabic poetry, a genre that would appear to have little in common with our semipopular narratives.

Let us note further formal similarities across various Arabic literary genres: frequent insertion of verse (sometimes poetry known from other poems, sometimes variations of lines found elsewhere; see Heinrichs); frequent passages in rhymed prose; direct and indirect references to the Qur'an; an ambiguous attitude toward what we now refer to as "plagiarism"; a tendency to report all information as coming from somewhere else, in what seems a reluctance to acknowledge the creative process, seen here with tales beginning, "it is said" or "reported," and so on. As a sort of summation, we might cite Julia Bray: "[M]edieval Arabic writings . . . are characterized to a very high degree by the repetition and reshaping of earlier narratives and their recombination in new patterns and series in such a way as to emphasise certain themes which, one may suppose, seem particularly significant to the reorganiser" ("Caliph" 160).

It is not merely a matter of shared formal components. The thematic elements, prominent in the frame tale and the initial story cycles, are common too in more so-called canonical literature: justice, punishment, fate, power and its abuses. The essays by Hamori are particularly pertinent (*On the Art* and "Comic Romance"). Finally, geographic, historical, and architectural details may reveal much about the background of individual tales, and here Jean-Claude Garcin's "historical reading" of the *Nights* is always worth consulting, bringing a social historian's eye to the collection.

In terms of both form and content, then, there is no reason to consider the *Thousand and One Nights* (and other stories such as those of *Tales of the Marvellous* or the *Hundred and One Nights*) as something apart from the rest of Arabic literature. The similarities are much greater than the differences.

In reading the *Nights* as Arabic literature, it is primarily the latter that stands to benefit. Its inclusion as a central (or at least nonmarginal) element widens the scope of the field, adds more narrative sources, and moves us away from the rarefied world of the poets and litterateurs while still—and this is essential—demonstrating the diffusion of elite themes and qualities into different genres and registers.

Comparing the reputation of the *Nights* in Arabic and in translation, it may appear that the former is one of disparagement, the latter of success. But this is not entirely correct. If premodern Arab Islamic writers were critical, it is nonetheless the case that the Arabic *Nights* were widely copied and widely read. And if European readers devoured the first translations, they had their share of critics as well, and we would do well to ask why so many translators felt the need to improve the *Nights*, to make it useful or morally beneficial, and why it has been largely relegated, outside of academe, to the world of children's entertainment. To its credit, the *Nights* itself contains hints of this ambiguity: in some manuscripts, the king is ready to execute Shahrazad on the thousand-and-first night, not least out of excruciating boredom. (The great Orientalist Antoine-Isaac Silvestre de Sacy remarked that at this point the king was surely not the only one feeling that way [52].)

The premodern critiques are no doubt perfectly valid: the *Nights* probably do appear in a less flattering light when viewed by one steeped in classic Arab Islamic literary culture. But the same might go for one steeped in European literature. Whatever specific Arabic qualities may be lost in translation, the popular and unpretentious character of the *Nights* remains constant, across time and across cultures.

NOTES

1. Kilito's Arabic text was also consulted in preparing the translation (*Al-Adab wal-irtiyāb* 50).

2. This passage from Ibn al-Nadīm is often cited from the translation by Bayard Dodge, who renders the last phrase, "bārid al-ḥadīth" ("a silly book"), as "without warmth in the telling" (Fihrist *of al-Nadīm* 2: 714). *Bārid* literally means "cold," but it is occasionally used in literary criticism to mean "vapid" or "insipid."

3. Even this is in fact a generic title, but in Orientalist circles, in any case, it has become associated with this particular manuscript and its edition.

4. The reliance on a limited repertoire of motifs is especially evident in the *Hundred and One Nights*.

The *Thousand and One Nights* and Rethinking Arabic Literature

Wen-chin Ouyang

Muḥammad ibn Isḥaq ibn al-Nadīm famously wrote of the Arabic *Thousand Nights* (*Alf laylah*) as a translation of a storybook originally written in Persian and known as *Hazār afsān* (*A Thousand Stories*), a book of fictional tales (*khurāfāt*) told at night (*asmār*).[1] By the time Ibn al-Nadīm included that description in the catalogue, *Fihrist*, of the extensive holdings in his bookshop in tenth-century Baghdad, Arabic writers, whom he described as versed in *bulaghā'* and *fuṣaḥā'* (i.e., the literary arts), had already polished the *Nights*' language and begun to write in a similar vein. *Hazār afsān*, said to have been written for a Persian princess by the name of Humani, daughter of Bahman, begins with a king, who beds a different woman every night and kills her at dawn, marrying a princess by the name of Shahrazad, who is both "intelligent and wise" ("lahā 'aql wa dirāyah") and starts telling him stories at night that stop mid-track at dawn. He stays her execution so as to find out how the story will end the following night. This goes on for one thousand nights, until Shahrazad bears the king a child. When she confesses her machinations, rather than punishing her for her deception, the king finds himself in love with this wise woman and remains married to her. The king has a housekeeper (*Qahrimāna*) by the name of Dīnārzād, who is in cahoots with Shahrazad.

Of course, Alexander the Great, Ibn al-Nadīm let it be known, was the first person in history who turned to storytelling at night during his military campaigns. He had among his entourage clowns and storytellers, who were there not to entertain but rather to help him stay awake and keep watch. Kings after him used *Hazār afsān* for similar purposes. The book contained fewer than two hundred stories, for each would be told over a period of few nights. Its "insipid language" ("ghathth bārid al-ḥadīth"), Ibn al-Nadīm noted, did not prevent known literary figures such as Abū 'Abdallāh Muḥammad ibn 'Abdūs al-Jahshiyārī, the renowned tenth-century author of the *Book of Viziers and Secretaries*, from emulating its form and collecting Arabic, Persian, and Greek stories in one book, albeit eschewing the night-within-and-into-night structure of storytelling. Each night would rather contain a self-sufficient story. Al-Jahshiyārī collected 480 stories or nights, and these he copied by hand in around fifty folios, but he died before he could bring the number up to a full thousand.

Two other well-known works are mentioned in the same chapter (8) and section (the first of three) on nocturnal and fictional storytelling: *Sindbadnāma* (a.k.a. *The Seven Sages*) and *Kalīla wa-Dimna*. Ibn al-Nadīm then defers the discussion of these until the following paragraph on Indian storybooks. These two books, though said to be of Indian origin, were translated into Arabic from Middle Persian, by writers known for the beauty of their style, such as Ibn al-Muqaffa', whose

Arabic renditions of pre-Islamic Persian works are today considered an integral, even indispensable part of the classical Arabic literary canon, *adab*. The works of Ibn al-Muqaffaʻ, whether considered translations or adaptations, including the animal fables in *Kalīla wa-Dimna*, have become so assimilated into the fabric of the Arabic literary language that it is not possible to even think of Ibn al-Muqaffaʻ as a mere translator and his works as foreign and, as such, uncanonical.

Ibn al-Nadīm's survey of translated storybooks already drops hints of the divergent destinies of the *Thousand and One Nights* and *Kalīla wa-Dimna*. The anonymity of its translator and its "insipid language" seem to have relegated the former to the "popular" field of Arabic cultural production, together with the "epics" (*sīra*), whereas the latter, thanks to its famed translator and the acclaimed elegance of his style, is elevated to so-called high literature as epitome of the "mirror for princes" genre. The *Thousand and One Nights*, despite its popularity even among the cultural elite, was of no literary consequence until the twentieth century, after the work had acquired the status of world literature in Europe, and when fiction, particularly the novel, rose to prominence in the Arabic field of literary production. The recent revisionist history of the *Thousand and One Nights*, whether theorized in fiction or argued in criticism, raises questions in regard to contemporary, perhaps even nationalist, canonization of classical Arabic literature and attendant classification, or categorization, of premodern Arabic writings into a variety of discreet literary fields based in periodization—classical, postclassical, and modern—or language register—classical, middle, and colloquial—where the postclassical and middle more often than not aligned with the Ottoman rule of the Islamic Caliphate (1362–1924) and, foreignized in nationalist historiography as non-Arab, are seen as a symptom of decline in Arabic letters.

Its lack of canonical status, however, did not negatively impact its popularity and the steady rise of its esteem among Arab writers and critics since the nineteenth century. It inspired Mārūn al-Naqqāsh, the Beiruti pioneer of Arabic theater, who wrote and staged *Abū al-Ḥasan al-Mughaffal and Hārūn al-Rashīd* as early as 1850. It is not clear whether he knew of the popularity of the *Thousand and One Nights* in Europe. He did spend a good number of years in Italy, and, even though the *Thousand and One Nights* was translated into Italian only in 1949 by a team of Arabists headed by Francesco Gabrieli, al-Naqqāsh could have very well got caught up in the *Arabian Nights* fever spreading like fire across Europe since Antoine Galland translated, or rather adapted into French, a body of stories from a fifteenth-century manuscript and other sources in twelve volumes between 1704 and 1717. The regular appearance of the *Thousand and One Nights* in nineteenth-century Arabic print culture, which has yet to be studied and analyzed, culminated in literary adaptations, such as Tawfīq al-Ḥakīm's 1934 play, *Shahrazād*, Tāhā Ḥusayn's 1943 novel, *Aḥlām Shahrazād* (*Shahrazad's Dreams*), and their 1936 coauthored novel, *Al-Qaṣr al-mashḥūr* (*The Enchanted Palace*), and in serious scholarship, such as Sahtr al-Qalamāwī's 1943 book, *Alf layla wa-layla*, based on her 1941 Cairo University doctoral thesis, supervised by Tāhā Ḥusayn. Since the second half of the twentieth century, and in spite of occasional bans in Arab countries, the *Thousand and One Nights* has been increasingly seen as an important work of Arabic literature. It is subject to infinite evocation, adaptation, and rewriting in poetry, fiction, theater, television, and cinema in the Arabic-speaking parts of the world.

Arabic scholarship today more readily accepts, or even owns, the *Thousand and One Nights* as a significant work of Arabic literature. 'Abdallāh Tāj's *Maṣādir "Alf layla wa-layla" al-'arabiyya* (*Arabic Sources of the* Thousand and One Nights) sees it as the library of premodern Arabic literature, in which all genres of Arabic writings are represented. If Tāj's work reasserts al-Qalamāwī's earlier observations of the plethora of Arabic and Islamic themes and motifs in the *Thousand and One Nights*, it additionally shows, through comparative analysis, where the *Thousand and One Nights* overlaps with various genres of Arabic writing and diverges in its engagement with the same themes and motifs. This view of the *Thousand and One Nights* within the Arabic literary context is made possible by an unproblematized reliance on the supposed final product of a long tradition of constant transformation, the so-called Zotenberg Egyptian recension, which does contain 1,001 nights and is reflected in print, with slight variations, by the editions known as the Bulaq (1835) and the Macnaghten or Calcutta II (1839–42).

The development of the text into these two apparently full versions from Galland's fifteenth-century manuscript and a variety of analogous manuscripts is at the heart of a key international inquiry that attempts to map the premodern global network of translation, adaptation, and creation, from East and South Asia to the Mediterranean, that produced the textual network—or a body of overlapping texts written in Middle Arabic—we can call the *Thousand and One Nights*. A parallel key international inquiry tracks the post-Galland global proliferation of the so-called Oriental tale, including "Aladdin" and "Ali Baba," two orphan tales traceable neither to oral nor written Arabic origins, and considers its impact on literature, the visual arts, music, theater, and popular cultures across the six continents of the world.

The *Thousand and One Nights* is in the state-of-the-art research a shape-shifting chameleon that survives and thrives in globe-trotting and crossing historical, geographic, cultural, linguistic, medial, and generic boundaries, and as such can serve as a key site for the interrogation of the boundaries between the canonical and popular, classical and modern, global and local, sacred and secular, oral and written, and literature and other cultural expressions in multilingual and multicultural fields of production in literary and cultural studies. The status of its text, be it the work, as varying collections of stories, or each story within each collection (and their development across genres, historical eras, and cultures), and the centrality of intertextuality in its composition, whether with religious texts (including the Qur'an and *Tales of the Prophets*), poetry, *adab*, travel literature, geographic and historical works, or pious and courtly storytelling, open vistas for rethinking the ways Arabic literature has been taught at institutions of higher education in the Arab world and outside.

At SOAS, University of London, the *Thousand and One Nights* is taught in two contexts: comparative or world literature and Arabic literature. In the first context it is taught as a foundational text in world literature. We look at the global circulation of the *Thousand and One Nights*—through translation and adaptation of stories (or a body of stories) in literary classics, world fiction, or cinema and television—and the impact of such circulation on modes of reading are considered and rethought. Orientalism, as a body of knowledge about the Orient and complex intercultural discourse, is at the center of this inquiry. In the second context, the very notions of *literature* and a *literary canon*, as secular, fixed, authoritative, and based in so-called high Arabic language, are explored through the prism of intertextuality and the attendant theories of textuality and intertextuality, orality and writing, genres, genre ideologies, and generic boundaries. Two lines of inquiry, both grounded in a common set of recurring, inexorably bound up aesthetics, ethics, and politics, are pursued: what the intertextuality between the *Thousand and One Nights* and other classical genres of writing tells us about premodern literary cultures of the Middle East and what the proliferation of premodern popular stories in contemporary fiction and cinema tells us about the abiding relevance of the set of recurring aesthetics, ethics, and politics today.

Literatures of the Near and Middle East is a first-year undergraduate course aimed at students of the BA in Middle Eastern Studies, an interdisciplinary degree that offers single as well as multiple language pathways with training in cultural and literary studies. This course looks at ancient Near Eastern literatures, particularly those written in Akkadian, Hittite, and Sumerian comparatively with medieval Middle Eastern literatures in Arabic, Hebrew, Persian, and Turkish, focusing on the city, cultural encounter, individual identity and imagined communities, gender, and representation within the writing systems, literary traditions, and genres of storytelling of the region. The *Thousand and One Nights* is taught in translation as a premodern Arabic literary work produced in regional collaboration within a broader global history. Attention is drawn to the role of Orientalism in elevating it to the status of world literature in the eighteenth and nineteenth centuries, and then to that of a so-called canonical compendium of storytelling in Arabic literature in the twentieth century. Through its overlap with the tales of the prophets, epics, and animal fables, its relation to biblical folklore; Indian and Persian traditions, such as *Kalīla wa-Dimna*; and Islamic legends are considered. A close reading of the "Mock Caliph," for example, allows for the exploration of the relation between urban space and the architecture of the story. In this story of Harun al-Rashid's nocturnal wandering in the medieval city of Baghdad, the planning of the round city serves as the blueprint for the tale's narrative movement (see the essay by Nadine Roth in this volume). More important, al-Rashid's encounter with the mock caliph on the river (Tigris) gives us a spatial configuration in the *Thousand and One Nights*: the land, or city, as reason and control and the sea as passion and lawlessness. Through the interplay between what goes on at sea and what happens on land, the notions of just rule and good citizenship are defined, tested, and confirmed.

The *Thousand and One Nights* is read in Arabic in Introduction to Arabic Literature, a second-year course in the BA Arabic degree program at SOAS that offers a survey of premodern and modern conceptualizations of literature and its role in society based in reading original texts at the appropriate level. The course is equally interested in the development of Arabic literature from pre-Islamic times to the present and in the role of cultural encounters in this development. "The Ox and the Donkey," the story Shahrazad's father tells her in admonishment in the frame tale, is read comparatively with "The Lion and the Ox" (Fishbein 62–145) and against the background of Ibn al-Nadīm's *Al-Fihrist* to highlight their shared history as translated texts and their common purpose as "education of the king" and "mirror for princes," which inform and underpin classical Arabic *adab* and its multicultural and multifaith sources and fabric, then interrogate the very categories into which they have been classified: popular storytelling expressed in Middle Arabic and canonical literature written in classical Arabic.

Culture, Society, and Politics in Classical Arabic Literature, a fourth-year course within the same degree program, also based in reading literary texts in the original Arabic, picks up the generic and didactic threads and expands on the ways the *Thousand and One Nights* engages dialogically with the tales of the prophets and mystical meditations through rewriting biblical folklore. It is seen as a site of confluence of the diverse cultures, religions, and literary traditions of the Middle East and of transformation during its travels from one cultural sphere to another, and across different genres in one cultural sphere. Solomon legends permeate the *Thousand and One Nights* stories, for example, and they give "The Fisherman and the Jinni," "The City of Brass," and "The Queen of Serpents" their fantasy, spirituality and adventure not to mention their jinn, demons, and treasures. Beneath these discourses on and allegories of political power, from model kingship in "The Fisherman and the Jinni" to its ephemeral nature in "The City of Brass" and "The Queen of Serpents," is a pious, mystical meditation on the wonders of the universe and God's creative powers. These stories bring together Arabic literature's internalization of its pre-Islamic literary traditions—Arabic, Greek, Persian, Sanskrit, and Syriac—and cultural heritage and religions—Christianity, Judaism, Zoroastrianism, to say the least—as well as its deployment of these to negotiate the tension between formal Islam and Sufism, between what is portrayed as mindless performance of prescribed religious duties and transcendental contemplation of God's might and grace. What are the ethics of good living? These are not defined by the exemplary conduct of the king or his subjects around political authority or their meticulous execution of religious instructions in their quotidian behavior, these stories suggest, but by going beyond structures of power and prescribed piety so as to be able to experience the omnipresence and beauty of divinity.

This tension between structure and the will to be free, expressed in the contrapuntal relation between *ʿaql* ("reason"), which structures thought, feeling, and conduct, and *hawā* ("passion"), which gives in to desire and leads to *junūn* ("madness"), in the *Thousand and One Nights* serves as the starting point for exploring theoretically the problem of classification or categorization and its impact on and limitation inherent in the reception of literature in the cultural institutions that devise a classification for intelligibility and then come to rely on this very invented classification. Arabic Popular Literature, an MA Arabic Literature course, takes advantage of students' assumed proficiency in the Arabic language and invites them to read more and longer stories from the *Thousand and One Nights* comparatively with texts from premodern genres, including historiography (*tārīkh*), tales of the prophets (*qiṣaṣ al-anbiyāʾ*), relief after hardship (*al-faraj baʿd al-shidda*), travel (*riḥla*) and cartography (*taqwīm, khiṭaṭ*), popular epic (*sīra shaʿbiyya*), and Arabic picaresque (*maqāmāt*), as well as modern short story, novel, and drama, to explore questions of genre ideologies, generic boundaries, and overlapping fields of literary production while tackling the major issues debated in Arabic literature, both past and present, such as ideal kingship, justice and law, the role of the individual in society, friendship, masculinity and femininity, and tradition and innovation.

A comparative reading of Solomon legends, with a focus on the loss of his ring and kingship for the duration of forty days, examining al-Ṭabarī's rendition, al-Thaʿlabī's *Qiṣaṣ al-anbiyāʾ*, and "Bulūqiyyah" in "The Queen of Serpents," shows the workings of genre ideologies in giving shape to each version of the story (or how form has content, according to Hayden White), as well as the transformations of biblical folklore in Islamic writings, from the condemnation of idolatry in al-Ṭabarī to a prophet's repentance as an expression of piety in al-Thaʿlabī to the transience of worldly power, including that of a prophet as mighty as Solomon, in "Bulūqiyyah." Reading the fourth voyage of Sindbād the Sailor intertextually with al-Tanūkhī's meeting between a Byzantine Christian grandfather and his Arab Muslim grandson (*Al-Faraj baʿd al-shidda*; 2: 29–31) showcases the intergeneric traffic in premodern Arabic writings, between the sacred and the secular and between classical and Middle Arabic, and the role of endurance and individual agency in the unfolding of destiny (Marzolph, *Relief*). Stories of adventures at sea, including "Sindbād the Sailor" and "Jullānar of the Sea," respond to religious discourses on passion, particularly desire, and its potential to unravel reason, therefore piety, as articulated in *Dhamm al-hawā* (*In Censure of Passion*) by Ibn al-Jawzī. Reading "Dalīla the Crafty" in the context of historical portrayals of its underworld knight-errant-like figures (*shuṭṭār* and *ʿayyārūn*), who come to the rescue of the wronged populace against corrupt and tyrannical officers of the state, and of their contemporary counterparts, such as the story of "Ḥasan and Naʿīma" in Egyptian ballads, provides an opportunity to explore the limits of the law in guaranteeing just rule in the premodern Islamic religious community (*umma*) or modern secular nation-state (*dawla*). Brotherhood, comprehended as the bond of loyalty defining the relationship among men, emerges in such instances as an alternative structure for community in the Arabic literary imaginary.

Gender and constructions of masculinity and femininity, so pervasive in discourses on community structured around sexual desire, understandably come to be central in any reading of classical and modern Arabic literature. Naguib Mahfouz's *Arabian Nights and Days* (*Layālī alf layla*), his rewriting of the *Thousand and One Nights* that tells the story of the stillbirth of modern democracy out of the ashes of King Shahriyar's monarchy, generates meaning by turning the familiar paradigm of educating desire into love into tales of misdirected desire and unrequited love. Hanan al-Shaykh's One Thousand and One Nights: A Retelling as an example of Arab women's response to centuries of male-centered Arabic and Middle Eastern writings, by contrast, completely eschews national allegory and instead dwells humorously on the pleasures of quotidian gender politics. In this al-Shaykh cleverly picks up on the capability for irreverence of the *Thousand and One Nights* and makes fun of all the earnest readings of religious, political, and moral discourses presumed inherent in its stories, just as the stories themselves mock *adab* and its pretenses. Even as the telling of stories in the *Thousand and One Nights* relies on language games to generate allure, it does not hesitate to parody the performativity of language exemplified by the picaresque *Maqāmāt*, in which the protagonist Abū al-Fath al-Iskandrī exchanges his eloquent words for money and worldly goods, and shows in "The Hunchback's Tale" that words, however eloquent they may be, are ineffectual prattle.

There is obviously more than one way of teaching the *Thousand and One Nights*. In the itinerary of the particular journey I guide, the work serves as a key site that opens out to an extensive intertextual network and brings into focus the conversations taking place among divergent texts in Arabic and between Arabic and world literature. More important, it marks the flexible entry points into this global textual network. It has been possible for me to offer this guided tour because of the strength of language training and literature program at SOAS. Yet small languages are fast disappearing from university curricula, and literature programs are being reduced to the bare minimum. Acquisition of transferrable skills is deferred to general courses on culture, literature, and film (of the Middle East and North Africa, South Asia, and Southeast Asia) taught in English and through English translation. As academics are being pushed back into this anglophone silo, our students are similarly being deprived of lines of escape from the isolation of an anglophone worldview and the attendant monolingualism.

By showing how multiple literary traditions around the world are connected and brought into dialogue with each other, the *Thousand and One Nights* provides a firm ground from which we can interrogate the conceptual categories and paradigms underpinning the division of labor in academic institutions and in regional or disciplinary approaches to research and teaching. Moreover, it opens our eyes to the centrality of languages, particularly multilingualism, and global humanities in how we work out the ethics of living for our everyday.

The intercultural context of the formation, circulation, and transmogrification of the *Thousand and One Nights* can be a point of departure from the silos of current teaching practices, structured, as it were, by national imaginings of community and monolingual definitions of language and literature, into a global vision of multilingual world literature.

NOTE

1. Ibn al-Nadīm's discussion of the *Thousand Nights*, *Sindbadnāma*, and *Kalīla wa-Dimna* may be found in *Al-Fihrist* [al-Mazandarānī] 363.

The Textual Tradition of the *Thousand and One Nights*: Teaching the Collection's Complexity

Ulrich Marzolph

When teaching the *Thousand and One Nights*, I sometimes start with a multiple-choice quiz game. Offering itself for a variety of purposes, this quiz aims above all to make me understand the extent to which the students are or are not acquainted with general knowledge I take for granted about the *Nights*. The one-page questionnaire I hand out to students contains a total of seven points, six of which are questions. The questions are supplied with a choice of four possible answers each, and students are advised that one or more of the given choices may apply. The questions are as follows:

> From which geographic region do the tales of the *Thousand and One Nights* originate? (Answer choices: India; Iran; China; Arabia)
> What is the name of the female person (sister, maid) that is together with storyteller Shahrazad? (Answer choices: Dinazade; Dinarzade; Dunyazade; Daryazade)
> How many tales do the *Nights* contain? (Answer choices: 100; 200; 500; 1,001)
> To which century does the oldest preserved manuscript of the *Nights* date? (Answer choices: ninth century; eleventh century; fifteenth century; eighteenth century)
> Why does Shahrazad tell the tales? (Answer choices: out of boredom; to satisfy the curiosity of her sister; because she wants to reform the murderous ruler; for money)
> Into which European language were the Arabic *Nights* first translated? (Answer choices: German; English; French; Turkish)

The first point on my form, instead of asking a question, invites students to name a maximum of five stories from the *Nights* they may remember.

The result of the short quiz is hardly surprising. It usually combines a wide range of vague guesses, some of them close to actual knowledge, with a few informed or correct answers given. In particular, the invitation to name stories from the *Nights* yields a telling result, since the response with an overwhelming majority regularly includes the triad of usual suspects: the stories of Aladdin, Ali Baba, and Sindbad.

I admit that, as a teacher, I sometimes feel tempted to judge the responses to my questionnaire as disappointing or utterly misinformed. But are they? And even though the responses may be wrong measured against the specialized knowledge held by the so-called expert, are they not equally right or valid in that they result from a process of cultural learning that, as far as the *Nights* is concerned, extends at least over three centuries? Against the backdrop of these questions, this essay considers what kind of knowledge about the genesis, history, and character of the *Thousand and One Nights* has been communicated to the public and who participated in this process. I am particularly concerned with the problems the supposed experts may encounter when aiming to convey their detailed understanding of the complex facts to the public.

Let me now sketch what I consider as general, or at least generally available, knowledge about the *Nights*.

The Thousand and One Nights: *Origins*

Antoine Galland's adapted French translation of the *Thousand and One Nights*, published in twelve volumes from 1704 to 1717, made available in Europe a Middle Eastern literary work that has contributed like no other to the constitution of Western culture—except the Bible, which, notably, is also a work of Middle Eastern literature. The tremendous success of the *Nights* is documented in innumerable reprints, translations, and selective editions. By way of imitations, adaptations, and literary works inspired by single stories, the *Nights* has become an invaluable constituent of world literature in European letters. As highly influential contributions of the so-called Orient to world culture, the stories have moreover served as a source of inspiration for numerous works of creative fantasy, above all in the areas of painting, dance, opera, drama, pantomime, music, architecture, and film. Since the European versions of the *Nights* and their worldwide appreciation employ the Orient as a matrix of Western imagination, the work has also contributed to the creation of a worldview that, through the often discussed publications of the Palestinian American historian of literature Edward Said, has become widely known under the label *Orientalism*—a reductive and biased worldview that Said saw as concomitant with colonial exploitation and imperial hegemony. And, finally, by way of some of the most popular stories included in the *Nights*, several of their scenes, images, and motifs have become an inseparable constituent of Western imagery. Here we should mention at least the flying carpet, the jinni imprisoned in a bottle that will fulfill the liberator's wishes when released, Aladdin's magic lamp (Marzolph, "Aladdin Almighty"), and the number 1,001 as a proverbial expression of infinity. For more than three centuries, the Western reception of the *Nights* has thus expressed the attractive, fascinating side of so-called Oriental culture, serving as the quintessential icon of a carefree and joyful life "as in a tale of the *Thousand and One Nights*."

What is this work that has resulted in such a dramatic international impact? What are the main characteristics of the conglomerate of stories that serve the female narrator Shahrazad to attract the cruel ruler's attention and fascinate him over a period of a thousand and one nights, that is, for almost three years? Where are the roots of this collection of tales, and how has it developed into the monument of transnational narrative we perceive today?

The ultimate origin of the *Nights* is obscured by history. Research has variously argued for an Indian or Iranian origin. Textual evidence has been taken to argue for the collection's Indian origin—or, to be more specific, for the Indian origin of several elements of the collection's constitutive frame tale. A commentary to the holy scriptures of the Jains mentions a tale in which a royal concubine tells a story or a riddle to the ruler for several nights, usually delaying the story's end to the following night. Shahrazad's action in the *Nights* thus echoes the ancient narrative stratagem of the cliff-hanger. Moreover, two of the shorter narratives included in the frame tale of the *Nights* possess an analogy in Indian literature: One is the story of the jinni who keeps his human wife imprisoned in a chest, a fact that does not prevent her from having sex with innumerable men; the other is the story of a man who understands the language of animals. One of the major obstacles in determining the relation of these texts to their later versions in the *Nights* is, however, the difficulty in dating early Indian literature.

The Story Collection in Persian and Arabic

The collection's presumed Iranian origin is attested by two short passages in tenth-century Arabic sources. More or less agreeing with each other, the Arab historian al-Masʿūdī and the Baghdad bookseller Ibn al-Nadīm mention a Persian book named *Hazār afsān*—a title that can be translated as *A Thousand Marvelous Stories*. The book's title in Arabic translation is given as *Alf khurāfah*, and it was commonly known as *Alf laylah* (*A Thousand Nights*). Although specifying the number of nights, the latter title does not supply a clue as to the number of narrated tales. The collection's frame tale as sketched by Ibn al-Nadīm is identical to that of the later *Nights* as we know the work today, and Ibn al-Nadīm also mentions a period of a thousand nights of storytelling. In addition, the names in the collection's frame tale appear to corroborate an Iranian context. King Shahriyar (whose name means "hero") belongs to the Sasanian dynasty (224–651 CE), the last pre-Islamic Iranian dynasty, which was vanquished by the Arabs in the seventh century. Shahriyar's brother Shahzaman (whose name means "king of the age") is the ruler of the city of Samarkand in central Asia. The name of the collection's main narrator, the vizier's daughter Shahrazad, is also Iranian, meaning "of noble appearance or ancestry."

The oldest preserved document testifying to the collection's existence is a paper fragment whose original writing has convincingly been argued to predate the year 879 (Abbott 138–44). The fragment's first page clearly shows the title *Kitāb fīhi hadīth Alf laylah* (*A Book Containing the Tale [or Chatter] of a Thousand Nights*), and its second page contains the beginning of the well-known frame tale in which the unnamed narrator's servant (or, in later versions, the narrator's sister) asks her to tell some tales. Relying on additional evidence from a variety of sources, the early textual history of the *Nights* has been reconstructed as follows: An originally Persian work was translated into an Islamized Arabic version before the eighth century CE, integrating narrative material from various other works. By the twelfth century, the work had acquired the title *Alf laylah wa-laylah* (*A Thousand Nights and a Night*), as documented in a note written by a Jewish bookseller in Cairo who lent the book to one of his customers around the year 1150 (see Goitein). Somewhat later, the history of Egypt compiled by Muḥammad ibn Saʿd al-Qurṭī mentions the collection's popularity in Mamluk Egypt (Chraïbi, Mille et une nuits 45–47). Although we can thus be fairly certain about the book's existence, we do not know much about the actual content of its early version except for the vague outline in the early paper fragment mentioning "striking examples of the excellencies and shortcomings, the cunning and stupidity, the generosity and avarice, and the courage and cowardice that are in man" (Abbott 133).

The content of the *Nights* only begins to show with the oldest preserved manuscript, the very one that the French Orientalist scholar Galland used for his adapted translation. Although the manuscript does not bear a date, its dating can be inferred from secondary evidence, the most important being a coin mentioned in the tale of the Jewish doctor in the cycle of stories connected with the supposedly dead hunchback (see Grotzfeld, "Age"). The so-called Ashrafī *dīnār* mentioned in this story was issued in the reign of Mamluk Sultan al-Ashraf Sayf al-Dīn Barsbāy (ruled from 1422 to 1437 CE) and later acquired such a great popularity that its name became a generic denomination. Since any text mentioning the Ashrafī *dīnār* as a regularly used coin is likely to have been prepared a considerable time after the coin was issued, the manuscript has been suggested to date from the middle of the fifteenth century.

The Galland manuscript today is preserved in the National Library of France in Paris. It consists of three volumes containing the stories up to the beginning of night 282, breaking off in the middle of the story of Qamar al-Zamān and Budūr. The manuscript thus consists of roughly a third of the total collection. In addition to the beginning of the frame tale, it contains a total of seven stories or cycles of stories. These stories or cycles of stories constitute the core corpus of the *Nights* (Chraïbi, Mille et une nuits 89–116), the compilation of whose oldest parts, according to current research, coincides with the so-called Baghdad period, or more or less the Abbasid dynasty before the eleventh century. In particular, the first stories are not told in a linear manner. They rather constitute diligently structured complex narratives changing between various layers that are, in their turn, told by different narrators. This characteristic feature relates particularly to the "Tale of the Hunchback," with a total of five embedded tales. The embedded "Tale of the Barber" again serves as a frame for several separately told tales: that of the barber himself and those of his six brothers. Considering this feature, the *Nights* presents itself as a story told by an anonymous (and presumably male) storyteller in which Shahrazad tells a story in which somebody tells a story that frames the story of yet somebody else. This variety of embedding and embedded tales has contributed to the attraction of the *Nights* for a reading (and listening) public. Both the so-called Oriental and the Western audiences will have been fascinated by the intellectual challenge posed by the collection's complex narrative layering.

In addition to the fifteenth-century manuscript that served as a basis for Galland, we today know of a dozen manuscripts that most probably were compiled before the end of the seventeenth century (Akel, "Liste"). None of these manuscripts is complete, and even the totality of fragments does not allow an unambiguous reconstruction of a standard set of narratives that might have been included in the Arabic manuscripts before the eighteenth century. Current research agrees that, besides the earlier formative Baghdad period, the so-called Egyptian period, coinciding with Mamluk rule in Egypt from 1250 to 1517 CE, contributed to the formation of the later repertoire of the *Nights*. Typical narratives from this period are tales of tricksters and thieves, such as the tale of clever Dalīla, which is taken to represent the popular culture of the Mamluk period.

Already this condensed survey of the historical development and repertoire of the *Nights* indicates an important aspect that has ruled the work's content before and after Galland: The *Nights* as we know it today is a work with a flexible repertoire of tales, a true shape-shifter. The tales of the ancient core corpus document a conscious composition by being linked to the frame tale through the concept that telling a story will save your life (Todorov 73–74). But the collection's younger versions, instead of containing a fixed set of narratives, rather offer a narrative frame that in its own right offers the potential to integrate narratives of the most diverse genres and origins. Consequently, over the centuries the *Nights* has integrated a large variety of narratives from just about each and every genre, including epics, tales of magic, religious legends, and animal tales, as well as jokes and anecdotes.

Manuscripts, Editions, and Translations

The *Thousand and One Nights* may allude to a specific notion, but it is not a single book. Each manuscript, each edition of the text, and each translation constitute separate and, at times, highly individual versions of a text or parts of a text. The total of the constituents of this conglomerate adds up to a much more complex phenomenon than any single version offers. Let me illustrate the complexity of the *Nights* with just a few examples from the three areas of manuscripts, editions of the text, and translations.

If we talk about manuscripts of the *Nights*, we might ask, What is so specific about the Galland manuscript that was edited by Muhsin Mahdi in 1984 (Thousand)? How do the manuscripts of the so-called Syrian branch differ from those of the Egyptian branch? What about the alleged Tunisian manuscript that served as the basis of parts of the Breslau edition prepared by Maximilian Habicht but has been proven to constitute a willful mystification? Should we include in our discussion the late-seventeenth-century Ottoman Turkish manuscript that already in Galland's day was preserved in the Royal Library in Paris and probably furnished some of the inspiration for his adapted translation? What about the early Turkish translations of the *Nights*, only one of which has been edited so far (Eğri) but some of which predate Galland by several centuries, thus in fact qualifying the claim that Galland produced the first ever translation of the Arabic *Nights* into another language? Should we take into account other anonymous Arabic collections of tales, some of which show a certain overlap with the *Nights*, such as the North African *Hundred and One Nights* that are built on a similar frame tale (Fudge) or the fourteenth-century Arabic manuscript of the *Tales of the Marvellous and News of the Strange* (Lyons) that contains several tales also encountered in the *Nights*? And what about the various versions of single tales, such as those of "The City of Brass" (Pinault 148–239) or "The Ebony Horse" (Bottigheimer), that have been preserved in other contexts, whether in learned or popular literature?

If we talk about the editions of the text, we might ask, Why are there two standard editions—those of Calcutta II and Bulaq—both of which contain more or less identical versions based on manuscripts that, to all appearances, are not available anymore, so that we are not in a position to judge the impact of editorial decisions taken in regard to content and language? Why does the Beirut edition, even though heavily censored, have its advantages for teaching? Should we also consider all the various Arabic texts, like versions of "Aladdin and the Wonderful Lamp," that are quite obviously translations from a European language and are sometimes published in separate booklets, but never as part of an Arabic edition of the *Nights*?

If we talk about translations, we might ask, What is so specific about the Galland translation that only partially relies on Arabic manuscripts of the *Nights* (Akel, "Quelques remarques" 211–13)? To what extent are the tales Galland added from the oral performance of the Syrian Christian storyteller Ḥannā Diyāb part of the *Nights* (Marzolph, "Man")? Why did Edward William Lane and Richard Francis Burton in their respective translations choose to treat morally disputable matters, in particular sexuality, in diametrically opposed ways? How could it be that the Joseph-Charles Mardrus translation inspired famous writers like André Gide and Marcel Proust, and why does its English version by Powys Mathers still hold a significant position in the book market, even though Mardrus took great liberties in including tales from sources that before him had never been connected to the *Nights*, such as anecdotes from chapbooks on the Turkish trickster Nasreddin Hodja or Egyptian fairy tales collected by a Western Orientalist scholar in the nineteenth century? What exactly is the difference between Husain Haddawy's translation and other English translations? Why is the German translation by Enno Littmann unanimously praised for its accuracy while such influential critics as Jorge Luis Borges characterized it as dull and uninspired ("Translators")? What is the advantage of the translation by Malcolm C. Lyons that, for the first time since Burton, renders the full text of the

Calcutta II edition in readable modern English? To this translation, Ursula Lyons supplied English versions of the original French tales of "Ali Baba" and "Aladdin," as readers would be disappointed not to find their most beloved tales.

Talking about manuscripts, text editions, and translations of the *Nights* is only a fraction of the total phenomenon. Particularly when considering the influence and repercussions of the *Nights*, we have to take into account a tremendous amount of eighteenth-, nineteenth-, and twentieth-century literature to an extent that, as Robert Irwin has adequately put it, in the end it would be easier to consider those authors (of English literature) that were not influenced by the *Nights* (Irwin, Arabian Nights 290–91). Moreover, what about theater, music, opera, ballet, drama, design, architecture, film, and so on? And what about the repercussions of the *Nights* beyond the West? The exploration of the *Nights* as a transnational collection has only begun (Yamanaka and Nishio; Marzolph, Arabian Nights *in Transnational Perspective*), and particularly its repercussions on Ottoman Turkish culture have only recently been explored (Proverbio; Thomann). Once you start occupying yourself with the *Nights*, the phenomenon appears to grow, like the jinni released from the bottle, until its size becomes frighteningly gigantic and clear definitions as to what belongs to the *Nights* and what does not become increasingly difficult.

There are various solutions to this situation. Teachers may decide to limit their interest to a clearly defined entity, such as a specific manuscript or a specific cycle of tales. This will enable them to produce focused courses, the results of which promise detailed insights into the character, context, and transmission of the limited samples of texts under consideration. Another solution offering itself is to practice a wide approach. In terms of teaching, this would entail regarding as relevant for the construction of syllabi and student assignments each and every cultural product that ever has been, currently is, or ought to be connected to the *Nights* in one way or another. A wide approach would incorporate more or less the whole area of how the so-called Orient is perceived by the West— either by way of the telling of stories, whether originating from the Orient or situated in the Orient in an Orientalist manner practiced in, say, the *Thousand and One Days* (Marzolph, *Relief after Hardship*)—or by way of the fairy tales written by Wilhelm Hauff (Polaschegg 398–449).

Countering Orientalist Stereotypes

To conclude, I would like to juxtapose two quotations from widely different, yet closely related contexts.

The first one is from the second edition of Irwin's *Companion* to the *Nights*. "Years ago," Irwin remembers,

> I used to play on a classic Williams pinball-machine, "Tales of the Arabian Nights." As I fired off one silver ball after the other, I would gaze at the

filmic iconography of *The Arabian Nights* spread out on the machine's gaudily painted playbar. That iconography, divorced and free-floating from particular stories, will register with people who have never opened the book of the *Nights*: the Roc's giant egg, harem girls in diaphanous trousers, hook-nosed men wielding scimitars, jinn, minarets, the Cyclops, the prince disguised as a beggar, the basket full of serpents, the rope which turns into a ladder, the all-seeing eye. This visual clutter of Oriental knick-knacks can be put to any purpose. In the West today, the *Nights* chiefly serves as a kind of reservoir of images and story-fragments that can be recycled in films for juvenile audiences. (vii)

He goes on to say, "In modern times, in both the West and the Arab world, the magnificent cultural riches of *The Arabian Nights* have been reduced to a scant handful of clichéd and kitsch-laden images" (viii).

The second quotation is from an interview with Jack Shaheen, author of *Reel Bad Arabs: How Hollywood Vilifies a People* and *Guilty: Hollywood's Verdict on Arabs after 9/11* and a winner of the American-Arab Anti-Discrimination Committee's Lifetime Achievement Award. Commenting on the national conversation on the Park 51 Islamic Community Center, Shaheen points out that anti-Muslim feelings in the United States

existed long before September 11, 2001. It's escalated after 9–11 and there are several reasons why it has escalated. One is the fact that we fail to distinguish between the 19 non-American Arab Muslim terrorists, and the seven-plus million American Muslims that had nothing to do with 9–11. Nobody talks about that and nobody talks about this not being an act of domestic terrorism. The destruction that took place . . . was not committed by American Muslims. So why are we condemning and attacking them?

Later in the interview Shaheen mentions that

in 2008, there were 28 million copies of one of the most racist documentaries ever made. It was called *Obsession* and it essentially vilified all things Islam. The major newspaper chains such as the *New York Times* inserted into their newspapers this hateful DVD [as a paid advertising supplement], giving the impression to some readers that the newspapers supported the theme of this documentary. Would any of these newspapers have distributed a hate documentary targeting Christianity, Judaism, or any other faith?"

These two quotations illustrate two sides of the same coin (see also Bacchilega 150–69). The Western perception of the Muslim world has long been dominated by stereotypical notions of the East as a sensual paradise, most aptly expressed in the notion of the *Arabian Nights*. In recent times, this image is tainted by partial and biased notions of the Muslim world as the ultimate harbor of terrorism that relentlessly rejects the basic values defining the West, such as individuality, equality, and freedom of speech. Needless to say, both views are equally simplistic in disregarding the complexity and diversity of the phenomena concerned. Both views single out specific aspects and posit them as the essential ones while consciously disregarding or suppressing others.

The devastating effect of this simplification can be demonstrated by a chain of misperceptions in such widely acclaimed productions as the 1992 animated Disney cartoon *Aladdin* (Marzolph, "Aladdin-Syndrom"). To the uninformed spectator, this Disney version is representative of the tale of Aladdin (though it is not), which is taken to constitute the quintessential tale of the *Arabian Nights* (to which it was only added by Galland). The *Nights*, in turn, is seen as an authentic representation of Arabic Islamic culture (which it is only to a limited extent), so that in the end the cartoon risks being understood as representing Arabic Islamic culture. Today's perception of the Muslim world works in similar ways. Here, the action of relatively small but highly organized terrorist groups cynically arguing with the core values of Islam is taken as representative of the whole of the Islamic community. Instead of striving to assess, understand, and eventually counterbalance the complex factors that nourish radical Islam and lead to the establishment of terrorist groups, public opinion prefers to succumb to the temptation of perceiving them as a kind of vermin the only treatment for which is physical annihilation.

Simplification, or maybe one should say oversimplification, is a road to bias. And bias might easily lead to denigration, contempt, and violent conflict. Neglecting that Muslim terrorists are not representative of Islam as a whole is equal to exploiting the world of the *Thousand and One Nights* as a legitimate playground for Western fantasy while disregarding the collection's highly complex history and diverse character. Uncritical praise is as misleading as uncritical vilification. Experts and teachers hold the key to preventing the solidification and further growth of such biased notions. As the international impact of the *Thousand and One Nights* is literally boundless, teaching the *Nights* is a position of significant responsibility.

The *Thousand and One Nights* as Urban Literature

Nadine Roth

Teaching the *Thousand and One Nights* in a core course on urban literature offers a unique opportunity to explore the roots of the story collection in the cities of the Islamic world, as well as to illuminate the importance of the *Nights* within the development of Western literary traditions. Particular stories from the *Nights* are familiar points of reference for many college students, but they are often surprised to discover how urban the tales are. Reading selections from the *Nights* alongside other urban fictions allows students to examine the distinctive values associated with city life across different cultures and time periods—fulfilling the key pedagogical goal of developing cross-cultural understanding within the core curriculum for students across all majors.

Built on an original core dating to the urban culture of the late medieval Islamic world, the tales of the *Thousand and One Nights* provide a valuable counterpoint to histories of urban fiction that rely on a Western narrative of modernity. In these tales, Middle Eastern cities burst with life—demonstrating their role in interregional commerce and social life and providing an important context for our discussions about the future of global cities in a new age of economic interdependence. The imagined cities of the *Nights* encapsulate memories of the golden age of Abbasid Baghdad, but these stories also offer a glimpse of the aspirations of subsequent generations of storytellers and listeners for prosperity and justice.

The Cities of the Thousand and One Nights

Scholars of the *Thousand and One Nights* have long understood the story collection to be a product of a distinctly urban ethos nurtured in the great cities of the Muslim world, beginning with the first compilations of the collection in Baghdad in the tenth to twelfth centuries. If the Abbasid capital—and its legendary caliph Harun al-Rashid—left a lasting impression in the original core of tales, the cities of Damascus and Cairo also left their mark in the centuries that followed. Tales added to manuscripts of the *Nights* during the collection's development from the fourteenth to the sixteenth century offer fascinating glimpses of the popular literature of the Mamluk period and some of the most vivid images of urban life in this period.

Without treating any tale as a direct representation of the urban world of Baghdad or Cairo, students can analyze the traces of the cities that shaped the lives of the many anonymous storytellers who contributed to the *Nights*, as well as their readers and listeners. Reading these tales in a course alongside other urban texts gives students the chance to extract a distinctive social imaginary that can be analyzed alongside more familiar city portraits in the work of Charles Dickens or Émile Zola. On the most basic level, students in this course are challenged to identify the essential qualities of a city in a distinct cultural context or historical period through their readings—whether those qualities lie in the presence of specific material features, the dominance of particular social classes, or the elaboration of certain structures of political control. Beyond this preliminary inventory of urban features, students are encouraged to apply Italo Calvino's notion of the city as a collection of desires and memories.

In tales such as the "The Hunchback," "Maʿruf the Cobbler," or "Mercury ʿAli of Cairo," the distinctive topographical markers of the urban—the city walls, the palace, the market, the khan, or the mosque—are easy to locate. The urban qualities of the *Nights* are even more pronounced when students turn their attention to the characters who populate the story collection—especially the merchants and artisans who are key to the commercial functions of these cities. Drawing from the contention of Aboubakr Chraïbi that the *Nights* can be considered a "mirror for merchants" ("Situation" 6), it is useful to spend some class time exploring the kinds of values that shaped the marketplace of the late medieval or early modern city. As plots turn on the making and losing of fortunes, the stories speak to the interplay of greed and generosity within the merchant class, patterns of mutual support in the face of financial risk, and various strategies to secure one's fortunes against the constant danger of deception.

This analysis of the social imaginary in the *Nights* offers a useful contrast to other literary texts students encounter in the course, which are more clearly the product of a single author's vision of a particular city (Zola's mid-nineteenth-century Paris or Virginia Woolf's early-twentieth-century London). Reading tales from the *Thousand and One Nights* in this context also offers an opportunity to disrupt conventional narratives in which novels of the city are strictly correlated with the development of the modern European city. Peter Caracciolo first suggested that translations of the *Thousand and One Nights* offered English novelists from Henry Fielding forward a prototype of a secular mode of fiction that could accommodate a dense experiential world filled with quotidian details of life in London. Robert Irwin has expanded further on this insight to emphasize the "documentary realism" contained within the early stories of the Arabic manuscript first translated by Antoine Galland, in which the stories gathered in the Hunchback cycle offer a remarkably "detailed evocation of everyday things" ("*Arabian Nights* and the Origins of the Western Novel" 146).

Following the lead of these scholars, students can be encouraged to read these descriptions against the cities of the eighteenth- and nineteenth-century novel. For instance, the detailed images of the luxurious offerings at the Baghdad market at the beginning of "The Porter and the Three Women of Baghdad" reveal a rich sensorial world reflective of trading networks within a broader Islamic world. They might be compared to the goods in Zola's Paris department store (inextricably linked to colonial power) or to the material environment of industrial London in Dickens's work. George Gissing famously asserted that Dickens had "put the spirit of the Arabian Nights into his pictures of life by the river" and "sought for wonders amid the dreary life of the common streets" (32). Students can search for echoes of the themes and narrative techniques of the *Nights* in Dickens's work, as well as in the London of George Eliot's *Daniel Deronda*.

The City as Labyrinth and Ruin

Beyond the many traces of the material culture of cities lodged within many of the *Nights* stories, some tales offer an opportunity for students to wrestle with the meaning of cities within the distinctive historical context in which the story collection was forged. The story I assign most often for this purpose is "The City of Brass," which draws on legends of a historical expedition under the Umayyad caliph 'Abd al-Malik ibn Marwan to narrate a classic journey to what appears to be a dead city. In this tale, a group of men are charged by the caliph to investigate reports that one of the copper jars in which Solomon had imprisoned the rebellious jinni had been found in a faraway land. Their journey takes them beyond the familiar landscape of Baghdad and Cairo through uninhabited territories containing mysterious omens and supernatural beings. When they finally arrive at a great walled city that has seemingly been frozen in time with its treasures intact, they are able to discover the source of its misfortune and learn an important lesson about the fragility of earthly riches.

In discussions of the story of "The City of Brass," students are encouraged to read both the journey and the city itself in metaphoric terms. This exercise dovetails with the challenges of reading a text like Italo Calvino's *Invisible Cities*—where a finely etched city image prompts speculative meditations on the nature of cities. Richard van Leeuwen's spatial analysis of "The City of Brass" is a useful guide to what might be achieved through careful consideration of this tale (497–99). Sited within a desolate landscape, the high stone walls and splendid brass towers of the city speak to the sharp divide between the strangeness of the lands through which the travelers have journeyed and the apparent security and order offered by the enclosed borders of the urban realm. In this respect, the tale speaks to the generic values associated with the city in this period: it is both a center of civilization and a realm of authority.

"The City of Brass," however, also offers the reader a classic example of an urban maze that presents the protagonists with a series of challenges that must be mastered if they are to enter into its confines and enjoy its riches. Since there is no visible gate of entry, the members of the expedition set to work building a ladder to scale the high city walls, but when the first man reaches the top, he seems willingly to leap to his death. The men discover that the walls have been enchanted so that anyone arriving at the top will see a vision of ten beautiful women and throw himself into their deadly embrace. It is the scholarly sheikh among the small band of travelers who avoids this enchantment by reciting the Quran and then proceeds to unlock one of the great towers and open the city to his friends.

As the group continues through the city, seeking to penetrate its mysteries, they encounter all the signs of a vital urban center—most important, a market bursting with goods and a palace filled with precious treasures—all apparently abandoned. When they arrive at the mysterious palace where the dead queen lies in state, the sheikh is once again called on to unravel the messages left for future visitors. Deciphering the inscriptions left by the dead, he discovers that the city was once the center of a powerful and flourishing empire, but all its wealth could not prevent catastrophe when famine struck the land. A message on a tablet of gold invites the visitors to partake of the precious treasures on offer as long as they do not touch the beautiful queen. Although one character finds himself unable to resist the temptations embodied by the queen—and is beheaded by her stone guards as a result—the rest of the group depart from the City of Brass with their camels loaded with gold and jewels and continue their search for bottled jinn.

"The City of Brass" provides one of the clearest instances in the *Thousand and One Nights* of a city designed to deliver a clear moral. If the dead city represents the fragility of human efforts and material wealth, the characters are seemingly rewarded for their ingenuity, faith, and moral strength. As students arrive at this conclusion, they can extend their analysis by drawing on other examples of ruined cities in the *Nights*, which repeat this motif while offering a variation on its significance. In "The Porter and the Three Women of Baghdad," the tale of the first woman describes the discovery of a seemingly abandoned stone city after her ship is lost at sea. In this case, the explanation for its destruction is delivered by one young man who has survived the city's doom: a population devoted to Zoroastrianism has been destroyed by God for failing to heed his call to embrace Islam.[1] Such stories bring students back to a consideration of a practice of urbanism grounded in the precepts of Islam, but "The City of Brass" also resonates with students attuned to the risks of environmental destruction and climate change and can stimulate further discussions of the future of contemporary cities.

This unit of study on the significance of these ruined cities in the *Nights* can be extended by drawing on a retelling of "The City of Brass" in a play by Naguib Mahfouz, *The Shaitan Speaks*.[2] In this retelling of "The City of Brass," Mahfouz weaves his own distinctive mixture of metaphysical speculation and political analysis to confront the dangers of authoritarianism and theological radicalism, and it offers a fascinating counterpart to the simpler structure of the *Nights* tale. In Mahfouz's version, the city is frozen in time because its queen demanded to be worshipped as a god, and when the members of the expedition get a glimpse of that lost world, it is clear that corruption and the active repression of political criticism had been the norm.

The Ethics of the City

Few tales of the *Thousand and One Nights* deploy urban archetypes in as didactic a fashion as "The City of Brass." In most of the collection, the city is simply the familiar and accepted territory of social life, and it offers both material and moral challenges to its many protagonists. Many of the stories featuring urban locations include examples of the conventional villains of popular fiction—kidnappers, con artists, and evil magicians. In "The Story of As'ad and Amjad" (added to "Qamar al-Zaman and Budur"), for instance, the city is filled with dangers and temptations that the brothers must somehow survive to find their happy ending. In other stories, the protagonists themselves are marginal characters who make a mockery of conventional social norms as they make their fortunes through ingenuity and wit. Utopian notions of the city as a transparent space guided by a singular religious or political authority are noticeably absent in these scenes, and tales of thieves and rogues challenge students to consider the ethical principles these urban spaces actually reflect.

For those readers seeking symbols of authority in the cities of the *Nights*, the series of tales featuring the Baghdad of Caliph Harun al-Rashid are of particular interest. In a number of stories putatively set in the Abbasid capital, Harun walks the streets of his capital disguised as a merchant to see for himself the condition of his people and to rectify any wrongs they may have experienced at the hands of his officials. In "The Three Apples," for instance, the caliph ventures into Baghdad to overcome his melancholy and finds the body of a murdered woman in a fisherman's catch. His demand for justice ultimately leads to the revelation of the circumstances of the crime. Whereas the caliph's appearances in *Nights* stories such as this one hint at the existence of a coherent order of justice within the city, other tales like "The Sleeper and the Waker" link Harun to episodes in which social categories are challenged and taboos broken.

The persistent elevation of tricksters and thieves as protagonists in the tales suggests that the urban realm is a far murkier moral territory, in which intelligence and sheer bravado often win out. Scholars have suggested that the stories added during the Cairo phase of the collection's development reflect the Egyptian popular literature of that period, which often celebrated the figure of the rogue against the apparent corruption and incompetence of officials. In stories such as "Dalila the Crafty" or "Mercury 'Ali of Cairo," it is the petty criminal who proves capable of outwitting all comers who emerges as the hero. The cities inhabited by these characters problematize the conventional boundaries that divide the private from the public sphere and challenge the trusted procedures of the marketplace.

The appearance of a new translation of "Dalila the Crafty" by Yasmine Seale in Norton's *Annotated* Arabian Nights offers an opportunity to explore this genre within a broader analysis of urban spaces (169–99). In this tale, Dalila launches her criminal escapades when she hears that the caliph has rewarded two "masters of guile and ruse"—Ahmad the Plague and Calamity Hasan—by making them watchmen of Baghdad (171). Observing this apparent reversal of expected patterns of authority, Dalila seeks to win back the status and income she has lost with the death of her husband by carrying out a chain of spectacular swindles. An accomplished "master of ruses and rackets" (171), Dalila assumes a series of disguises and bluffs her way into the homes and shops and palaces of Baghdad—stripping her victims of their goods, clothes, and dignity as she goes. With a keen eye for identifying a mark and a talent for subterfuge, she passes smoothly through the protective boundaries of the city—sneaking into the wali's harem at one point and escaping the custody of her guards at another. She even finds a way to talk herself out of crucifixion—as she persuades an inexperienced bedouin on his way to the big city to take her place in the expectation of receiving a treat of honey fritters. In the end, Dalila's reading of the obverse logic of the path to success in this fictional Baghdad proves correct, and she is rewarded by the caliph with a salary and a position as the portress of the caliph's khan and keeper of his carrier pigeons.

The achievements of Dalila as a trickster are matched by those of her daughter, Zaynab, and by her daughter's suitor, Mercury 'Ali, in another of the stories that seem to have been particularly beloved by Cairo audiences. As expressions of a popular culture that valorized the ingenuous strategies by which the socially marginal could challenge established urban elites, these stories speak to both the social and financial insecurities and to the dreams of good fortune and social ascent that resonated among the populace of Cairo. The prevalence of masquerades in the stories seems to suggest a remarkable fluidity of identity in the sprawling cities of the formative period of the compilation of the *Nights*, cities crowded with artisans, merchants, and travelers. In fourteenth-century Cairo, whose population is estimated to have been around 300,000, the opportunities to take on new social identities and the dangers of falling for the ruses of the clever con artist seem to live on within these entertaining tales of tricksters and rogues. There is little trace of the moral realm of the city in these Cairo tales, and Harun's role as the bringer of justice is decidedly muted by his apparent preference for a criminal class in stories like "Dalila the Crafty."

In a course that adopts a comparative methodology, these images of urban disorder can be usefully supplemented by readings from the fiction of Naguib Mahfouz that explore social tensions in the lives of Cairo's diverse population and, in some cases, draw inspiration from the *Thousand and One Nights*. Students seeking a modern comparison might examine the portrait of the marginalized residents of the city in *The Harafish* or the tensions within a Cairo neighborhood experiencing the pressures of economic and political change in *Midaq Alley*. Mahfouz's rewriting of certain tales from the *Thousand and One Nights* in *Arabian Nights and Days* is perhaps the most obvious extension of lines of inquiry regarding political authority and urban corruption in the story collection. The sweeping portrait of persistent social disorder and ineffectual leadership in this novel offers a more pessimistic perspective than the crowd-pleasing escapades of antiheroes like Dalila.

Magic Doors and Interstitial Spaces

Within a course on urban literature, the distinctive blend of supernatural elements and realist conventions within the stories of the *Thousand and One Nights* can be challenging for some students who are accustomed to seeking authenticity in narrative texts. Distracted by plots in which a protagonist is lured from his shop by a sorcerer or suddenly transported to a strange land by a jinni, some readers forget that these characters still operate within the distinctive codes of an urban merchant class. Pointing students to Mahfouz's blend of the supernatural and the realistic in *Arabian Nights and Days* may help broaden their understanding of this genre, but students often spy even closer parallels with contemporary literature that integrates elements associated with the genres of science fiction or fantasy. The recent short story "The Merchant and the Alchemist's Gate" by Ted Chiang, for instance, integrates time travel into a tale evoking the Baghdad and Cairo of the *Thousand and One Nights*.

The tales of the *Thousand and One Nights* are filled with narratives in which different spatial and temporal realms intersect to drive the plot in unexpected directions. Within the stories presumed to have been added during the Cairo period, one could consider the blend of realism and fantasy in "The Tale of Ma'ruf the Cobbler." In this tale, the cobbler's shop is clearly inscribed within the recognizable historical geography of Mamluk Cairo at a particular location just outside the Zuweyla Gate. Constantly criticized and abused by his wife, the cobbler eventually flees the city into the liminal realm that lies beyond its walls, and it is there that he encounters a resident jinni (fig. 1) who immediately transports him to a distant town called Ikhtiyan al-Khutan. The story builds on the contrast between the realistic environment of Cairo and the supernatural domain of Ikhtiyan al-Khutan, where the cobbler's gestures of generosity and kindness, as well as the intervention of a jinni of the ring, result in his rise to wealth and power as the husband of the princess and the eventual king.

If the possibility of merging distant temporalities is embodied in the object lesson of "The City of Brass," the possibility of moving into mythical or supernatural realms through the simple artifice of a magical door or a subterranean tunnel marks many of the more fantastical stories in the collection. In "The Man Who Never Laughed Again," for example, a young man squanders the fortune that he has inherited from his father and is forced to take a job as the servant to eleven old men who are living out their days in a somber mansion. As the men die one by one, the young man is warned that he must never open the single locked door in the house. When he inevitably gives in to temptation, he finds himself magically transported to a distant ocean. In the journey that ensues, he travels to the island of the Amazons and enjoys an idyllic existence until he once again opens the wrong door.

The intersection of the realms of the supernatural with the more mundane concerns of everyday life in the stories of merchants, artisans, and even caliphs

Figure 1. Fernand Schultz-Wettel, from *Tausend und eine Nacht* (*A Thousand and One Nights*), Neufeld und Henius, Berlin, 1914.

is part of the continuing appeal of the *Thousand and One Nights*. The political potential within this matrix of storytelling motifs can identified in more recent writing about the challenges of urban life. Paulo Lemos Horta, for instance, argues that the juxtaposition of realist and utopian dimensions within the stories of the *Thousand and One Nights* can be likened to the interpenetration of spatial regimes that Ato Quayson identifies in postcolonial narratives set in contemporary African cities ("Beyond the Palace").

In my own experience teaching city novels, I have noticed that students find echoes of the narrative patterns of tales from the *Nights* in many novels that mix elements of realism and fantasy to explore contemporary political issues. Mohsin Hamid's *Exit West* offers perhaps the most direct parallel to the magical passages of the *Thousand and One Nights* in a narrative that wrestles with the difficult realities of global migration. As the city in which the novel's young protagonists live disintegrates into war and oppression, they seize the opportunity offered by the appearance of magical doors into distant lands where they will join a diverse community of migrants from other foreign countries and cultures. This wondrous passage between East and West is, however, only the prelude to the more sustained struggle to build a future in another land and cope with the loss of one's homeland. Interposing the utopian promise of instant mobility with the harsh realities of the lives of migrants, the novel offers students a chance to explore the continued potential that lies within the narrative patterns of the tales of the *Thousand and One Nights*.

NOTES

1. A similar plot element appears in the story of "Abdallah ibn Fadil and His Brothers."
2. *The Shaitan Speaks* has not been published in an English translation. I teach from a version translated collectively by the students at New York University, Abu Dhabi. On Mahfouz's rewriting, see Fudge ("Underworlds").

The *Nights* as Crime Fiction: Teaching "The Tale of the Murdered Girl"

Roger Allen

"The Story of the Three Apples" (in Arabic, "Ḥikāyat al-tuffāḥāt al-thalāth"), also known as "The Story of the Murdered Young Woman" or "The Tale of the Murdered Girl" (in Arabic, "Ḥikāyat al-ṣabiyah al-maqtūlah"), is found in the sequence of stories that makes up the tale collection known as *Alf laylah wa-laylah*, or the *Thousand and One Nights* (Mahdi, Thousand 219–25; Haddawy, *Arabian Nights* 150–57).[1]

As an enormous and ever-increasing repertoire of research has now shown (see the works-cited list for this volume), this world-renowned tale collection, the *Thousand and One Nights*, needs to be regarded and analyzed as two separate collections. The earlier of the two is of Indo-Persian (and later Arabic) provenance; it dates from unknown beginnings to a period no later than the fourteenth century and contains some 282 nights ("The Story of the Three Apples" is placed between nights 69 and 72). The later compilation is a much larger collection assembled as a direct consequence of the earlier collection's translation into French by Antoine Galland between 1704 and 1717, its subsequent translation into multiple European languages, and its rapidly increasing popularity in Europe and beyond (Mahdi, *Thousand* [1995]; al-Musawi, *Scheherazade*). Through the addition of multiple tales and tale types from a wide variety of sources (including, for example, animal fables), the later collection process managed to bring the number of nights up to 1,001, although in the collection's original title, 1,001 served not as a specific number but as a notion suggesting merely a very large and open-ended collection of tales. The Arabic versions of this larger and later collection were first published in the nineteenth century. As the discussion below illustrates, the major themes of this particular story and others from the earlier collection are linked to those of the frame story with which the tale collection begins. Thus, the texts that will be used in this essay are those of the earlier collection (and the corresponding English version). Although the story is also included in the earlier parts of the larger and later collection (and its many translations), the addition of multiple tales tends to de-emphasize the thematic linkages to the frame story that are a specific feature of the original collection.

Following an introduction to the story itself—its structure, its characters, and its layering—the discussion will move on to possible modes of analysis that might be used in a classroom context.[2]

The Story

A major feature of "The Story of the Three Apples" is the number of layers it contains, often linked to the characteristic identification of "nights" segments.

Those subdivisions in the story come to an end at a crucial point in the narration and provide a linkage back to the frame story, as part of which our celebrated narrator, Shahrazad, daughter of the king's minister (vizier), is telling her stories to King Shahriyar and her own sister Dunyazad. The king has been out to take revenge on all women because he has caught his wife in flagrante with one of the men enslaved in the palace. As a result, he has taken to marrying a virgin girl every night, enjoying her sexual favors, and slaying her the next day. It is when his minister, Shahrazad's father, informs the king (and his own daughter) that the supply of virgins is running low that Shahrazad volunteers to be married to the king, taking her sister with her to his quarters. Her strategy is to postpone an apparently inevitable death by telling stories. To this point in the collection's narratives, she has avoided the unfortunate demise of many of her predecessors. The threat of impending violence and death and the potential application (or misapplication) of kingly authority, however, are a constant feature of the narrative atmosphere. Thus, each night (or perhaps early morning) the frame story explains that Shahrazad brings her narration to a close at a crucial point in any particular story so that the king will have to wait in patience till the following day to hear the conclusion of any tale—a very early example, one might suggest, of the principles governing contemporary soap operas.

The first of this particular story's layers involves Shahrazad's narrating its context and incidents to the king; she is portrayed as orchestrating the course of the episodes and determining the places where they are to be deliberately interrupted. The second layer introduces the reader to another ruler and his minister—namely, the renowned caliph Harun al-Rashid and Jaafar al-Barmakī. These two characters are actual historical figures, but it seems fairly clear from historical accounts that the picture painted in this and several other tales in the *Thousand and One Nights* is not intended to offer an entirely accurate portrait of the famous 'Abbasi caliph whose period of rule (786–809) is remembered for its thriving cultural and scientific atmosphere. To be sure, Jaafar, the caliph's closest confidant—according to the historical record—was to become a victim of his family's downfall, being beheaded in 809 on orders of the caliph (apocryphally he was having an affair with 'Abbasa, the caliph's sister). Certainly in this particular story the portrait of Jaafar, wise counselor and family man, contrasts completely with that of Caliph Harun, issuer of snap judgments and questionable decisions. Presumably, with the linkage of the themes in the stories of the original collection to its frame narrative in mind, King Shahriyar, the narrator Shahrazad's audience, is supposed to listen to the story, take note of such behavior, and avoid such practice in his own decision-making.

At the beginning of the story, the two men are indulging in one of Harun's favorite activities (at least, in the *Thousand and One Nights*)—namely, touring the streets of the caliph's capital, Baghdad, in disguise. The caliph's motivations in so doing are described in admirable terms: good deeds performed by his officials are to be rewarded and bad deeds punished. As the story proceeds, however, those laudable principles are not reflected in the caliph's decisions. During their tour of the city, the two men come across an old man fishing in the River Tigris—and here the different versions of the story vary widely in the amount of detail provided; Edward William Lane's version of the story (as part of his translation of the later collection), for example, contains a nine-line poem (Thousand and One Nights 120). The fisherman (also depicted as an unemployed teacher) has been fishing for some time with no luck. When the caliph asks him to try one more time, the fisherman hooks on to something, and a heavy chest is pulled out of the river. The chest is now opened, and the narrative tension mounts as layer upon layer of the contents is removed by the caliph's eunuch, here as elsewhere in the collection called Masrur (meaning "delighted"): "inside the basket was a stretch of carpet and, beneath it, a shawl folded in four, and, beneath it, a young woman like pure silver, killed and cut in pieces" (Seale, *Annotated* Arabian Nights 162).

At this crucial juncture the sixty-ninth night comes to an end. The mystery has now been set: a body has been discovered, dismembered even. Who is the victim, who is the killer, and what is the motive? Here are all the elements of a mystery story. The seventieth night opens with the caliph in a fury, addressing his minister and counselor as "dog of Viziers" (162). He is concerned, of course, about the young woman's death, but he is much more worried about his own responsibility on the Day of Judgment for the commission of this crime in the community of which he is the ruler. Jaafar is given three days to find the killer; if he fails, he and forty of his relatives will be condemned to death by crucifixion. So much, one might say, for the caliph's good intentions. Jaafar is no detective, however, and after the three-day period he informs the caliph that he has failed to find the killer. A public execution is now announced throughout the city, but before the sentence can be carried out a young man comes forward and confesses to the murder. A much relieved Jaafar is about to take the man before the caliph when an old man comes forward and confesses that he is the killer. Jaafar has now to take both men before the caliph. Presented with the dilemma of two confessed killers, the caliph announces glibly that both should be killed. It is Jaafar who has to explain to him that one of them would be justly killed, the other unjustly—further impairing the caliph's record on Judgment Day. The young man now gives a detailed description of the way the corpse was arranged inside the chest, whereupon the caliph, now convinced that the young man is indeed the killer, asks him to explain his conduct. As the young man is poised to answer, the seventieth night comes to an end, and Shahrazad lives another day.

The seventy-first night takes us into a third layer of the narrative, in that the young man provides an extensive account of the circumstances leading up to the discovery of the chest in the river. The young woman was his wife, and the old man is her father and his uncle. In other words, in a society where the marriage of cousins was a regular way of maintaining family cohesion, she is an ideal partner. Not only that, we also learn she has borne him three sons and has been in every conceivable way a dutiful and loving spouse. Some parts of the mystery are now resolved, but the major question remaining concerns motivation. It is the answer to that question that involves the three apples of the story's title.

When the wife falls sick, she asks her husband to bring her some apples—an extremely rare and valuable commodity. He travels to Basra in the South, procures three apples from the caliph's own orchard, and brings them back to her. One fateful day, while sitting outside his shop, he sees an enslaved man carrying an apple. Asked where he has obtained the apple, the man replies that he got it from his mistress and provides enough details to convince the husband that it is his own wife with whom the man has consorted. When his wife cannot explain why there are now only two apples, he attacks her with a knife, kills her, and cuts off her head. The details of the earlier unwrapping of the layers inside the chest are now repeated in reverse as the husband describes how he placed the separate parts of his wife's body into the chest and threw it into the river. When the husband returns home, however, it is to find his son weeping. In the fourth layer, the boy informs his father that he stole one of his mother's apples and told the very same man who accosted him in the local market where it had come from. The man snatched the apple, ignored the boy's pleas to give it back to him, and left. The husband now realizes, "I knew I was wrong to kill my wife" and notes that the fault rested with the "slave [who] had lied" (167). At this point one must assume that, once again, King Shahriyar, the narrator Shahrazad's audience, is listening to this account of violence against a wife and an enslaved man's role in bringing it about—as had been the case with the king's own wife in the frame story. Husband and uncle/father-in-law spend three days weeping over their shared loss. This is the "story of the murdered girl," and, as the caliph is about to react, the seventy-first night comes to an end.

The seventy-second night returns us to the second layer of the narrative. It opens with Jaafar being once again ordered by the caliph to bring the culprit—this time the miscreant from the market—to justice, again on pain of death should he fail to do so. Thus, for a second time in this narrative the caliph's loyal minister is placed into his failed detective mode. This time, however, he readily acknowledges the impossibility of his task and prepares himself to meet his apparently inevitable fate at the hands of the caliph. Having prepared his will, he awaits the arrival of the caliph's retainers. Sure enough, on the third day they arrive and Jaafar bids farewell to his family, coming last to his youngest daughter. In a depiction of the minister that creates a significant contrast to that of the caliph, he embraces the daughter who is described as being his favorite child ("whom he loved more than the others" [167]). Hugging her to his chest, he feels something bulging from her pocket. It is now the little girl's turn to offer a fifth layer, one that clarifies some of the uncertainties left from the short narrative of the wife's son in the fourth. She tells her father that she has had to purchase the apple, which has the caliph's name on it, from a man enslaved in their own household, Reyhan. Reyhan responds to Jaafar's questions by giving an accurate recounting of his own conduct, a sixth narrative layer—"the story of the apple," as the man himself states to conclude his account. Once again, Jaafar's hopeless quest has resulted in a fortunate conclusion.

Jaafar now takes Reyhan to the caliph, who is duly amazed; indeed, he bursts into laughter "until he fell on his back" (168). The caliph commands that this remarkable story be recorded in writing, but in a surprising move Jaafar now informs the caliph that, although the events of this story are indeed amazing, he will tell his master a yet more amazing tale, "The Story of the Two Viziers," but only on the condition that the caliph agrees to pardon Reyhan. The caliph agrees, replicating exactly the posture of King Shahriyar in the frame story: if the next story is indeed remarkable, Reyhan will be pardoned; otherwise he will die. In other words, Raihan's life now depends upon successful storytelling.

In spite of the ruthless violence against the young wife and the highly questionable decisions made by the caliph, the inexorable logic of Shahrazad's narration—the need to keep telling amazing and interrupted tales or be killed—demands that the stories follow one another, each more amazing than the last. And in this particular sequence, it is Jaafar the minister who is now narrated by Shahriyar as telling the next story—a direct continuation of the seventy-second night.

Teaching "The Story of the Three Apples"

While it is clearly possible to prepare a teaching module devoted to this story that is based solely on a reading and discussion of the text itself, the complexity of the collection's cultural provenance and reception may lead some teachers to favor an approach that begins by offering some background material. There is, needless to say, a plethora of options, and I will refer here to only some of the more obvious examples (all of which I have myself used in classroom presentations).

At the most general level we can begin by noting that there exist numerous studies devoted to the vast influence that the collection has had on European culture and its modes of expression and performance. These modes, to offer just a few examples, include music (Nikolai Rimsky-Korsakov and Maurice Ravel, both of whom composed pieces entitled *Scheherazade*); literature (Johann Wolfgang von Goethe's poetry collection *West-östlicher Divan*); painting (an entire school of Orientalist art, with Eugène Delacroix's *Les femmes d'Alger* as one of the most notorious examples); fashion (harem pants and veils that certain Gulf airlines still favor for flight attendants' uniforms); pantomime (where the two favorite presentations—at least per my own childhood experiences in England—are based on the tales of "Aladdin" and "Ali Baba," long thought to be French fakes with no authentic provenance in West Asia [see the essay by Paulo Horta in this volume]); and the much-criticized Disney and DreamWorks cartoons featuring Aladdin and Sindbad the Sailor—the original version of the latter set of tales being a separate collection of Persian origins but included by Galland in his translation of the original the *Thousand and One Nights* collection into French.

Discussion of these specific instances of cultural influence may conveniently lead to further explorations of issues connected with the more general context of the impact of such trends on a broader social and cultural scale. Significant among those trends would be the emergence of the concept of a *mission civilisatrice* during the eighteenth century and into the nineteenth and twentieth centuries, leading to assertions of cultural advancement and backwardness and the imperative of so-called development, which were to serve as partial motivations for the colonial (and evangelical) excursions initiated by European powers during those centuries. Such perspectives can be fruitfully explored in conjunction with anticolonial perspectives found in works such as the Sudanese author al-Ṭayyib Ṣāliḥ's famous novel, *Mawsim al-hijrah ilā al-shamāl* (*Season of Migration to the North* [see Saleh]) and many studies of such reactions to colonialism (such as Bill Ashcroft's *The Empire Writes Back*).

The linkage of this particular story to the frame story of the tale collection as a whole (illustrated in the analytical summary above) provides the opportunity for other types of preliminary investigation. The theme of decision-making by the ruler, here illustrated by the caliph's often instant and ill-advised comments and verdicts, can be seen as a vivid illustration of the tradition associated with the "mirrors for princes" genre, texts that offer sage advice to rulers as to how to make wise decisions. Although Aristotle's advice to the young Alexander the Great is usually cited as one of the original examples of the genre, the Arabic tradition has its own precedents, among them the collection of animal fables known as *Kalīlah wa-Dimnah*, a work translated from an Indo-Persian original entitled the *Panjatantra*, in which a pair of jackals offer advice to a ruler, duly illustrated by a number of animal fables.

On a more theoretical and textual level, the linkage between this story and the collection's frame narrative can serve as the basis for a discussion of the narrative technique of framing, both as a structuring device (demonstrated above in the consistent return to the first narrative level at the end of each night) and, as noted in the same analysis, as an illustrator of the thematic linkages that bind the story together.

I now offer two possible modalities whereby this story can be analyzed and discussed in a classroom setting. Whereas the first follows the sequence of the narrative itself, the second endeavors to highlight the complexity with which the narrative is assembled by making use of the writings of the French narratologist Gerard Genette, found in their most accessible form in his (translated) work *Narrative Discourse*, where he explores the impact of the twin categories of *histoire* (the order in which the events of the story occur) and *récit* (the order in which they are presented in the narrative), based in turn on earlier theorizations by members of the Russian formalist school.

I have previously described the summary of the story included above as "analytical" because, although it recounts the sequence of events as they are narrated in the story itself, it also points out several features that can be the focus of further discussion. The most obvious, and the continuing linkage that ties this tale, and by implication all the tales, to the frame story, is the subdivision of the narrative into a number of "nights" units, each of which involves the role of the collection's narrator, Shahrazad, in determining when a crucial juncture in the narrative has been reached; at that point she is described as bringing her narration to a close in keeping with her continuing strategy of postponement in order to stay alive. The way in which these several postponements within this particular narrative create their momentary tensions (in narrative time rather than in the implied daylong time for the narrator, Shahrazad) is, of course, an intrinsic feature of mystery stories, of which this would appear to be a relatively early example. Once the chest has been pulled out of the river and has revealed its horrifying contents, the questions posed by the need to identify both the victim and her killer become the driving force in the story and also its structure. Here, one might parenthetically suggest, a murder mystery that began with "John Smith did it" would at the very least entail a radical departure from the structural logic of the vast majority of mystery narratives. In this particular story, the buildup of tension and the need for its resolution are further enhanced by the narrative layers that have already been identified. The second of those layers provides us with a hapless caliphal minister whose life is spared only at the very last moment, when not one but two men come forward to confess to the crime. The tension created by this complicated situation is resolved only when, in the third layer, the husband of the murdered woman provides enough detail to convince the caliph (and us) that the identity of the killer has now been clearly established. Yet even now the questions concerning the missing apple remain unresolved; for that, the narratives of the woman's son and Jaafar's daughter are required, and the serendipity of the culprit's identity is finally revealed—much to the caliph's amusement.

Another mode of analysis involves an examination of the way in which the various personalities who feature prominently in the narrative are characterized. Most vivid here is the clear contrast in the story's description of two of the principal participants, the caliph and his minister, Jaafar. In spite of the caliph's expression of good intentions at the beginning of the story's second layer ("to question the people about the conduct of my administrators, so that I may dismiss those of whom they complain and promote those they praise" [Haddawy, *Arabian Nights* 150]), he is shown to be both irascible and impulsive. His primary victim is, of course, Jaafar, his own minister, but his snap judgments (at one point, ordering that both confessed killers be put to death, for example) are clearly not those of a ruler who contemplates the appropriateness, not to mention the legality, of his decisions. The behavior offers a clearly negative "mirrors for princes" message that is not lost, one presumes, on Shahrazad's primary listener, King Shahriyar. Jaafar is presented as a kind of foil to his caliph. He is, of course, the primary target of the latter's wrath, being twice threatened with death (and, as already noted, the actual Jaafar al-Barmakī was indeed executed on the orders of Harun al-Rashid). Right at the end of the narrative, it emerges that he is a family man who loves his little daughter best of all, a nice domestic touch totally absent from the rest of the story, not least with regard to the family that includes the husband and father of the murdered woman. But even before that, it is Jaafar who habitually points out to the caliph the inadvisability of his decisions, not to mention the negative effect they may have on his accountability on the Day of Judgment. In this context of Jaafar's portrayal, it must be observed that the version of this story found in the earlier collection of the *Thousand and One Nights* that I use as the textual source for this essay (Mahdi, Thousand) emerges as a shorter, more stripped-down narrative than the ones included in the later and longer collection. In Lane's translation of the later version, for example, the contrasting images of the caliph and Jaafar are further amplified. The caliph invites anyone from among the population of Baghdad who wishes to witness the crucifixion of Jaafar and his relatives to come and entertain themselves. While the caliph's retainers await his orders to carry out the sentence, both the earlier and later versions record that "the people wept for Jaafar and his kin" (Seale, *Annotated* Arabian Nights 163).

The way the killer husband and his murdered wife are depicted provides a further example of this mode of characterization through narrative. The young man whose last-minute confession spares the lives of Jaafar and his relatives is elaborately described: "moon face and dusky eyes, lily brow and rosy cheek and downy chin, and a mole like a disc of amber." By contrast, his uncle and father-in-law is simply "an ancient man" (163). His murdered wife is given a similarly elaborate portrait: "my cousin (this old man is her father and my uncle). I married her when she was still a virgin, and in eleven years we were blessed with three sons. She loved and served me, and I found no fault with her and loved her dearly" (164). This, then, is a young and handsome couple, an ideal match within the societal norms of the time, all of which makes the commission of such a grotesquely violent crime inexplicable. The attitude of the woman's father, who is portrayed in economic terms as weeping for his daughter, along with her husband, for three days, seems not a little subdued, given the awful circumstances involved.

At the end of the story, the crime remains unpunished. Jaafar secures a pardon for Reyhan, whose actions have triggered the entire tragedy. The succession of stories has to continue in spite of such a heinous crime.

Turning now to the second modality noted above, if we apply Genette's notion of *histoire* (the chronological sequence of events) to the text of this story, then we might create a new opening sentence along these lines: "In the city of Baghdad during the reign of the caliph Harun al-Rashid there lived a young couple with their three sons. One day, the wife fell sick and asked her husband to bring her some apples." This is indeed the initial situation and event that is to trigger the entire account represented by this story. It provides confirmation of the importance attached to this particular family as reflected in the two titles by which this story is known (cited at the very beginning of this essay). Genette's other analytical concept, the *récit* (the order in which the events are narrated), places the same section of the narrative into its third layer, the middle of the text, thus providing a good illustration of a major principle of mystery narratives, the postponement of resolution.[3] As noted earlier, we find out who committed the crime from the husband's confession, but the entire mystery is resolved only at the end—as one hopes and expects from a mystery story.

The comparison of the application to this story of these two analytical approaches elaborated by Genette, *histoire* and *récit*, shows clearly that the former reflects the titles in prioritizing the events concerning the young couple and the three apples, whereas the latter is primarily focused on the caliph and his minister (although the sheer coincidence of the thief's turning out to be a man enslaved in Jaafar's own household is certainly a convenient connecting device). It is, of course, the *récit* that is represented by the story as it has come down to us. One might conclude by suggesting that, in spite of the horrific nature of the young woman's murder and the insane jealousy of the husband (amplified by his reaction to the enslaved man's account—something that would certainly resonate with vengeful King Shahriyar), the circumstances and consequences of the murder are somewhat tangential to the overall sequence of the narrative—at least insofar as it is treated within the text itself. This is certainly a tale involving violence against women, but its primary (and initial) focus is on the conduct of the ruler.

"The Story of the Three Apples" is relatively short in comparison with some of the other tales in the *Thousand and One Nights*, and yet, as I have tried to demonstrate in this essay, it allows for a pleasing variety of approaches and interpretive strategies. The joint themes that link it to the collection's frame story—the appropriate (and inappropriate) behavior of rulers and the treatment of women in society—allow for the combination of this story with a huge number of other narratives devoted to the same and akin topics. In spite of the tale's relative brevity, the element of mystery and its eventual resolution can furnish the teacher with still further means by which to link this narrative product of bygone centuries with much literature from subsequent eras.

NOTES

1. I have often thought that the most frequently encountered English title of the collection, the *Arabian Nights*, is something of a misnomer in view of the Indo-Persian provenance of the original version and its subsequent translation into Arabic.

2. I have myself used this tale for a number of years in an introductory comparative literature class (Narrative across Cultures) at the University of Pennsylvania. The focus of the course has been on world narratives in a variety of genres. In this particular case the title of the session has been "framed narratives," and this story has been combined with Mark Twain's "The Celebrated Jumping Frog of Calaveras County."

3. As already noted, Jaafar does not even try to investigate the murder, and his discovery of Reyhan as the thief who steals the apple is purely coincidental. Erle Stanley Gardner, the creator of the series of novels (and television series) devoted to the successes of the renowned detective Perry Mason, regularly challenges his readers at a certain point in the narrative to guess who the criminal is, pointing out as he does so that all the evidence needed to identify that person is already available.

THE TALES AS WORLD LITERATURE

"Ali Baba" and "Aladdin" as Modern World Literature
Paulo Lemos Horta

The teaching of "Aladdin and the Wonderful Lamp" has been revolutionized by discoveries made in the past half decade with regard to the tale's known storyteller, the Syrian Hanna Diyab, now confirmed as a creative agent behind the story he gave the French translator Antoine Galland in Paris at the end of the first decade of the eighteenth century. As a result, the teaching of "Aladdin" emerges as a case study that offers particular challenges and opportunities for any instructor seeking to do justice to a tale that travels between cultures.

For over a decade, I have taught Diyab's tales within the context of a course that explores how the corpus of the *Thousand and One Nights* has served as a point of encounter between Middle Eastern literary traditions and the cultural politics of Western literary and artistic production and translation. The course examines the processes of cross-cultural exchange through which the tales were adapted for distinct audiences in medieval Egypt and Syria, modern Europe, the Americas, and the Middle East. Topics of discussion include how the nucleus of tales gathered in the Arab world was shaped by the forces of commerce, urbanism, science, and faith; and how familiar tales such as "Aladdin" and "The Story of Ali Baba and the Forty Thieves," which lack authoritative sources in Arabic, were added by Diyab and Galland. Students also consider the central role that translations and translators of the *Nights* have played in anchoring discussions of Orientalism and cosmopolitanism by Edward Said and Kwame Anthony Appiah, respectively.

The course has been housed in programs of literature and world literature that question the supremacy and boundaries of paradigms of national literature in the study of literature.[1] In this context I consider the original cycle of Arabic tales that constitutes the core of the story collection and also tales that were added in European translations, which have been the domain of courses on French or English literature, Orientalism and imperialism, or media and cultural studies. They seemed at the time of this course's first design paradigmatic examples of tales that gain in translation, lacking an original manuscript or text and having entered European and world letters through inclusion in Galland's French version of the *Thousand and One Nights*. They fit right in with notions of world literature in vogue in the first decade of the twenty-first century that emphasized circulation à la Pascale Casanova or Franco Moretti and, in David Damrosch's definition, thrived outside its culture of origin. Excluding such tales for lack of an "authentic" Syrian original was not an option. Rather, the challenge has been to apply the tools of literary history, comparative literature, and translation studies to disentangle the intricate and complicated patterns of conflict and collaboration that enabled the addition of such tales to the French translation produced by Galland.

While genealogies of "Aladdin" and "Ali Baba" have always referred to the elusive figure of Hanna Diyab, recent research has made it possible to demonstrate more decisively his role in stitching together the tales and bridging the Arabic and European origins of the story collection. The recent identification and publication in Arabic, French, English, and German of Diyab's memoir, the *Book of Travels*, show the Syrian to be an author in his own right. Diyab's engagement with traditions of travel writing and autobiography within the Arab world challenges us to rethink assumptions about the essentially French provenance of the mislabeled authorless or orphan tales. In the tales he gave Galland, Diyab exhibits some of the same techniques as in his *Book of Travels* of half a century later: not only a characteristic way of reassembling elements of known tales to make his own but also the embedding of tales within tales to create suspense, not unlike Shahrazad in the *Thousand and One Nights*.

We know that Diyab must have been a captivating storyteller for Galland to refer to his tales as beautiful in his diary (Horta, *Marvellous Thieves* 18), and there is evidence that in his youth Diyab was not only a consummate oral storyteller but also a budding author, as suggested by the precision of some of Diyab's observations of Paris recorded fifty years later. Given this new understanding of the Syrian French context for the origin of these tales, they are likely to figure alongside the tales of the *Nights* taught in a much wider variety of classroom contexts in the future. Diyab's expanding corpus of writing would fit a wider palette of definitions of world literature, one as likely to be predicated on practices of ethics and migrancy as on concerns with circulation. The revelation of an expanding corpus of manuscripts by Diyab will pique the interest of area specialists beyond the great books, comparative, and world literature frameworks that have propagated the teaching of the *Nights* in the North American academy.

Teaching Editions of "Aladdin" and "Ali Baba"

The revolution in the understanding of the genesis of the tale has also represented a boon in the materials available to instructors interested in teaching "Ali Baba" and "Aladdin."

Editions of the *Nights* intended for the classroom typically do not feature the tales added in French. Anthologies of world literature, such as the popular Norton survey, sample the original core cycle of tales as representative of medieval Arabic literature. The Norton Critical Edition of the *Arabian Nights* does likewise (see Heller-Roazen and Mahdi). As Husain Haddawy explains in his introduction to the deluxe paperback Norton edition, the tales added in French are considered part of the grime that the diligent editor and translator of the *Nights* must remove (Haddawy, *Arabian Nights* xvi). Although Haddawy begrudgingly agreed to include "Ali Baba" and "Aladdin" in a separate volume ("*Sindbad" and Other Popular Stories from the* Arabian Nights), he did not withdraw the verdict that dismissed the stories as a kind of fraud of literary history, best excised from memory.

Norton has nonetheless been quick to reevaluate these added tales following the publication of Diyab's travelogue and the recent reappraisal of Diyab's own literary contributions in studies, including *Marvellous Thieves: Secret Authors of the* Arabian Nights. My new edition of the *Nights* inclusive of all Diyab's tales was published under Norton's Liveright imprint in 2021 (Seale, *Annotated* Arabian Nights). The volume includes my introduction explaining Galland's debt to Diyab and the hybrid nature of the tale, signaling the flexibility of stories that could be taught as products of Syrian, French, or Syrian French culture, or of Mediterranean exchange. After the relative indifference to the tales among modern translators dubious about their authenticity, this edition affords the ideal opportunity for their rediscovery in the classroom.

Ursula Lyons, who appends an indispensable note on the difference in pace and psychology between the tales received in Arabic and those added in French, has also produced an excellent translation of "Aladdin" from Galland's French for Penguin, in the version included in Malcolm C. Lyons's translation from the Arabic. Ursula Lyons's version has the virtue of fully restoring the agency and voice of Aladdin's mother, undercut in all other extant modern versions. For the college or high school instructor, the only quibble here is that the use of bulky paragraphs makes it hard for instructors and students to find episodes and passages and pick out the dialogue in the long story. For the stand-alone Liveright edition of "Aladdin," I divided the tale into twelve chapters, gave them titles, and broke out dialogue into separate paragraphs, making it an easier text for students to navigate in class discussions and to employ in comparative research involving other versions and film and stage adaptations (Seale, Aladdin).

The Storyteller and the Translator

The emergence of Diyab as a literary figure in his own right now allows for a deeper exploration of the stories as examples of cross-cultural collaboration, introducing students to the research skills needed by the literary historian.

Diyab's memoir, produced in Aleppo near the end of his life, contains a lively account of his youthful journeys from Aleppo to Paris in the company of a French treasure hunter named Paul Lucas. New translations such as those by Paul Lunde and Elias Muhanna provide an opportunity to explore the writing skills of the author who provided Galland with the text of "Aladdin" in 1709. Diyab's account of his arrest by Parisian authorities for being an associate of a suspected jewel thief stands out as an episode displaying the use of embedded anecdotes to heighten the suspense in the narrative.

There are several episodes from Diyab's *Book of Travels* that can be profitably analyzed against episodes in "Aladdin" in the classroom: Diyab's first tomb-raiding excursion with Lucas, which yields a ring and a lamp; the presentation at Versailles, with its bejeweled princesses; and Diyab's visit to the opera, where he marvels at the appearance and disappearance of the palace. Whatever the relationship of Diyab to the text of the story Galland would claim in his diary to have received from him—whether he was author, compiler, or previous owner—these episodes attest at a minimum to the resonance of the tale with Diyab's own travels with Lucas, whom I and others have likened to the Maghrebi magician (*Marvellous Thieves* 58).

In the classroom, juxtaposing episodes from Diyab's *Book of Travels* with "Aladdin" affords the opportunities to explore the tantalizing possibilities of literary production in a cross-cultural context. In what ways might the story of the tailor's son reflect Diyab's concern for the socially marginal figures of beggars and condemned prisoners, displayed in the travelogue's descriptions of Paris? The editor of Diyab's work in French comments on the particularity of the Syrian traveler's description of the sympathy of Parisian crowds for condemned prisoners and antipathy toward executioners, given much historical record demonstrating the opposite (*D'Alep à Paris* 320–21). It is striking that when Diyab tells the story of Aladdin's march to his own execution, the crowds similarly side with the young protagonist. Given that Diyab composed his memoir of his travel to France half a century later, in the mid-1760s, it is difficult to guess the vector of possible influence, whether his experiences on the streets of early-eighteenth-century Paris influenced the narrative of "Aladdin" provided to Galland, or Diyab's preference for tales of the unpredictable fates of the socially marginal shaped the recollections of his experience as a young man.[2]

The relation between the stories offered to Galland by Diyab and the versions of the tales Galland included in *Les* Mille et une nuits: *Contes arabes traduits en français* (*The* Thousand and One Nights: *Arabic Tales Translated into French*) also affords a fruitful exercise in acknowledging the limits of what can be known. Galland received a text of "Aladdin" from Diyab, but students could gain a sense of Galland's own literary process by examining the translator's handwritten notes from the storytelling performances of Diyab relating to "Ali Baba" (Galland, *Journal* 1: 359–63; see also Seale, *Annotated* Arabian Nights 533–38). In the classroom a comparison between these jotted notes—a few short pages in the case of "Ali Baba"—and the published version—close to forty pages for the story—brings into relief the differences between Galland's record of Diyab's tale and the version ultimately published by the French translator. The summaries recorded from Diyab would appear more tolerant of moral ambiguity, whereas Galland exhibited a strong preference for sharply delineated heroes and villains. Richard Francis Burton, among others, observed the evident interpolation by the Frenchman of morals at the end of "Aladdin" and other tales. Yet until and unless there is confirmation of a Diyab manuscript for "Ali Baba," we can only speculate about Galland's precise contributions to the final version of the tale. What is certain from a consideration of sources for the tale's component parts—the clever servant, the magic cave, and the band of thieves—is the brilliance of the storyteller who first stitched it together.

Diyab's Tales and the Nights

Given the hybrid nature of Diyab's tales, a vital task in the classroom is to assess the affinity of the tales with both the Arabic core of the *Thousand and One Nights* and the emerging corpus of French fairy tales into which they were incorporated. A good way to accomplish this is to present students with the contrasting commentaries on Aladdin by Marina Warner (*Stranger Magic*) and Robert Irwin (Afterword). In her work, Warner emphasizes the tales as creatures of Galland's Paris and the undercurrents of modernity circulating in the early eighteenth century. Irwin, answering Warner, rejoins that many of the allegedly French qualities of the tales can be traced to elements borrowed from the original cycle of the *Nights*. Putting the two novelists and *Nights* scholars into conversation is a good way of inviting students into the denser field of scholarship.

Reading "Aladdin" against Arabic popular literature, Irwin protests that the dissonance of this tale with regard to the *Thousand and One Nights* has been greatly exaggerated (Afterword). The Arabic story collection possesses an array of lazy young men undeserving of the marvelous changes in fortune, one of whom employs a jinni to build a palace by magical means in order to woo a beautiful princess. Warner is on equally strong ground in identifying the deep resonance of "Aladdin" with the fairy tales of social elevation in vogue in Paris at the start of the eighteenth century (360–61). If Irwin notes the specific resonance between Aladdin's lamp and the raised lamps of the mosque, Warner in turn interprets the flight of Aladdin's palace within a distinctive eighteenth-century Parisian fascination with the possibilities of flight.

Students should be encouraged to investigate the nature of the tale's appeal in both eighteenth-century France (where it benefited from the phenomenon of Charles Perrault's *Tales of Mother Goose*) and England, from the early bootleg Grub Street versions of the *Thousand and One Nights* in London. "Aladdin" was often published separately. Some of these inexpensive chapbooks sported neoclassical palaces on their covers, and the ease with which this story was adapted to the urban landscape of Paris and London speaks to the near universal appeal of this tale of wish fulfillment. Encompassing both our wildest longings and our deepest uncertainties, the tale speaks to both the childhood dream of adventure and the terrors of coming of age. "Aladdin" would be bound within popular collections of fairy tales alongside other staples such as "Jack and the Beanstalk" and has a varied history beyond the frame of the *Thousand and One Nights*.

The tale was popular among those who, like Diyab himself, peopled the margins or lower stations within European society. Folklore scholars suggest that Aladdin quickly made the leap from the page to oral storytelling, as servants or other lower-class literates memorized the tale and recounted it to others. Ulrich Marzolph notes that, although it is rare to find direct accounts of oral transmission of published fairy tales, the preface to a nineteenth-century German collection of fairy tales does just that in the case of "Aladdin." It recounts the case of a maid who had been given a copy of the *Arabian Nights* by her employers. She liked "Aladdin" most of all and after many readings learned the story by heart. She loved to recount the tale when she visited a nearby town, and a generation later a storyteller was still retelling the tale he had heard from her. In Europe most of the forty distinct oral variants of "Aladdin," Marzolph argues, can be traced back to the text published by Galland from the tale gifted him by Diyab—attesting to the story's ability to quickly penetrate popular and oral culture in Europe.

Orientalism

In the classroom "Aladdin" can illustrate a history of circulation prior to the modern age of Orientalism that Said dates to Napoleon's invasion of Egypt in 1798 (50), and any instructor concerned with history will want to differentiate both these Orientalist moments. The Orientalism that governed the original reception of the tale in France was one defined by the acquisition of rare curiosities and the consumption of luxury goods from the Levant, as reflected in the role of the young Galland as a collector of manuscripts in the Ottoman Empire and Paul Lucas's commission as a procurer of curiosities for the royal court. Diyab's journey to Paris in the service of Lucas can be seen as a function of these expeditions to gather knowledge and precious objects. The story elements of "Aladdin" were well suited to meeting the thirst of a European readership entranced by the riches on offer in the palaces and markets of the Middle East. The extreme luxury of the palace constructed by the jinn to establish Aladdin's claim to the princess's hand, as well as the treasures of the cave of wonders (as in the tale of Ali Baba), all spoke to the Orientalist obsessions of court society in Galland's day—a phenomenon very familiar to Diyab, given his time with Lucas.

Students can be invited to explore how, once modern French and British imperial interests more directly shaped the production and reception of the *Nights* from the start of the nineteenth century, versions of "Aladdin" reflected the distinctly imperial pomp of the era and the imprint of the experience of invasion and occupation of Cairo and India from the French to the British. When the Victorian explorer Burton settled on translating from South Asian vernacular versions of "Aladdin," his stance accurately reflected the shift in British imperial interest in the tales of the *Thousand and One Nights* and in the so-called Orient more generally. Both the Arabic texts of the Calcutta I and Calcutta II editions of the *Nights* were the product of British colonial institutions and educational policies elaborated in India in the first half of the nineteenth century, as was the first English translation of the *Nights* from Arabic by Henry Whitelock Torrens. Small wonder that in Burton's translation the already confused geography of a tale bearing distinctly Arab and Muslim mores in a Chinese setting acquired the further backdrop of his own formative experience of British India. It is no coincidence that this imperial cocktail resulted in the lavish settings and scene changes in the high imperial pantomime versions of "Aladdin," with its pastiches of the Orient, anticipating Disney's Agrabah.

One way of excavating the imperial uses of "Aladdin" in the classroom is to encourage students to research the digital image archives made available by the Bibliothèque nationale, the Victoria and Albert, the British Museum, and other institutions and museums. "Aladdin" made the leap to the stage before the close of the 1700s, and it is instructive to compare the illustrations, set designs, and costumes of editions and stage plays of that century with the decidedly more exotic fare that followed in the next century in the high age of modern French and English imperialism in the Middle East. "Aladdin" has become such a staple of the pantomime stage to this day, where only "Cinderella" rivals it in popularity, that it is tempting, though inaccurate, to attribute the tale's global popularity to the phenomenon of the Victorian panto adaptation. Aladdin was already embedded in European culture before the late Victorian extravaganzas that boasted luxurious scene changes and imperial pomp and ceremony.

Given how deeply the tale burrowed into European culture, students would do well to look beyond the blanket backdrop and bluster of imperialism to disentangle the political ideals in an age of liberalism that provided the impetus for directors to adapt "Aladdin" to the stage. Adam Oehlenschläger's 1805 theatrical adaptation of the play proved a landmark in modern European literature, posing a counterpoint between Aladdin (embodying a positive Romanticism) and a new character, Muhraddin, that would recur as a structuring device in no fewer than thirty-six Danish novels in the century that followed, as Richard van Leeuwen has found. If in the earliest iterations Aladdin is a passive romantic figure, disconnected from reality, in later work he can be energetic and in charge of his own fate. Victorian Orientalist pantomime versions of "Aladdin" in Britain likewise could channel liberal ideals, as in adaptations, as Warner has noted, that advocated for the abolition of slavery (365).

"Aladdin" on Film

The apparent power of Disney to dictate the canon of popular culture across the globe may lead teachers to believe that the multinational conglomerate headquartered in Burbank, California, is responsible for the popularity of the tale of "Aladdin." Yet the *Thousand and One Nights* and "Aladdin" were vital from the earliest experiments in cinema in France, the United States, and India (see Irwin, "*Thousand and One Nights*"). Key points of reference can be found in Lotte Reiniger's 1926 *Die Abenteuer des Prinzen Achmed* (*The Adventures of Prince Achmed*), the oldest surviving animated feature-length film, which employs the tale of Aladdin for one of its five acts, and Raoul Walsh's and Alexander Korda's films of *The Thief of Bagdad* (1924 and 1940, respectively), which have engendered a series of direct and indirect imitations, including clear legacies within Disney's animated and live-action films, both titled *Aladdin* (1992 and 2019).

If, like late imperial pantomime, Disney's versions of "Aladdin" are partly to blame for an Orientalism that threatens to reduce the Middle East to a garbled "Agrabah," I have found it most useful to tackle this syndrome head-on in the classroom by engaging the live-action film version of 2019 that students are most familiar with. There is no shortage of scholarship detailing the service performed by the Disney animated 1992 film for the interests of the United States in the Middle East—notably Michael Cooperson's "The Monstrous Births of 'Aladdin'" and Sut Jhally's documentary *Reel Bad Arabs: How Hollywood Vilifies a People* (see also *Edward Said on Orientalism*, by Jhally). In my experience these debates on cultural appropriation and whitewashing in American education need to be updated, and instructors should reconsider the decision to focus on a 1992 film more central to their own formation than to that of their students. Students are particularly savvy when it comes to debates on Orientalism in media and film and come to class already well versed in the controversies associated with the blockbuster Disney live-action remake of "Aladdin" (2019).

This film attracted headlines for expanding Jasmine's agency and role, giving her a new solo, and expanding the range of her significant relationships to include a close friendship with Dalia, a newly introduced handmaiden. Students should be encouraged to discuss how far Hollywood has come or has yet to come. The 2019 film proves a complex case study in the classroom, as signaled by the mixed reception among reviewers, academics, and cultural and social activists upon its release. Much of the initial wave of thought pieces and academic interventions, based entirely on the trailer and publicity for the film, was negative and dismissed the film's politics, assuming it to be a shot-for-shot remake of the animated classic. Yet only a few weeks into its release, journalists were discussing the elimination of the racial stereotypes of the original animated film and the unprecedented box office success of a film with nonwhite leads, including popularity among Latino and African American audiences. Newspapers now published lists of things the live-action remake had done better in the area of cultural representation than its animated precursor.

Mainstream outlets from *Time* and *Life* magazines to *The Guardian* even heeded developments in scholarship to ask if "Aladdin" could now be attributed to the Syrian Diyab, dislodging long-standing assumptions of the complete inauthenticity of the tale and opening room for a reevaluation. Referring to this new scholarship, the Lebanese American critic Mary Kay McBrayer found herself open to rediscovering the story in Yasmine Seale's rendition ("It's written beautifully, every line is poetry"). These developments prove the relevance of new resources available for the teaching of "Aladdin."

Since "Ali Baba" and "Aladdin" bring with them the dangers of overfamiliarity, the trick is to encourage inquiry into cross-cultural misapprehension and communication. It helps that the past decade of research into the origin of the tales has uncovered Diyab's agency. The discovery of Diyab's memoir of this traveler's journey from Aleppo to Paris has afforded a critical reappraisal of stories long dismissed as cultural appropriation. Students' enthusiasm can be channeled into an investigation of the full complexity of authorship within the unequal relationship of a French translator and a Syrian storyteller and on recuperating the history of the reception of "Aladdin" within modern European and world literatures.

NOTES

1. I have taught courses on the *Thousand and One Nights* in the literature and creative writing program at New York University, Abu Dhabi, and at Harvard University's Institute for World Literature's summer school.

2. "In searching Diyab's memoir for clues about the creation of the orphan tales, the chronology of these events is striking. Diyab encountered the splendors of Versailles several months before he began telling Galland his tales in May 1709—opening up the possibility that the deep impression made by the ladies of Versailles shaped the stories that he contributed to the *Arabian Nights*. However, the influence may also have run in the other direction. When Diyab composed his memoir some fifty years later, he may have reused the stock phrases with which he had described fictional characters of ravishing beauty and wealth in tales like 'Prince Ahmad' to describe the French princesses of Versailles" (Horta, *Marvellous Thieves* 47).

Travels with the Tales of Sindbad

Maurice Pomerantz

Sindbad may be among the few figures from the *Thousand and One Nights* who is even better known than Shahrazad. He is the prototype of the intrepid seeker who recounts the heroic tale of his escape from shipwreck, impossible horrors, and monsters. He is the voyager who returns with a marvelous tale.

Traversing cultures, languages, and time, the Sindbad tales have manifested a similar propensity to travel. Sindbad's adventures have become the inspiration for countless children's books, movies, and comics. As Wen-chin Ouyang recently observed, "Where would *The Thousand and One Nights* be today had it not been for Sindbad the Sailor?" (Ouyang, "Whose Story" 133). In this essay, I share my approach to teaching the tales of Sindbad in undergraduate courses on Middle Eastern literatures in translation and on the *Thousand and One Nights*. My teaching has been informed by the work I have done as a scholar on the migration and travel of stories in premodern Arabic literature. I am particularly attentive to the fact that the tales of Sindbad, and many of the disparate materials from the *Thousand and One Nights*, have been primarily studied by scholars interested in their circulation following their so-called discovery and translation by European Orientalist scholars and others. Although this emphasis has done much to show how central these materials were in the formation of European identities, it has also had the unintended effect of foregrounding the European imagination of the East over the study of the East's imagination of itself. But even more so, the focus on the tales' circulation in Europe has taken precedence over inquiry into the lives these tales had prior to their recording by Galland. Where was Sindbad before he became such a famed figure of the *Thousand and One Nights*?

Another World Literature: The Travels of Premodern Arabic Literature

The alleged modern discovery of the tales of Sindbad was the result of the work of one man, Antoine Galland. The Sindbad stories were not among those found in the fifteenth-century codex of Syrian provenance that forms the basis of the *Mille et une nuits* (*Thousand and One Nights*)—the so-called Galland manuscript (Marzolph and van Leeuwen 2: 535). Rather, it was Galland himself who had found manuscripts of the stories during his travels in Turkey. Galland was so enamored of these tales that he translated them in full and later added them to the third volume of the *Mille et une nuits* that he published in 1704 (see 3: 228–91). Galland had witnessed the popularity of the *Mille et une nuits* and hastened to add these further tales of daring adventure.

The history of Galland's edition and translation of the *Mille et une nuits* has been well documented. But what can we say about the history of the tales of Sindbad prior to this encounter with its European translators? What evidence is there for the tales of Sindbad prior to their discovery by Galland?

Sindbad between History and Romance

Early estimations of the tales of the *Thousand and One Nights* and the tales of Sindbad emphasized their qualities as entertainment (Warner 20–21). Scholars soon began to consider the information that was contained therein more seriously, however. The English poet and antiquarian Richard Hole pointed to the possible affinities between Sindbad and other ancient epic literatures. Particularly important was the figure of the man-eating giant in Sindbad's third voyage, which echoed Odysseus's encounter with Polyphemus in book 9 of the *Odyssey* (Montgomery, "Al-Sindībād" 445). Such readings often suggested that Arabic literature was a cultural way station that transferred knowledge from Greco-Roman antiquity to the present. Late-nineteenth- and early-twentieth-century Orientalist readings of the tales began to focus on geographic details as a source of possible historical realia. These details suggested that the Sindbad tales were based on real accounts of sailors who had braved the Indian Ocean and returned to the ports of Basra and Baghdad to tell their tales (Hennig 196–99). To these scholars the stories were factual accounts that possessed a mythical residue of the great mercantile explorations undertaken by Muslim traders in the Indian Ocean during the height of the Abbasid caliphate.

The tales did not only reveal geographic knowledge, however. Folklorists have detected that certain Sindbad tales reflect stories that were long in circulation (Zipes, *Irresistible Fairy Tale* 8). For instance, the "living island" motif—in which a protagonist standing on an island realizes it is in fact the back of a large sea creature—is, as one scholar puts it, "as old as maritime literature itself": the motif is first attested in Chinese literature in the fourth century BCE and in the *Physiologus*, a work of Greek literature of the second century CE (Tuczay 285).

The Anglo-Norman *Legend of Saint Brendan*, which dates from the twelfth century CE, provides an interesting counterpoint to the Sindbad tales. The tale recounts the voyages of Saint Brendan "the navigator" for seven years and includes such marvels as a mysterious deserted castle, an island of birds, and an island of giant sheep. The voyage comes to an end when the travelers find a crystalline column and visit the mouth of hell. Among the many marvels described therein is the famed account of Brendan's feast on the back of a whale. The Anglo-Norman *Legend* records how, after a perilous journey across the sea, all but one of Brendan's companions disembark on a great island, where they begin to feast. Soon after they light a fire, they feel the island beginning to move and scurry back to the boat, where a lone abbot remains:

Brendan said to them: "Brothers, do you know
> Why you have been afraid?
> It is not land, but an animal
> Where we performed our feast,
> A sea fish greater than the greatest.
> Do not be astonished by that, gentlemen.
> God wanted to lead you here for this
> Because He wanted to instruct you.
> The more you will see His wonders,
> The better by far you will then believe in Him;
> The better you will trust Him and the more you will fear him,
> The more you will obey his command.
> First in rank the divine king made
> This sea fish above all others."   (Mackley 272–73)

Reading this tale in class, we discuss how the Anglo-Norman *Legend* is, like the tales of Sindbad, seemingly predicated on the production of wonder in the service of reflection. They point to the form of the wonder tale central to the narrative logic of the Sindbad tales.

Tales Wondrous and Strange

Arabic literature was often a site where the flotsam and jetsam of oral folk material was retrieved by literary artists. German scholars of medieval Latin and vernacular literatures described this process as *Verschriftlichung* (Ziolkowski 40). Thus, the Sindbad tales possess folk motifs similar to those of other tales from around the world, such as the *Legend of Saint Brendan*.

The tales also, however, possess some features typical of Arabic and Persian literary storytelling traditions. The capacity to astonish and amaze was a fundamental quality of tales known as *'ajā'ib*. The production of "wonder" (*'ajab*) is a basic feature of tales such as the *Nights* (Mottahedeh). The term *'ajā'ib* in particular was found in geographic texts, yet in Arabic and Persian contexts it is not strictly limited to the "fantastic" but also encompasses the astonishment that an onlooker might have when encountering a great mosque (Hees 104–06). Moreover, the term in premodern Arabic and Persian contexts is not in opposition to scientific realia. Rather, it was understood that "astonishment" with the world (*ta'ajjub*) was something that provoked and inspired further exploration of it.

This spirit of exploration and adventure deeply imbues many of the Sindbad stories. In my teaching of the tales, I find it instructive to think with students about the various ways the wondrous and exotic figure in the narrative structure. For instance, during the second voyage, Sindbad expresses his wonder at seeing the giant Rukh bird: "My wonder increased, and I recalled a story I heard from tourists and travelers that there is on certain islands an enormous bird, called the Rukh, which feeds its young on elephants, and I became certain that the dome I saw was one of the Rukh's eggs and wondered at the works of God the Almighty" (Haddawy, "*Sindbad*" 15). Later in the same voyage, Sindbad similarly expresses wonder at an "enormous serpent" that the Rukh bird took in his mouth (15). The tale reaches its climax in the bizarre account of the mountain of diamonds. Sindbad reports having heard that this mountain is so treacherous that merchants who deal in diamonds use a ruse to obtain them, taking a freshly slaughtered sheep and throwing it down from the top of the mountain, whence diamonds stick to it. They then wait for eagles and vultures to swoop down and grab the meat, bringing it and the diamonds back to the top of the mountain.

What is striking about both these instances is that they not only generate astonishment on the level of the strange and wondrous events themselves (which are surely bizarre) but also offer further evidence of the veracity of these astonishing events. Moreover, Sindbad's tales are seemingly designed with a frame that too is meant to provoke wonder. As Sindbad the Sailor begins recounting the tales to Sindbad the Porter, the former tells the latter to focus on the tales:

> Porter, my story is astonishing, and I will relate to you all that happened to me before I attained this prosperity and came to sit in this place, where you now see me, for I did not attain this good fortune and this place save after severe toil, great hardships, and many perils. How much toil and trouble I have endured at the beginning. I embarked on seven voyages, and each voyage is a wonderful tale that confounds the mind, and everything happened by fate and divine decree, and there is no escape from that which is foreordained. (Haddawy, "*Sindbad*" 5–6)

Sindbad the Sailor makes it clear to his namesake, Sindbad the Porter (in itself a bizarre coincidence!), that his tales of wonder will be astonishing. Each tale is likewise an occasion for wonder that may confound him, and by extension all other listeners to the sailor's tales. This type of layering is a feature found in other sections of the *Thousand and One Nights* and is also common to Arabic and Persian *adab* collections that play on the reader's recognition of a well-defined narrative form to create new narrative effects.

Traveler's Tales

The ideas of recounting tales about wonders and distant lands bring the fictive tales of Sindbad into dialogue with a long-standing literary form in Arabic: the traveler's tale. In my classes I have contrasted Sindbad's tales with selections taken from the large corpus of writings by Muslim geographers and travelers.

In discussing the harrowing scenes from the fourth voyage, in which Sindbad is, according to a local custom, buried alive with his wife, I have had students read passages of a similar live burial taken from a report found in the early-tenth-century geographer Ibn Rusta. He writes, "When a leading man dies, they dig a hole as big as a house in which they bury him dressed in his clothes and wearing a gold bracelet, accompanying the corpse with food, jars of wine, and coins. They bury his favorite woman with him while she is still alive, shutting her in inside the tomb, and there she dies" (Ibn Rusta 146; Montgomery, "Ibn Rusta's Lack" 76). This coincidence between the reportage of a supposed actual practice among the Rūs and a fictional tale should pose questions about the nature of these categories in premodern Arabic literature.

Even more dramatic a comparison is Ibn Baṭṭūṭa's famed account of the ritual self-immolation of a young woman (suttee), which also seems to have parallels to Sinbad's fourth voyage. In this passage, Ibn Baṭṭūṭa rationally frames the practice in terms of Islamic practice, then quickly moves to a detailed description of the suttee ritual. As Ibn Baṭṭūṭa has it, Brahmins surround the women, and a band of trumpets and drums precede her as she is led toward the pyre. Ibn Baṭṭūṭa's account begins with a dispassionate description referring to suttee as an "honorable act" (*mandūb*) and not "required" (*wājib*). His horror colors the eventual reportage, describing the location in which the suttee takes place as "a location as if it were hell." At the end of the account, Ibn Baṭṭūṭa states that he almost fell off his horse, swooning from witnessing the scene (209–13). Such a progression from dispassionate factual reportage to horror maps in interesting ways onto the emotional register of Sinbad's tales and how they might have been received by their audiences.

Between Tales and Maqāmāt

For a long time, scholars were convinced that the tales of Sindbad represented a popular form. This non-elite literature, known in Arabic as *khurāfāt*, was filled with the fantastic and unbelievable and thus not suited or suitable to the tastes of "men of learning" (*'ulamā'*). In their language, taste, and style, such works were popular and were not a part of the canonical works of premodern Islamic learning (Irwin, *The* Arabian Nights: *A Companion* 81).

Students of the *Thousand and One Nights* and Arabic literature of the Mamluk and Ottoman periods are increasingly discovering the important role elite scholars played in the composition and dissemination of this literature. In the case of the Sindbad tales, I have shown that Sayyid Abd al-Raḥīm al-ʿAbbāsī, a major scholar of the sixteenth century, retold what must be considered to be a prototype of Sinbad's fourth voyage while he was resident at the court of Sulaymān the Magnificent (Pomerantz). Al-ʿAbbāsī was in turn editing and modifying a tale told by the tenth-century Baghdadī scholar al-Tanūkhī. Ulrich Marzolph has found yet another version of the same motif in the early-twelfth-century Persian compendium *Mujmal al-tawārīkh wa-l-qiṣaṣ* (Marzolph, "Scholar" 292 and "Early Persian Precursor").

Tale-telling was long a part of the learned man's repertoire and was associated with many important personalities (see Orfali and Pomerantz 13–27). Many writers found occasion even in the course of their scholarly work to tell tales of the type defined above as *khurāfat*. Indeed, the form of the *maqāma* utilized by al-'Abbāsī lasted for nearly a millennium and was practiced across all regions of the Muslim world.

In my classes I like to demonstrate how fluid the boundaries between elite and popular literature were and how frequently the literature of elites is in fact a rewriting of stories and motifs that were popular and folkloric. As is the case in European literature, oral and written cultures were for a long time in conversation with one another (Heath xvii).

Cultural Mobility

One widespread assumption of world literature is that it is mainly with the advent of the modern world system of the sixteenth century that stories began to travel across the globe. It should come as no surprise, however, that numerous literary forms in Arabic literature were on the move during the premodern period, and the Sindbad tales surely display evidence of being part of this circulation (Pannewick).

Literary history of the premodern period often drew on a vast store of oral literary motifs, and writers and storytellers combined and refashioned tales. The tales of Sindbad do more than simply reflect the patterns of distant trade and adventure. Rather, they are also representative themselves of the travel of literary forms. The tales were in some sense already part of far-flung literary traditions when Antoine Galland first obtained manuscripts of the work.

CONTROVERSIES

Shahrazad's Gender Lessons
Suzanne Gauch

What does Shahrazad teach us about gender? Most immediately, this question often leads to debates about Shahrazad's putative feminism or arguments about the status of women in the time periods or places represented by the *Thousand and One Nights*. Like everything else about the tales, however, their representations of women, gender, and sexuality are neither straightforward nor consistent. The *Nights* lend themselves to inclusion in classes ranging from introductory literature to women's literature and feminist theory courses, and even certain film courses. Shahrazad's lessons are complex and contradictory, bound up with race, ethnicity, and social status, and with the benefit of some well-framed questions, adaptations, and more recent feminist writing, students will discover their own riches for the study of women's agency, gender dynamics, and perceptions of women's sexuality in the tales—across the ages and in the here and now.

Of course, Shahrazad's voice looms large. Not only does she insist on speaking up despite her own father's efforts to keep her quiet for her own presumable good but she also finds myriad ways to keep holding the room through audience engagement rather than force. Students are sometimes impatient with Shahrazad's apparent concessions to power or critical of stratagems easily coded as feminine wiles and apt to compare her unfavorably to the sword- and power-wielding heroines of, say, *Game of Thrones*. Drawing their attention to a less obvious parallel—namely, present-day advice, tips, and guidelines for women who seek to be heard in male-dominated workplaces, corporate environments, and politics—offers some critical perspective on the frameworks that continue to regulate whether and how women are listened to and heard. Such advice abounds in popular media, whether on blogs or in newsletters or newspaper pieces for women in business and the public sphere, as much as in evaluations of women's performances on reality television competition shows or political debates. Asking students of any level or in any type of course to compile a list of such sources will show them how abiding and inflexible these constraints on women's speech remain. A related creative assignment might ask students to transpose Shahrazad's approach into a scenario where she must challenge an abusive power structure by making a boss, opponent, or mansplainer listen, first writing and then performing their scene. Yousry Nasrallah's 2009 feature film, *Tell Me a Story, Sheherazade* (*Ehki, ya Shahrazade*), dramatizes one such scenario, and with a bit of prompting, students will readily find their own.

Instructors may take a more explicitly literary approach by asking students to comparatively analyze women's speech in narrative. The most obvious works for comparison are other premodern frame stories, whether Geoffrey Chaucer's *The Canterbury Tales*, Giovanni Boccaccio's *The Decameron*, or Juan Ruiz's *The Book of Good Love*. Questions they might consider include the following: What are the conditions by which women come to speak in each? How long are they granted an audience? What are the common framing and narrative elements in each case? What are the notable differences? Does the speaker's gender determine the content or focus of these stories in predictable ways? These questions can be placed into transhistorical contexts by asking classes to identify notable women narrators in literature written by women and men across the ages and dissect the premises of their speech and elements of their narratives. An assignment that prompts students to rewrite the framing story or one of Shahrazad's tales in the style of their favorite author will engage them in close comparative study of structure and content, as well as the construction of gender and sexuality. Preparatory readings for this exercise can include the fairy- and folktale refashionings of Helen Oyeyemi and Nalo Hopkinson, respectively, as well as those of Angela Carter, Anne Sexton, and Margaret Atwood, and students can be prompted to compare the portrayals, roles, and norms of femininity in the fairy tales and folktales these authors depict with those in different versions of the *Nights*.

Fatima Mernissi's ingenious examination of her aunt Habiba's retelling of the story of Princess Budur, the birdwoman, as a foil for Richard Francis Burton's rendering of the tale in his (in)famous translation of the *Nights* sharply highlights the varying value assigned to speech and writing by different cultures. Mernissi's work further serves as a jumping-off point for discussions of the relationship of author to narrator and character. The question of whether an author can and should write characters whose experiences of gender and race and cultural and sociopolitical realities deviate substantially from their own is a timely issue, and the *Nights* renders it more complex because of the tales' age and fantastical cast. To be sure, retellings of the *Nights*, whether by women or men, also lend themselves to feminist analysis, particularly those that delve into women's writing and speech, or *écriture féminine*, as developed by Hélène Cixous, Luce Irigaray, or Chantal Chawaf. Students might trace these to the embeddedness of the gendered mind-body duality in Western thought and reflect on whether the *Nights* disturbs this duality. Perhaps less conventionally, instructors may introduce a work like Edgar Allan Poe's "The Thousand-and-Second Tale of Scheherzade," which reflects the gendering of the so-called Orient by comparison with the technologically advanced West while also emphasizing the science-fictional dimension of Shahrazad's tales. This opens up consideration of how women's relation to science is portrayed over time, from the *Nights* until today. Students might research the obstacles confronted by women scientists, the ways their work is reported and recorded, and the erasures of their work in the past as much as today, or they might identify and examine Shahrazad-like characters in science fiction and fantasy works.

That is one cycle. Here is another: Shahrazad, you may recall, is not the first woman seen in the frame story of the *Nights*. That honor belongs to Shahzaman's wife, no sooner spied by her husband in the arms of her lover, "a kitchen boy" (Seale, *Annotated* Arabian Nights 6), than she is cut in two before she can utter a word. Several more women appear: Shahriyar's wife and her enslaved female attendants, quickly joined by their Black lovers. This second, still unnamed, queen speaks only to summon her lover. Although, she is slightly more defined than Shahzaman's wife, information gleaned about her is limited to her marital status, appearance (great beauty), and social rank (conveyed by her commanding tone), her character filtered wholly through her brother-in-law's judgment. Shahriyar and Shahzaman alike judge her instantaneously, and their determinations that she has violated her vows and status broach no mitigating circumstances. Even the more loquacious jinni's stolen bride, whom the two monarchs learn was abducted and raped by the jinni on her wedding night and held captive ever since, and who temporarily enslaves the pair when her captor falls asleep, fails to inspire any reflection on the complex interplay of gender, sexuality, class, race, and power in the two kings. All the brothers take from their terrifying confrontation is that wily women are capable of cuckolding even the most fearsome jinni. Shahriyar, assuaged, returns home, kills his wife, and begins marrying a virgin every night, and executing her the following morning, confident that he has found the key to managing women's rebellious sexuality.

These women are seen rather than heard, their stories cut short before they can be told, their perspectives and experiences effectively discounted. In many ways, they resemble what has happened to Shahrazad's character in adaptations of the *Nights* for stage and film. Students in the United States are familiar with the Disney renderings of "Aladdin and the Wonderful Lamp," and it can serve as an excellent starting point for discussions of how and why Shahrazad's model of womanhood vanishes or is radically altered in stage and film adaptations of the *Nights*. Students could be tasked with breaking down the gender tropes in adaptations of the "Aladdin" narrative—a tale that first entered the *Nights* when Antoine Galland adapted it from Hanna Diyab's text and that has characterizations in common with Western fairy tales—and contrasting them with those in the framing story of the *Nights* as well as with those in the less well known story cycles within it, whether "The Tale of the Porter and the Three Women of Baghdad" or "The Tale of the Hunchback." Marina Warner's examination of the popularity of stage adaptations of "Aladdin" in her volume on the cultural resonance of the *Nights* might be included by way of highlighting the tales' enduring popularity, as students examine how much of that popularity depends on its reproduction of certain conventions of femininity and masculinity, and its eschewing of women's sexuality.

Another exercise might ask students to compile lists of cinematic adaptations of the *Nights* in North America, Europe, or globally to examine how (and whether) they characterize Shahrazad. Does she vanish entirely? Is she reduced to a belly-dancing sex symbol or enslaved woman of the harem? Does she retain her voice? Is her role substantially transformed? Does her character change as cinematic versions of the *Nights* evolve? How do film versions balance spectacle with Shahrazad's overarching message—namely, that seeing alone never gives the beholder a full sense of how this picture came to be, that truly bearing witness demands patient and attentive listening, and that justice requires careful reasoning based on complete information? Beyond Shahrazad's character, one might delve into the gendered power dynamics of these adaptations, in addition to exploring whether and how they address race and social standing. Students might be challenged to write a screenplay or make a short video or podcast for a crucial scene that accords agency to the kings' wives, Shahrazad, or the jinni's enslaved woman and explain the logic of their choices. Along similar lines, they might set the tale in today's social context.

That is a second cycle. Here is a third: Shahrazad's tales, you may recall, are not for King Shahriyar's ears alone. Shortly into her first night with Shahriyar, Shahrazad begs the king to summon her sister:

> [W]hen the king took her to bed and pawed at her, she wept. When he asked why, she said, "I have a little sister, and I want to say good-bye to her before the night is done." The king sent for Dunyazad, who came and went to sleep under the bed. She woke when it was dark and waited for the king to finish with her sister. When they were done, Dunyazad cleared her throat and said, "Sister, if you are not sleepy, tell us one of your lovely stories to while away the night before I say good-bye at dawn. Who knows what tomorrow holds for you?" Shahrazad turned to the king and said, "May I tell a story?" "Yes," he said. And she said, "Listen."
>
> (Seale, *Annotated* Arabian Nights 19)

Sometimes Dunyazad's presence beneath the marital bed is ignored; sometimes it is made much of, its strangeness dissected, and the solidarity, common victimization, and eventual rivalry of the sisters explored, as in Assia Djebar's *A Sister to Scheherazade*. In any event, Shahrazad's request that her sister be summoned as the sex act begins and before the king can "finish with her" ensures that Dunyazad receives lessons in more than just storytelling. Although the scenario is most remarked for its break with the kind of Victorian sexual mores that many presume preceded present-day openness, it is equally if not more notable for the lessons in sex education it offers. Such lessons were widespread in the premodern era and have much to teach contemporary readers, as Carissa Harris's incisive study of sexual explicitness and obscene language in Middle English and Middle Scots literature in *Obscene Pedagogies: Transgressive Talk and Sexual Education in Late Medieval Britain* demonstrates. In essence, Shahrazad is speaking out about rape, a theme that especially resonates with today's students, for that is really what the king does to every virgin he marries, silencing his crime by subsequently executing his victim. By bringing Dunyazad into her nuptial room, Shahrazad offers her sister an explicit preview of her eventual fate, for surely the king acquiesces with the understanding that the younger sister will become his new bride on the following night. This effectively conveys the message that only by forming an alliance can they bring about an end to the prevailing cycle of rapes and femicides.

Instructors familiar with medieval tales and stories that show variations on this scenario may lecture on the comparative historical and sociopolitical circumstances surrounding their emergence. Once again, the erasure or highlighting of the circumstances in which Shahrazad delivers her story in various renderings of the *Nights* in different geographic regions should prove instructive. Shahrazad and Dunyazad's alliance and tactics might also be compared with those employed by anti-rape groups and in sex education throughout time, including at high schools and on college campuses today. Study of transcripts of legal cases, whether premodern or modern, in which the defense argues that the victim's foreknowledge minimizes the offense might prove equally instructive. The Me Too movement and its emphasis on speaking out and women telling their stories presents an especially effective model for comparison.

Although Shahrazad does not prevent her own rape, she does succeed in preventing the definitive silencing that would follow it, for Dunyazad is a quick study. King Shahriyar, on the other hand, learns much more slowly, requiring many—or, better said, infinite and continuous—stories of women (and men) responding to injustices, follies, and seemingly arbitrary violence in the broadest possible array of ways. One such tale, notable for its frank presentation of women's sexuality, linking of alcohol consumption with loss of inhibitions, depiction of the close intertwining of sexual domination and social power, and representation of an apparent sadomasochistic play, is the "Tale of the Porter and the Three Women of Baghdad."

In it, a porter waiting for work in a marketplace in Baghdad is approached by a richly attired woman, who bids him carry the elements of a varied, fabulous feast to her home. Arriving at a mansion with his goods and seeing that he is the only male present, the porter ingratiates himself with the three mistresses of the house and is given permission to stay and party with them. As the evening progresses, his wildest hopes are realized as he and the three women lose all their inhibitions to drink, with the result that he is able to flirt with and fondle them to his heart's content. When one of the inebriated women strips herself naked and leaps first into the pool and then into his lap, he can scarce believe his luck—until she begins to question him:

> "My lord, my love, what's this?" "Your womb," he said. "Whoa! You have no shame," she said, and cuffed him on the neck. "Your mound," he said. And one sister shouted, "Ugly word!" and nipped him. "Your cunt," he said. And the other sister hammered at his chest to cries of "Shame!" and knocked him back. (Seale, *Annotated* Arabian Nights 87)

The abuse continues until he finally capitulates and asks them what its name is, and the girl replies, "Basil of bridges" (87). When the porter accepts and repeats this name, drinking resumes until the next girl takes her turn. Beyond the power of self-naming that each girl claims, there is that of self-knowledge. When the porter arrived at the home of the three ladies, he assumed himself their master of sorts by simple virtue of his maleness, a presumption of superiority borne out by the young woman's interpellation of him with the words "my lord, my love." Yet just as quickly, his superiority and authority are challenged by blows and physical abuse that leave him bruised and weary. Although the porter regains his poise when he names his own organ in a way that would make it the vanquisher of the girls and persuades them to allow him to stay the night, as the story progresses, he is increasingly relegated to the back burner, and he has been allowed to leave by the time the ladies and dervishes are married off (some to one another) by the caliph.

Showing students how the porter's interactions with the three ladies of the house consist of give-and-take in word and deed and are marked by constant negotiation for access (to the house, the food, the wine, the women) opens up a contrast with the appearance of the three dervishes and their introduction of a more rigid paradigm of social interaction. The dervishes immediately speculate about the porter's identity and what has happened. Interestingly, the porter sides with the ladies, chiding the men to remember the inscription over the door: "Speak of what concerns thee not and burning ears shall be thy lot" (90). When the three ladies commence their strange nocturnal activities, only the porter is called on to assist them. Is this because of his lower social standing or because he has earned the ladies' trust? The other men also prevail on him to break the pact of silence they have all taken, but he does so by emphasizing that he is but the conduit of the other men's curiosity.

Multilayered and complex as it is, this tale (or story cycle) juxtaposes several models of men and women negotiating gender and power relations through preparations for sexual encounters and within those encounters themselves. Students might compare the relationship established between the porter and the three ladies in the frame with those established between the three ladies and their lovers and husbands in their respective tales, and with those in the stories of the three dervishes, detailing the codes and assumptions at work in each.

There are plenty of contemporary narratives that parallel these, and students should be encouraged to bring in examples they find relevant and decode them. Broader study of the marriage plot, and what it means that the women's sexuality is relegated to the bounds of marriage at the tale's end and that the porter escapes this, opens up a wealth of new avenues and cycles of study. In a version of the exercise with which this essay began, students might write mock letters to advice columnists on behalf of the various characters, and exchange and answer them while maintaining the persona of one of the characters. Lending itself to many strange permutations, such an exercise reveals much about the gendered power dynamics that shape memorable stories, and encourages students to borrow something of Shahrazad's voice.

Reading Race and Racism in the *Thousand and One Nights*

Rachel Schine

Often, the question of how to teach Arabic literature today in an American classroom is one of how to sympathetically and complexly interpret the experience of a grossly misrepresented other. But how do we then frame texts that convey a portrait of the other's others, exposing aspects of systemic practices of dehumanization as they occurred within a foreign culture—ones that may echo uncannily and painfully with students' experiences? How do we teach the racism of the *Thousand and One Nights*?

In class, I use the notorious frame tale of the *Thousand and One Nights* to sketch out a reading practice that encourages students to examine textual features such as stereotyping and symbolization as a set of political processes rather than solely literary choices. This interpretation prompts students to read reductive practices in a text—the underwriting of characters, the use of stereotypes, or the application of euphemism and allusion to displace subjectivity—as acts of epistemic violence that we should interrogate as such, instead of attempting to look behind or reclaim something from them. That is, a major technique of epistemic violence used by racializing texts is thinning the descriptions of othered characters while giving normative characters dynamism, substantive motivations, and historicized backgrounds. It is fruitful when teaching a text in which this occurs to pose the question of thinned characters or groups, "What has been taken away from you, what kept, and why? What are we meant to see and feel of you and what not?" It often is less useful to try to force such attenuated half beings within a work of fiction to speak for themselves because the text itself strategically forecloses on their having much to say without our reading added meanings into the work.

Many American students have a strong sense of literary canon in which the intellectual output of white people matters and the literature of people of color does not, as well as a robust—if proprioceptive rather than thought-through—sense of the systemic racism that has given rise to such conceptions. Recent debates have done much to critique such formulations of canon in national and global terms. In addition, the peoples historically marginalized from achieving canonicity at the level of authorship make their presences known in the canon's content, sometimes without readers or authors even recognizing this to be the case. Toni Morrison has dubbed the often overlooked prevalence of Black people in much American literature an "Africanist" presence, which draws on the "denotative and connotative blackness that African peoples have come to signify" (6). This significance is a product of Black people's often unnamed ubiquity in the nation's historical narrative and the constitutive effect this has on the white author's world. Through the surrogacy of Black figures in a text, authors explore the moral and social quandaries of white characters using an expansive symbolic vocabulary in which blackness adumbrates anxieties, taboos, and desires.

The *Nights* tales also have a multifarious Black presence encoded in the texts. This can be read against much of the text's putative setting in the Abbasid era, during which spheres of courtly, military, and domestic life featured a substantial Black African underclass. Critical engagement with the whys and hows of the Black presence in the *Nights* can place the text at once on firmer historiographical footing and into clearer conversation with the contemporary ethical aim of teaching ourselves to read racism critically. As I attempt to demonstrate in class, using contemporary sources on race such as Morrison's text and the works of Sara Ahmed and Adrian Piper as companions to portions of the *Thousand and One Nights* equips students to uncover its discursive analogues across time and space.

I have selected these texts in particular for their resonance with aspects of the contemporary Western racial experience, the accessibility of their language and style, and the fact that each critically addresses whiteness. Through the prism of whiteness studies, the *Nights* may be taught as a text that—much like its particular brand of racism—is at once familiar and defamiliarizing and can be played illustratively off many students' experiences of themselves. I frame my reading with three overarching questions that one could apply in the classroom: Why is Shahzaman's world so dark? How are white women and Black men relatively positioned? What is the politics of the frame tale's resolution?

Why Is Shahzaman's World So Dark?

It is widely presumed that the stories of Shahzaman and Shahriyar—the two cuckolded brothers whose personal crises catalyze Shahrazad's entrance into the king's harem—run in perfect parallel: each one's wife sleeps with an enslaved Black man and is caught by her spouse in flagrante delicto, whereupon each king kills the two lovers. The wiles of women are exposed, and the brothers duly become more judicious (and, in Shahriyar's case, murderous) about whom they take to bed. We find in varied editions of the *Nights*, however, that, whereas the identity of Shahriyar's cuckolder is explicit, Shahzaman's queen's lover is referred to only as a servant (see Materials). He is instead racialized through a number of cues in Shahzaman's portion of the text.

Shahriyar sends for his brother out of longing for his company, and Shahzaman provisions himself and prepares to set out. He is compelled to repair to the palace, however, where he finds his wife in bed with a man from among the kitchen hands, locked in an embrace. Seeing this, Shahzaman's world "[goes] dark," and he becomes afire with rage (Seale, *Annotated* Arabian Nights 6; Mahdi, Thousand 1: 57).[1] He exacts his wrath by killing both his wife and her paramour. Color eddies around the edges of Shahzaman's story. The color of the man whom Shahzaman's wife embraces is not mentioned but is nonetheless folded into the darkness surrounding the story—Shahzaman arrives home at the blackest hour, midnight, and his world blackens on seeing the couple in the act; he himself is the singular, blazing object in the blackness, his head aflame with anger.

Action in Shahzaman's vignette continues to be enacted by groping one's way through various kinds of shadow: after witnessing the nocturnal lovemaking of his wife and her lover, Shahzaman draws his sword and smites the two, then drags them from the palace, throwing the corpses into the depths of a trench, where they are enveloped by a doubled darkness, obscured by both the night and the ditch. Shahzaman's murder of his spouse results in a form of reflexive bodily mortification on his part. Deprived of the ability to fulfill one appetite, he loses all others and is unable to eat or drink when he arrives at his brother's home. His body wastes away and his complexion pales. The shadow and pallor that characterize Shahzaman's section of the tale may be read as a précis to the starker, black-white scheme that pervades the portion featuring Shahriyar's wife and her retinue. As the narrative builds, bodies and objects attain more definition and vibrancy. As one instance becomes embedded in a trend, essentialisms crystallize.

Later, on seeing his own brother's wife committing adultery (this time at midday) with the enslaved Black man Masud, who awaits his lover in a tree in the palace courtyard, Shahzaman's appetite returns, and with it his own health and color is restored at implicit cost to the vitality of his soon-to-be-killed Black counterparts. The return of Shahzaman's joie de vivre signals a fuller awareness of his world and discernment of its pleasures and pains: when the king begins again to consume things, he does so after bodies of women and enslaved people—themselves treated as consumable properties—have transformed from indistinct shadow forms with secretive natures to objects held up to the light for his scrutiny.

Shahzaman's vignette relies on a narrative strategy of using a Black presence to launch an actualization of the self. Morrison asserts that if one combs through American literature, one finds many articulations of an Africanist representation that acts as way of evoking suppressed elements of the author's consciousness: "The fabrication of an Africanist persona is reflexive; an extraordinary meditation on the self; a powerful exploration of the fears and desires that reside in the writerly conscious. It is an astonishing revelation of longing, of terror, of perplexity, of shame, of magnanimity" (17). Though the palimpsestic nature of the *Nights* makes it impossible to read Africanist presences therein as meditations on a single "self," they nonetheless may still function as epiphenomena of collective consciousness; this is especially true of elements of the text that carry across several versions and multiple centuries, which speaks to their sustained salience. Morrison similarly emphasizes that Africanist presences are housed not merely within individual novels but within a "national literature," and part of their power is derived from aggregation and canonization.

Morrison's human Africanist presences may also be supplanted by a disembodied but suggestive blackness, as with a specter, a darkness, a depth, or a shadow, meaning that signs and signifieds are, in effect, reversible: black bodies may be called to mind by the depiction of darkness, just as a metaphorical darkness can be elicited through mention of a Black person. The pervasive symbolism of night and shadow in Shahzaman's vignette constitutes one such Africanist presence, and this representation carries with it a particular sociopolitical background. The fact that the black color of Shahzaman's foe can be implied through the proxies of darkness and depth leads us to conclude that the assumed audience of this vignette must have had sufficient exposure to Black people to render such allusive language successful at conjuring black bodies in the mind's eye, yet this exposure must have also been of a profoundly inegalitarian nature, given the negative connotations of the symbolic web in which Black people are enmeshed and their characters' lack of substance—or indeed any superficial characterization beyond their complexion—in the text.

We may ask students, then, what makes blackness such a potent signifier here and use this as a springboard for discussing the symbolization and mythologization of Black people in the Arabic-speaking world, where they were historically subsumed under terms such as *sūdān* and *ahl al-sūdān* ("Blacks" and "people of the lands of the Blacks"), *banū ḥām* ("tribe of Ham"), or *zunūj* ("Zanjis")—to say nothing of *'abīd* ("enslaved people"). These epithets cut across massive variations of ethnicity and territory of origin stretching, per Arabic geographic and climatological tradition, from West Africa to Southeast Asia across the known world's southernmost extents. They most often reference peoples from sub-Saharan Africa, the Sahel, and various Indian Ocean islands in popular literature. Why in the *Nights* do we encounter dark-skinned people as "Black people" but not as members of variegated ethnic formations? Why do the concepts of Black and enslaved people appear so nested? With the help of Morrison, teaching Shahzaman's vignette as an allegory of a naive king's incipient worldliness—enacted through the emergence from a metaphorical darkness into light—can take place while emphasizing the real, historical source of that symbolic darkness's literary efficacy.[2] We see blackness's role in fashioning the very idea of a world about which a ruler can come into knowledge.

How Are White Women and Black Men Relatively Positioned?

In "A Phenomenology of Whiteness," Sara Ahmed sets out to "re-pose the question of whiteness as a phenomenological issue, as a question of how whiteness is lived as a background to experience" (150). In so doing, she constructs a portrait of white mobility in which white people, by nature of being society's default, can proceed through daily activities with their actions unquestioned by others and with relatively little attention paid to their own physical form and the impression (or nonimpression) it makes on others. She contrasts this with Frantz Fanon's representation of Black individuals as always operating under a "third-person consciousness" and tailoring their movements to fit within white society's parameters of comfort and conformity, lest they become even more visible and thus more threatening. By enforcing such behaviors for nonwhite people, whiteness becomes an institution and vice versa: "Spaces are orientated 'around' whiteness, insofar as whiteness is not seen. . . . The effect of this 'around whiteness' is the institutionalization of a certain 'likeness,' which makes non-white bodies feel uncomfortable, exposed, visible, different, when they take up this space" (157). The frame tale of the *Nights* at once complements and complicates Ahmed's conclusions because the orientation of the environment and patterns of normativity within the society of the *Nights* are, naturally, structured along lines of gender and class as well as race (these are added variables that Ahmed does not examine at length). The correspondent normative standard in the *Nights* is set by kings whose relative lightness of color is indicated not only by their brides' coloring and their extreme animus toward blackness but also through geography: the two are associated with Sasanian Persia and are said to reign over India, China, and Samarkand. While these places would have connoted exotic lands for an Arab and Arabized audience of the *Nights*, the allusion to the kings' Persian heritage invokes a long history of referring to Persians collectively as light-skinned, either *aḥmar* ("red") or *abyaḍ* ("white"). Throughout the Arabic-speaking world, these terms often refer not to relative appearance but to privileged lineage and perceived origins, showing that whiteness is a construction of heritable power and access, not a merely or solely visual category. The two are not mutually exclusive, though: travel literature of the early medieval period renders the complexions of Chinese and Central Asian peoples as close to the ideal of being light-skinned and rosy-cheeked (cf. Abū Zayd al-Sīrāfī's *Accounts of China and India*), though, as mentioned, parts of India are portrayed as having darker-skinned peoples.

Emblematic of the kings' idealized physicality is the instance where Shahzaman's color returns to normal as he convalesces, but whatever his normal may be, it is presumed to be common knowledge and left unelaborated. Though the two kings form a stable top tier, the arrangement of social positions beneath them is less readily inferable. Playing the *Nights* off Ahmed's essay lets us examine how bodies that are differently gendered and raced move relative to one another and are surveilled and controlled in the frame tale; this facilitates a discussion of the institutions that determine these relationships in the text.

We may begin by probing Ahmed's idea that whiteness is inherently invisible, habitual, and institutional by asking whose whiteness is remarked on and whose is not in the *Nights* and why this might be so. In doing this, we find that whiteness tends to arise explicitly only in contradistinction to blackness: whereas the whiteness of the kings goes unnamed, that of their wives and maidens earns emphasis because of their contact with Black people. This is compounded by the fact that women, as a function of their gender, are also subject to libidinous inspection, such that we not only are told of their skin color but also, in the case of Shahriyar's wife, hear of her comeliness, the contrastive blackness of her irises (described as *aḥwar*), and the sway of her gazelle-like gait (Seale, *Annotated* Arabian Nights 7; Haddawy, *Arabian Nights* 7; Mahdi, Thousand 1: 59). Are white women, then, invisible? Are they able to move freely? If not, are they able to maneuver with relative freedom vis-à-vis Black people in the text?

Freedom of movement, of course, presupposes freedom itself, and so the respectively bound status of wives and concubines and of Black enslaved people places them on similar footing at the outset, and the comparability of these conditions is worth discussing (cf. Ali). Nonetheless, differences do emerge between the two. In pursuing this line of inquiry further, Ahmed's point that disruptive bodies inherently attract more notice when they enter a space than when they already are contained in—and thus disciplined by—a given space is instructive. Ahmed asserts, "[W]hen the *arrival* of some bodies is noticed, when an *arrival* is noticeable, it generates disorientation in how things are arranged" (163; my emphasis). In the frame tale, white women must scheme and plot routes to minimize the noticeability of their entrances and exits when they wish to pursue their agendas, utilizing secret doors, operating under the cloak of night, or springing themselves from lockboxes in the case of the *'ifrīt's* captive; this operates to ironic effect, making their movements all the more dramatic. Black men, meanwhile, transgress boundaries in the text by concealing themselves and sheltering in place, fading into the landscape, like Masud in his tree, or by hiding in plain sight, like the cross-dressing Black so-called harem girls, whom I discuss shortly. This suggests that, whereas women are particularly visible only when in certain types of motion, Black men are noticeable qua their bodies' very presence. That is, their arrival itself constitutes an unwelcome revelation, whereas for women the quality and conditions of their arrival become part of its effect. This is in keeping with the fact that Black men are cast as physically threatening in the narrative, but women are represented as intellectually subversive, and the reader is duly warned of their guile.

Yet although women are conniving, they are depicted as a necessary evil; when Shahriyar's enslaved concubines are slain, they must be replaced with new women, and consequently new precautions are put in place. Meanwhile, the Black men receive no such attention or censure but instead disappear from the narrative entirely, and we are left to assume that they, like Shahriyar's wife and maids, have been disposed of. In this light, we see that Ahmed's point about the reification of whiteness's organic belonging in the world rings true: in order for white bodies to draw fire, they must be doing something to warrant this and, in turn, to warrant their removal. Black bodies—in whatever condition they appear—are remarked on, and their absence leaves no ostensible vacuum in the world of the text.

Having posited that whiteness is the default setting for bodies within the frame tale of the *Nights* and a basic condition for their freedom and mobility, we may ask students two types of questions. The first concerns the context of the *Nights* and the second their own position as it relates to the text: What does it mean that the protagonists of the *Nights* are implicitly presented as white? Has the definition of whiteness changed over time or from place to place, and how? Would you say these Arabic texts are artifacts of so-called white culture—why and why not? Such a discussion may be particularly productive if placed in relation to Orientalism and histories of the racialization of Arabs and Muslims in the West. After all, Ahmed's essay ultimately urges readers to make their institutions' whiteness visible as an object of critique.

What Is the Politics of the Frame's Resolution?

I end with the conclusion of the frame tale itself. When Shahriyar is apprised of his harem's subterfuge by his brother, he demands visual confirmation. The two stake out the palace's inner garden, and Shahriyar is able to witness firsthand the ten Black "maids" and ten white ones—though in the earliest manuscript of the text, the women are "unmarked" except as enslaved, and Mahdi inserts their colors in brackets (Antrim, "Qamarayn" 22; Mahdi, Thousand 1: 59)—walk into the garden along with his queen, whereupon half disrobe, revealing their blackness and manhood simultaneously, and begin to make love to the women. This combined disclosure distills in a double entendre. In the act, the bodies of the Black, enslaved men (*'abīd sūd*) cast a twofold shadow that echoes the image from Shahzaman's vignette; they are said, slangily, to fuck the maidens, but more literally to blacken them (*sakhkhamūhum* in the Mahdi edition, from *s-kh-m*, meaning "blackness"; though they are simply said to "mount" the women in the translations by Seale [*Annotated* Arabian Nights 7] and Haddawy [*Arabian Nights* 11]), obliterating whiteness from view. Seeing this, "Shahriyar's mind nearly left him," indicating not only his profound anger but also the overturning of his episteme: what he had known to be real proves not to have been so (Seale, *Annotated* Arabian Nights 10; Mahdi, Thousand 1: 62). The enslaved men here become representative not so much of dominance in and of itself, but rather the flux and subversion of dynamics of domination; in embedding themselves with the women of the harem, Shahriyar's enslaved men govern his world in ways he cannot detect.

Shahzaman and Shahriyar experience a twofold revulsion at the divulged passing of the enslaved Black men, first on the level of gender and then on the level of their race's gendered implications: the seemingly sexually available and docile tacitly Black women of Shahriyar's harem suddenly become marked Black men who, in exerting sexual dominance over the white women therein, mimic and undermine Shahriyar's actions (Seale, *Annotated* Arabian Nights 7; Haddawy, *Arabian Nights* 11; Mahdi, Thousand 1: 62). That is, the inversion of the Black enslaved men's gender gives their race new significance, particularly with respect to the reproductive output of Shahriyar's harem. When Shahriyar, to stymy this, decides to bed and kill one virgin per night, this is not only a reaction against the guile of women but also a means of distancing himself from the potential for his future partners to have been "blackened" like his prior concubines.

In murdering them immediately after consummation, he forecloses on the potential for further generation or mixing once the women leave his chambers.

Though the terms under which they conceal themselves are gendered, the fact that the enslaved Black men can hide so thoroughly and yet, once exposed, exert such a totalizing blackening on the people in their midst may be read as a metaphor for racial mixing, ambiguity, or obscurity, brought about through the introduction of a foreign element into one's ancestral line that, even when superficially muted, can exert socially tangible effects. In Islamic legal contexts, children belong to the "marriage bed" (*firāsh*) unless proven otherwise. Nonetheless, in premodern cultures where notions of biological atavism, superfetation, and contamination of the womb through the wayward mixing of bodily fluids held sway, uncertainties about one's genealogy produced appreciable anxiety.[3]

In the United States, the particular principle of even very distant genealogical blackness carrying an irreducible social connotation has historically been termed the "one-drop rule," as Adrian Piper explains in her semiautobiographical essay, "Passing for White, Passing for Black," where she argues that, "according to this long-standing convention of racial classification, a white who acknowledges any African ancestry implicitly acknowledges being black—a social condition, more than an identity, that no white person would voluntarily assume, even in imagination" (18). "Passing" is a way of undermining rigid systems of racial classification, which for Piper is intimately linked with class. One who is able and chooses to pass operates in society while being perceived as a member of a race other than one's own, and thus accesses socioeconomic privileges enjoyed disproportionately by certain racialized groups over others. According to Piper, coming into awareness of an instance of passing both elicits an at times violent emotional response and compels white people to "[consider] the probable extent of miscegenation." This can lead them to confront the possibility of being Black themselves, a reality whites resist and reject in ways that manifest as "hatred of the self as identified with the other" (19–20).

This resistance stems largely from the fact that treatment of Black people in the United States has rendered blackness a "social condition, more than an identity," and the precarity of social status to which whites would make themselves vulnerable in acknowledging Black ancestry is thus the crisis in potential; more interiorized disturbances are mere side effects vis-à-vis the systemic ramifications of making alternate possibilities for relationality known. Piper's work invites us to consider how those with other histories and literatures have confronted the prospect of social transformations that redound to questions of race and/as class. We may read Shahriyar's outrage at the enslaved Black men's gendered passing and his harem's resultant mixing as a reaction not only against seeing himself placed in a position analogous to that of enslaved Black men but also against a future in which the indeterminacy of sovereigns and enslaved people will become reified as a fact of biology—as the "womb kinships" and patrilineal inheritances characteristic of legitimate heirs in Muslim family structures become increasingly misaligned (Kia, *Persianate Selves* 136). Shifting articulations of power are already latent in the wives' legal trespass—namely, sexually accessing enslaved people in ways that only male heads of household are permitted to do. All this presents uncomfortable prospects for Shahriyar, amplified to chimerical proportions when he is subsequently forced into sex with the captive mistress of a giant, black *'ifrīt*, only to realize that in addition to being his bedmate, the woman has defiantly had intercourse with scores of other men. She has taken a trophy from each in the form of a ring. This forfeiture of opulence in the aftermath of increased sexual proximity to a powerful black being recasts the threat of mixing in a more explicitly material idiom. We may thus ask students to consider the biopolitics of Shahriyar's solution in terms of the text's implied ideal world: How are differently raced and classed people permitted to interact? What ambiguities and uncertainties does the text make space for? How fixed are social roles, and what influence do racialization and ancestry have on this?

And so in the classroom one may frame race in the *Thousand and One Nights* through highlighting themes in the frame tale itself, from Shahzaman's vignette to the precipice of Shahrazad's entry into the text, and comparing these with a number of critical theories on race that are particularly conducive to undergraduate learning. The function of Shahrazad in the *Nights* is regarded by many as that of a healer and teacher—she shows the king that not all women are immoral and slowly rebuilds his ability both to take delight in the world and to trust. But we may ask students when reading through the framed tales that Shahrazad proceeds to tell the king to keep thinking about what sort of world he is being delivered, by way of ascertaining the conditions of his (and the implied audience's) comfort and amusement. In essence, if these stories are supposedly for a white king Shahriyar, who are they against? Reading the text with race in mind engenders a complex engagement with the source that resonates with the complexities of our present.

NOTES

1. On this passage, see also Ghazoul, *Nocturnal Poetics* 26.
2. Supplemental readings on medieval and early modern Afro-Arab relations and the trans-Saharan trade in enslaved people include Gomez; Hunwick; El Hamel; Savage; Wright; Lovejoy; Gaiser.
3. On notions of reproductive biology in the medieval Arab Muslim world, see Kueny; Musallam.

Race, Gender, and Slavery in the *Arabian Nights*

Parisa Vaziri

As is well known but infrequently marveled at, the frame story of the *Thousand and One Nights* begins with an interdiction on "interracial" sex.[1] The text's frame story and its one unchanging feature pivot on the transgression of female adultery translated from Persian into Arabic in the eighth century: Southwest Asian women making love with enslaved Black men.[2] Lost from the abbreviated popular memory that magnifies Shahrazad's inexhaustible rhetorical talents are the plot machinations leading up to her marital entrapment. Prior to their marriage, Shahriyar, the Persian king of Indochina, and his brother Shahzaman witnessed Shahriyar's wife sleeping with an enslaved Black man and thereafter lost all faith in female righteousness:[3]

> The men mounted the women, then the lady of the house called out "Masud! Masud!" and out of the tree a slave came down to join her. He raised the lady's legs and entered her, and they went on making love (the men to the women, Masud to the mistress) until half the day was gone.
> (Seale, *Annotated* Arabian Nights 7)

After witnessing the queen from over a fence making love to Masud in this salacious garden orgy, Shahriyar vowed to kill every virgin in his kingdom. When the vizier in charge of presenting Shahriyar with his victims ran out of virgins to sacrifice to the king, the vizier consented to allow his daughter Shahrazad, by her own request, to marry Shahriyar.

Sensuality saturates the tales, demoting the *Nights* from the respectable literary category of *adab*, designating the classical canon, to second-rate "literature of pleasure" (Miquel 8–10). For feminist scholars like Fatima Mernissi, the centuries-long disdain for what would eventually emerge as one of the most fascinating texts for the modern global imagination grew out of a gendered paradox: a simultaneous dismissal and fear of female *khurāfa* (superstitious tales) combined with an elitist disregard for the life of the everyday illiterate masses. It is precisely a queer liminality as middle object that inspires the *Thousand and One Nights* with pedagogical value. Its questionable status as a cultural prestige object as well as its sheer breadth and transgression of geographic and temporal specificity render the *Nights* a repository for the tortuous, global history of fantasy. Its enigmatic appearance and evanescence throughout medieval history analogize it to unconscious thought (Beaumont 17). That sexuality and blackness are thus so unambiguously foregrounded in the text's frame and subsequent tales lends itself to charged questions about how one might teach the *Nights* against the thorny but unavoidable themes of gender and race—more specifically, antiblackness—precisely as they manifest in a collective fantasy whose greatest mystery lies in the problems of origin and historicity.

In this essay, I outline how the articulation of misogyny in the *Nights* is imbricated with manifestations of antiblackness that complicate easy assumptions about the imaginary or real worlds the text purportedly reflects, and indeed about the color of its debatable feminism. In tandem, I suggest a few ways one might creatively thematize this imbrication in two advanced undergraduate classroom settings: the first, a theoretically oriented course on comparative slavery intended for students interested in the history of slavery and race, and the second, a cultural studies course focused on representations of gender and race.

Comparative Slavery and the Limits of Historicism

The eroticism of the frame tale resounds throughout and affects every tale in the *Arabian Nights* corpus. In "The Tale of the Enchanted Prince," a woman again cheats on her king-husband with a Black man: "I saw my wife standing before a man, rough-looking, sitting on a reed mat, dressed in rags. . . . the world went dark before me and I forgot where I was" (Seale, *Annotated* Arabian Nights 68). The woman transforms the king's lower body into black marble when he discovers her and slashes her Black lover's throat. Unremarkable details imperceptibly absorb and rearrange the bodying tropes "female" and "black" throughout the *Nights*. For example, in the frame tale, Shahzaman returns to his palace in the middle of the night because he forgets a bead. In the ancient Near East, suggests al-Munsif bin Hasan, the bead symbolized the vagina and forgetfulness symbolized blackness (70). Daniel Beaumont points out that most studies that highlight gender violence in the text elide the figure of the enslaved person, which he, like Hasan, finds central to the text's comprehension (43).[4] The calamity of sexual encounters between Muslim women and (religiously unmarked) Black men that the *Nights* evokes should sound familiar to a Western audience, for the relation between a white (Christian) female and a Black male is one of the most recurring phobic tropes of American history. In the Southwest Asian context, this trope may feel displaced, yet it attests to a much longer history of African slavery in the Indian Ocean. Although its relation to constructions of gender and racial blackness has yet to receive adequate theorization by scholars of race, this sense of displacement forms an original site of inquiry for pursuing such a research agenda (see Vaziri).

The prevalence of various enslaved figures throughout the *Nights* attests to the ubiquity of slavery during the Abbasid period, the backdrop against which the *Nights* is thought to unfold. As Fuad Matthew Caswell notes in his study of the *qiyān* ("enslaved singing girls") in the early Islamic world, a market selling enslaved people thrived in every city during the Abbasid period and the institution of slavery played a singular role in the construction of social distinctions, especially gender, a fact that scholars like Mernissi and Abdelwahab Bouhdiba have interpreted in dubious ways (Myrne 61; see also Ibn al-Sāʿī; Bray, "Men, Women and Slaves"). On the other hand, and important for our purposes, the contorted textual history of accretion and attrition of the *Nights* forbids any quaint notion of historical context; most critical scholarship on the *Nights* agrees on at least this guiding precept.

With regard to the study of slavery, the superposition of historical contexts only heightens the difficulty of temporal (and geographic) specificity. A distinct, but not disconnected, history of African slavery in the Western world no doubt saturated the imaginations of European compilers and translators of the *Nights* in the eighteenth and nineteenth centuries. Thus, Richard Francis Burton in his English translation adds a note to the lovemaking scene between Shahriyar's wife and Masud explaining to his readers that "[d]ebauched women" prefer Black men because of a sexual endowment Burton personally attests to (1: 6). The white male anxiety and fascination with Black sexuality, mediated through the figure of the "debauched" white woman, translate uncannily across time and space. For Burton's hyperbolic language does not undermine that this fascination is inscribed into the so-called original Syrian fifteenth-century manuscript. Frantz Fanon's psychoanalytic investigations into negrophobia and negrophilia suggest just such an enigma of the origin of antiblackness; the imago of the *nègre*, for Fanon, is originary in this enigmatic sense that eludes simple historicization and that the textual history of the *Nights*—in French, Arabic, English, in the eighteenth, nineteenth, fifteenth, and eighth centuries— uniquely crystallizes.

The textual formation of the *Nights* is thus an exemplary site for teaching the complex configuration between sexuality, blackness, and slavery. Though a range of studies can help teachers historicize the medieval Islamic world and histories of slavery in which the transcription of the *Nights* unfolds, the *Nights* demands thought models capable of confronting, rather than disavowing, the limits of historicism—or the idea that historical context alone can fully reveal a truth or even ground history's epistemological privilege.

The following assignments should be spread over the course of a number of class sessions, or an entire semester, and can culminate in a research-driven final paper for a course on comparative slavery. Organize students into groups and assign to each group a period of slavery in the western Indian Ocean to research: examples can include slavery during the Byzantine, Abbasid, Mamluk, Safavid, or Ottoman periods. Have groups present on a number of predetermined themes or figures as they manifest in their assigned periods and regions. These can include various enslaved peoples (Circassian, Turkish, African, South Asian, Persian, etc.), as well as individual figures (the *jāriya*, or enslaved harem woman; the *qayna*, or singing enslaved girl; the *kul*, or high-status servant, such as the eunuch; or the *mamlūk*, or enslaved military man). This assignment can demonstrate to students the breadth of the meaning of slavery in the Indian Ocean world and generate questions about how to approach the relationship between slavery and race, as these terms are understood today.

Two additional sessions can help clarify how to treat this breadth in light of the more familiar history of African chattel slavery in the Atlantic world. In the first session, have students read "The Story of the Two Viziers, Nur al-Din Ali al-Misri and Badr al-Din Hasan al-Basril" and "The Inspector's Story," paying attention to the role of eunuchs in these narratives. In "The Two Viziers," for example, the eunuch is charged with the care of Ajib, the estranged son of Badr al-Din, and ultimately of reuniting the two, whereas in "The Inspector's Story," the eunuch acts as a go-between between Zubaida's maidservant and the steward or inspector. Throughout the history of Mesopotamian civilization, eunuchs traditionally guarded women's quarters, and fragmented evidence from the eleventh century, and more concretely from the sixteenth century forward, suggests rulers preferred Black eunuchs in particular for their perceived ugliness and "coarseness" (Babaie et al. 17). In class, ask students to discuss with their assigned research team how various figures of enslaved people (such as the eunuch) problematize normative sex-gender codes.[5] To facilitate and deepen the comparative dimensions of the discussion and encourage reflection on the purpose of such comparison, the instructor can prepare a lecture on contemporary approaches to thinking of slavery as a violent process of "ungendering."[6] Does this critical term operate in the assigned slavery contexts, and if so, how? How does it charge or inflect the question of comparison in the study of comparative slavery? What other elements of historical context does one need to take into consideration?

The second session might be conceived as part of the comparative slavery course but could work equally in the cultural studies model described below. The instructor can project famous odalisque images from the history of Western art, such as Jean-Auguste-Dominique Ingres's *La Grande Odalisque*, *Odalisque with Female Slave*, and *Turkish Bath*; Henri Adrien Tanoux's *Odalisque*; Jean-Léon Gérôme's *Slave Market* and *The Bath*; any of Henri Matisse's innumerable odalisque paintings. In class, ask students to choose one image and write a visual analysis. The visual analysis should include the students' interpretation of the position inscribed for or by the spectator in the painting. In group discussion, have volunteers present their analyses. How does the figure of the enslaved white woman (odalisque) in the imagination of European art history contrast with the image of the enslaved person, male and female, Black and white, in the *Nights*? Gérôme's *Moorish Bath* depicts an enslaved white female in partial profile hunched over on a seat at the bath, her back to the viewer, while on her left, an unabashedly naked enslaved Sudanese girl holds a brass basin of water attentively near the enslaved white woman. A similar dynamic colors *The Bath*, in which a Black woman with her breasts exposed stands and scrubs the back of a pale white woman seated on a chair, whose nudity is hidden from the viewer. Both instances describe a racialization of the female enslaved body that students can contrast against their historical research and classroom discussions on race, gender, and the position of the enslaved person in the western Indian Ocean.

Sex, Race

The tension over the feminism of the *Nights* is one of a number of reasons that recommend it as an object for the diachronic study of gender and sexuality in a cross-cultural context. As an example of how one might populate a *Nights*-based syllabus session to reflect the challenge of the diachronic and transgeographic, one could situate the frame tale of the *Nights* alongside diverse cultural objects that interrogate racialized sexuality. I describe two such possible objects here for a cultural studies course on representations of race and gender. Amiri Baraka's play-turned-film *Dutchman* explores the charged sexual dynamic between a white woman, Lula, and a Black man, Clay, whom she seduces, as they ride on a New York subway in the 1960s. The dialogue between them intends to trouble the binarism implicit in theories of patriarchal oppression, alluding to the history of white female incrimination of Black men during the high lynching era of Jim Crow.

After having students read the frame tale of the *Nights* and watch *Dutchman*, ask students to form small groups and discuss how representations of sexuality resonate in the two texts. The sea jinni scene from the *Nights* hyperbolizes female heterosexual voracity. Feminist commentaries by Afsaneh Najmabadi and Fedwa Malti-Douglas respectively highlight this point. In a reversal of the tree-falling scene between Masud and the queen, the promiscuous woman from the sea entices Shahrazad and Shahzaman to come down from the tree and have sex with her. In *Dutchman*, Lula, Eve-like, consumes apples in succession and carelessly chucks their cores on the subway floor as she shifts around in her minidress, revealing bare legs to Clay. After having students note and discuss the representation of female sexuality in the two texts, ask them to reflect on the racial dynamics in the frame tale of the *Nights* and in *Dutchman*. Both feminist interpreters of the *Nights* and those that counter their arguments regularly omit that the authority handling the textual circulation of the *Nights* is not just male but also racially unmarked. Encourage students to reflect on the way historical distance and author positionality shapes similarities and differences between the two texts.

Near the end of her music video "Shahmaran," the Iranian-Dutch singer Sevdaliza lies on a black leather couch wearing a clear synthetic face chain and a plastic and metal seamed bikini ("Sevdaliza—Shahmaran"). Parched, the Black man whose journey the camera tracks throughout the video inches toward her before he bends down to dip his sweat-beaded face in the pool surrounding her. The futuristic Eastern-inspired cinematography complements Sevdaliza's music style—trip-hop and experimental pop. As a nonnarrative form, the music video can be a useful complement to a film like *Dutchman*; Baraka's underlying politics are far more transparent than Sevdaliza's. Ask students to watch "Shahmaran" and reflect on the historical motifs that Sevdaliza draws on (the enslaved Black man, the exotic supine female body, the magnetic climax of forbidden interracial sexual encounter, the desert). What elements of the form of "Shahmaran," including its genre, lyrics, platform, and female authorship, complicate the viewer's expectations about its meaning?

These few approaches to teaching the *Nights* do not exhaust the many ways instructors can creatively engage the text to open questions about the comparative study of gender, race, and slavery. What becomes clear through this rich pedagogical source, the *longue durée* of Near Eastern and European contexts with which it obliquely engages, and the generic ambiguity of the textual formation of the *Nights* is the sheer complexity involved in treating the question of historical context. The vast temporality and geography of the *Nights* demands a reckoning with *how to think* history.

NOTES

1. It is difficult, despite its obvious hazards, involving especially the long-standing orthodoxy about the origins of the concept of race, to find an adjective other than this one to describe the intercourse between Persian or Arab women and Black men. And yet even to formulate the problem this way is to presuppose a series of racial certainties.

2. Pier Paolo Pasolini's 1974 version, *Il fiore delle* Mille e una notte (*The Flower of the* Thousand and One Nights), vividly captures the erotic nature of the tales.

3. Name spellings and geographic references come from the Seale and Haddawy translations of Muhsin Mahdi's text. At least one version of the *Nights*, albeit not an authoritative one, describes the cook Shahzaman finds in bed with his wife as Black. The Seale and Haddawy translations do not, whereas the Macnaghten text does.

4. Beaumont himself virtually ignores the question of enslaved figures' blackness, focusing instead on a psychoanalytic reading of the enslaver-enslaved dialectic.

5. For the history of eunuchs in the Near East, see Ringrose; Marmon. Marmon points out that eunuchs literally inhabited and were associated with vestibular spaces in a variety of Islamic architectural settings (8).

6. Spillers's iconic essay "Mama's Baby, Papa's Maybe: An American Grammar Book," which engages Middle Passage historiography, would be an ideal text to introduce with regard to the question of slavery and gendering.

The *Thousand and One Nights* in World Film History

Samhita Sunya

Among the most prominent explorations of the interface between cinema and the *Thousand and One Nights* have been several incisive critiques of Hollywood's long history of "brownface," or racialized caricatures of Arabs, alongside depictions of the Middle East in colonial and neocolonial Orientalist clichés of harems, carpets, camels, and so on. The current stakes of engaging students in such conversations—especially in the United States—remain informed by the post-9/11 contexts of invasions of Iraq and Afghanistan led by the United States in the ongoing war on terror, within a much longer history of visual representations that have propped up Islamophobia in the West. Yet *A Thousand and One Nights at the Cinema*, a course I developed for my home department of Middle Eastern and South Asian languages and cultures, is geographically vast, aesthetically rich, and stylistically diverse. Genealogies of Hollywood cinema's stereotyped portrayals of Arabs, Muslims, and the Middle East, as noted in Jack Shaheen's pathbreaking work (*Reel Bad Arabs*), constitute one certainly very crucial node of engagement, within a globally expansive, prolific screen history of the *Nights*.

My course unfolds as an account of the persistent and perhaps unparalleled on-screen presence of the *Nights* in manifold historical and geographic contexts, from the earliest moments of cinema through the present day. The course underscores the way cinematic iterations of the *Nights* have congealed into a genre of their own; catapulted explorations of the fantastic, iterated as the sensuous wonders of technology; platformed Orientalist desires and stereotypes, themselves inextricable from histories and legacies of imperialism; and engaged in metacinematic reflections on audiovisual storytelling itself. In this essay, I briefly detail my approaches to setting up my students' engagement with the *Nights*, before focusing on a subset of films from beyond Europe and the United States that illuminate the manifold, global arcs of both cinema and the *Nights* in negotiating twentieth-century modernity.

To build students' awareness of the *Nights*' long history of tellings, retellings, and translations, to the extent that the identification of any singular textual, cultural, or geographic source is impossible, I assign students a series of essays that explore histories and origins of the *Nights*. I emphasize punctual moments in the history of the *Nights* that include the efflorescence of medieval Islamic city centers like Baghdad and Cairo and the eighteenth-century publication of Antoine Galland's French edition of the *Nights* as well as the technological shifts and material practices that informed the tales' circulation, from manuscripts to the advent of printing to the role of storytellers and genres of theatrical performance in medieval city centers. I thus ground the course's cinematic explorations of the *Nights* within a long history and wide geography of the *Nights*' heterogeneity, translation, and circulation across manuscript, print, performance, and audiovisual media.

Offering students an introductory glimpse into the centuries-old textual, performance, and visual histories of the *Nights*, I proceed chronologically from the earliest moments of cinema—for example, Ferdinand Zecca's *Ali Baba et les quarante voleurs* (*Ali Baba and the Forty Thieves*) and Georges Méliès's *Le palais des* Mille et une nuits (known in English as *The Palace of the* Arabian Nights)—through more contemporary films that draw on the *Nights*. This chronological rather than geographic ordering conveys a sense of the twentieth-century ubiquity of the *Nights* and cinema, as both were well traveled, quick-footed, and highly malleable. As the course proceeds, I offer intermittent lectures on elements of film form, including mise-en-scène cinematography, editing, and sound. I intersperse a few literary adaptations of the *Nights*, such as Edgar Allan Poe's short story "The Thousand-and-Second Tale of Scheherazade," as a way of highlighting the metatextual proclivities that cohere through the frame tale and the figure of Shahrazad; Hanan al-Shaykh's absorbing retelling of the *Nights*, as a way of imparting a sense of the bawdiness and adult-oriented themes of the Arabic versions from which al-Shaykh's retelling ensues; and Salman Rushdie's novel *Two Years Eight Months and Twenty-Eight Nights*, as a way of calling attention to not only the historical inextricability of the *Nights* from medieval Islamic philosophical and theological debates but also the distinct phenomena of the text's predilections toward visually evocative genres of fantasy, sci-fi, and stylized action reminiscent of comic books.

Action and Adventure Genres: Ali Baba and the Forty Thieves

In a chronology of moving-image adaptations of the *Nights* that begins in the early moments of cinema at the turn of the century, I teach Homi Wadia's *Alibaba aur chalis chor*, a Hindi-language *Ali Baba and the Forty Thieves*, after two versions of *The Thief of Bagdad*—Raoul Walsh's 1924 silent-era feature from the United States followed by Alexander Korda's 1940 British-American coproduction. The two versions facilitate discussions of the intervening advent of synchronous sound as well as Technicolor. At this juncture of the course, Wadia's black-and-white feature yields fruitful discussions of four themes: the rapid global transition to sound films by the early 1930s, in comparison to the much less even, much more gradual transition to color film stock; the genealogies of song-dance forms in Bombay and other South Asian film industries; comparative histories of film genres and the *Nights*; and the shifting repertoire of tropes that marked out fashionable modes of Orientalism as modern, urban phenomena in both Euro-American and non-Western cultural productions.

To initiate a discussion of the transition to sound film, on the one hand, and to color stock, on the other, I ask students to speculate in small groups over reasons for the former's much quicker uptake. In ensuing conversations, we inevitably come to discussions of language, dialogue, and music. I highlight the importance of synchronized sound recording (sync sound) for postcolonial industries whose films with lower production values could gain a competitive advantage over Hollywood or other foreign films by producing films in the languages of their local audiences. I mention the importance of music in the talkie era of Bombay cinema, particularly, as the catchy songs were broadcast via radio to advertise films among audiences who spoke different languages. When I ask the class to reflect on their overall experience of the film, most students respond by characterizing *Ali Baba*'s song-dance sequences as sites of pleasure and entertainment.

I invite students to consider the Orientalist tropes and exoticized settings in the two *Thief* films and *Ali Baba* in order to point to the former films' tendencies to link the genre of the *Nights* with generically Arab tropes and geographies; the latter film includes vaguely Persianate images and geographies as well—however imprecise and however muddled with a broader mishmash of Oriental motifs. Turning to the insights of Rosie Thomas's chapter "Thieves of the Orient," from her book *Bombay before Bollywood* (31–65), and Anupama Prabhala's "Around the World in Eighty Minutes," I ask students to reflect on the historical links and the distinctions between the role of the *Nights* in the Hollywood genre of the swashbuckling adventure comedy, on the one hand, and in the Bombay genre of the fantasy film, on the other. Such a discussion helps students think through the transnational movement of films—and film genres—alongside a comparison of the material practices of different film industries at specific historical junctures.

For the final portion of the discussion, I play the song-dance sequences "Dekho jii chaand niklaa" ("Look, sir, the moon has emerged") and "Ae sabaa unse kah zaraa" ("O gentle breeze, why don't you tell her") from *Ali Baba*. I ask students to write down all the sounds they hear while these clips play. This exercise is aimed at directing students' attention toward the aural stereotypes of vaguely Middle Eastern–sounding melodies that accompany the jazzy vocal style of the singers and cabaret-style belly dance performance by the elaborately costumed heroine in "Dekho jii," in addition to the orchestra and plucked lutes featured in the interludes of the "Ae sabaa" duet. Elements associated with the modern entertainments of theaters and night clubs are somewhat paradoxically motivated by the ostensibly premodern mise-en-scène of the *Nights*. Frequently tied to genres of fantasy, moving-image adaptations of the *Nights* have in this way tended to showcase audiovisual spectacle and the technological marvels of moving-image media.

Issues of Access: **Night of the Hunchback**

In a marked departure from the frequently spectacular proclivities of *Nights* films, the Iranian filmmaker Farrokh Ghaffari's 1965 film *Shab-e-Ghuzi* (*Night of the Hunchback*) is a black comedy that transplants the tale from the *Nights* to contemporaneous Tehran. A film that unfolds in a distinctive combination of expressionist and noir styles, Ghaffari's *Night of the Hunchback* depicts an urban milieu teeming with paranoia and mistrust among individuals who are shown to be chronically cold and calculating. Incidentally, Ghaffari had planned the film as a period piece to be set in Baghdad during the reign of Caliph Harun al-Rashid, though the setting was changed in response to an objection by censors. Held to have been among the first films that inaugurated an auteurist Iranian cinema, Ghaffari's film, like several other Iranian films that preceded the 1979 revolution, has yet to be officially distributed in any digital version, much less one with English subtitles.

As a particularly striking instance of a film whose legacy does not correspond with its accessibility, *Hunchback* presents an opportunity to engage students in a discussion of a key problem of film historiography and pedagogy—that is, to use Julian Stringer's formulation, the tendency for distribution histories to stand in as production histories (135). How do we account for the fact that film pedagogy is shaped largely by films that happen to be readily available, often as a result of garnering acclaim at Euro-American film festivals in the case of non-Western films? As teachers, can we find ways of critically engaging with films that are no longer extant, inaccessible even if extant, available only in low-resolution versions, or unsubtitled in our languages of instruction?

Although I raise this discussion in every course that I teach, my determination to include *Hunchback* in *A Thousand and One Nights* at the Cinema yielded a very special and effective strategy, dependent for its success upon the kindness and enthusiasm of my colleague who coordinates the Persian language program in our department. Although I assign most films as take-home viewings, I scheduled *Hunchback* as an in-class viewing. Resorting to a low-resolution, unofficial, unsubtitled *YouTube* version (now defunct) in the absence of an alternative, I played *Hunchback* for my students while my colleague eloquently narrated live translations of the dialogue.

When possible, such a strategy is rewarding because it makes for a memorable group viewing and offers a poignant "Exhibit A" for the complexities of access and translation that inevitably and indelibly shape film historiography and pedagogy. In addition, the neo-*benshi*-style delivery of live translations occasioned a return to earlier discussions of so-called silent cinema as a misnomer, given the musical and other accompaniments that shaped experiences of cinema prior to the advent of sync sound in the late 1920s. The art of *benshi* in Japan, for example, featured performances of live narration during a film screening. Its practitioners were revered as stars in their own right and crucial to shaping an audience's interpretation of a given film.

I have required students to read al-Shaykh's retelling of the "Night of the Hunchback" tale from the *Nights* prior to the in-class screening of Ghaffari's *Hunchback*. They are then already familiar with the plot, such that—in combination with the live translation in the case of the unsubtitled version—the film remains intelligible despite the low quality of the image. Furthermore, the students' prior familiarity with the story aids their reflections over the fact that *Hunchback*'s contemporaneous audiences, too, may have been familiar with the story. In addition, students see that the engagement with the *Nights* in Ghaffari's film is distinct from many other *Nights* films, in that *Hunchback* adapts a specific tale in a more gritty and realistic—albeit darkly satirical—mode, instead of conjuring a generalized world of the *Nights* as a spectacular, exotic, audiovisual milieu unto itself.

Hunchback's titular character is a performer whose face is smeared with ash, constituting a performance of blackface that rarely goes unnoticed by students. I have more recently addressed this by passing out printed copies of Beeta Baghoolizadeh's short piece "The Myths of Haji Firuz" as an in-class reading, which students first discuss in small groups. The piece introduces histories of blackness and slavery that are specific to Iran, which helps students think more critically about descriptions of enslaved characters in the *Nights* and better understand the global histories and ongoing legacies of both slavery and antiblackness.

Sexualized Experiments: Yamamoto's Thousand and One Nights

The first film in Mushi Productions' *Animerama* trilogy of animated films with mature themes, Eiichi Yamamoto's *Senya ichiya monogatari* (*A Thousand and One Nights*) was the first X-rated animated feature to receive a (limited) theatrical release in the United States. It did quite poorly at the box office in the United States, perhaps because of American audiences' tendencies to associate animated films with children's content. My own students, too, have found Yamamoto's film exceedingly uncomfortable—far more uncomfortable to watch, in fact, than Pier Paolo Pasolini's *Il fiore delle* Mille e una notte (*The Flower of the* Thousand and One Nights; known as *Arabian Nights* in English), despite the latter's much more graphic live-action nudity and sex. I teach the two films together to emphasize that both endeavored, at least in part, to recover the intense sensuality of older versions of the *Nights*, in contrast to later sanitized versions of the *Nights* that had been circulating as children's tales. Yamamoto's film includes scenes of sexual violence and incest, in addition to being charged with an intense voyeurism. Feminine figures repeatedly find themselves on display as sexual objects before masculine figures within the film, often unknowingly or unwillingly. Crucially, the film does not necessarily normalize this misogyny, in that every male character, including the protagonist Aldin, is presented as unequivocally flawed. In other moments, the film is erotically suggestive through visual styles that are highly abstract and psychedelic. Some students surmise that their discomfort may stem from being unaccustomed to animated adult content that is neither irreverent nor humorous, in the vein of more contemporary Adult Swim television shows.

In order to ensure a productive conversation that acknowledges the validity of students' discomfort with the film, I begin with a rationale for its inclusion in the course. I note the film's uniqueness as an adult animated version of the *Nights* and its emergence from a 1960s rock-and-roll-driven psychedelic audiovisual culture and global youth culture of experimentation. As Sofia Samatar has argued, the exotic lure of the *Nights* from a Japanese perspective was in fact oriented through the *Nights*' association with the West. Thus, even as the mise-en-scène of Yamamoto's film reiterates clichéd tropes of an Orientalized, generically Middle Eastern setting, the referent for this mise-en-scène—as indicated by the film's bluesy, guitar soundtrack and its psychedelic animation style reminiscent of contemporaneous works such as the *Pink Panther* animated shorts—is a repertoire of largely Euro-American cinematic iterations of the *Nights*.

Having offered this explanation, I ask my students whether they would include Yamamoto's film on their syllabi if they were to teach the course. In this way, I invite my students to reflect on their discomfort and make space for them to process its gender politics, among other issues that they may be hesitant to raise otherwise. The exercise is productive for generating sincere reflections from students, several of whom respond by both acknowledging their deep discomfort with the film and avowing its importance in critical conversations, often deciding on this basis that they, too, would include it in a syllabus.

Excavations of Folklore: **Ashik Kerib** *and* **The Dove's Lost Necklace**

Ashik Kerib and *The Dove's Lost Necklace*, although marked by wholly distinct styles and production contexts, are both films whose respective engagement with the *Nights* is yoked to dreamy, cinematic excavations of folklore. The films' ethereal worlds are narratively and formally rooted in arresting visions of landscapes, produced as reservoirs of esoteric knowledge whose echoes linger in storytelling, music, architecture, decorative arts, and, in the case of *Dove*, calligraphy. I teach the films back-to-back, which yields robust comparative analyses of their respective auteurs' distinctive styles and the films' metacinematic layers.

Both *Ashik* and *Dove* are cinematic invitations to wander about with a childlike sense of wonderment, whereby the enchanted world of fairy tales seeps into and is indistinguishable from that of the everyday. A discussion of the larger oeuvre of the films' respective auteurs allows students to apprehend the stakes of their formalist approaches. Like *Ashik*, a Soviet-era Georgian-Azerbaijani feature made as a children's film, the other films in Sergei Parajanov's Transcaucasian trilogy are set in borderlands of the region and invoke Armenian, Georgian, and Azeri stories, visual motifs, and settings. Eschewing any straightforward cultural histories of these contexts, the stakes of Parajanov's works lie, nonetheless, in a formalist approach that draws inspiration from the folklore and artistic genealogies of their locations. His films overall, in this manner, extol the heterogeneity and distinctiveness of their respective contexts (Armenian, Georgian, Azeri, Ukrainian), against the state-imposed homogenizing project—rhetorical and otherwise—of the Soviet Union.

Dove, too, unfolds in a world of children's fairy tales that occurs at a cultural crossroads: primarily medieval Andalusia, an Islamic civilization that stretched from Arabia to Iberia, and secondarily Samarkand, the legendary Silk Road hub that lies in present-day Uzbekistan. The young character Hassan's quest for the princess of Samarkand in his search for love and inspiration is metacinematic. This quest, as discussed by Roy Armes, reflexively inscribes the filmmaker Nacer Khemir's own wanderings through the rich past of a cosmopolitan, transcontinental Islamic cultural history of architecture, literature, and arts in seeking inspiration for a cinematic labor of love. Similarly, the wanderings of *Ashik*'s eponymous minstrel in search of love and inspiration reflexively evoke the filmmakers' search for the same through local fairy tales and folklore, which crystallize in *Ashik*'s formalist approach.

Much time can be spent on carefully peeling back the layers of both films, in terms of examining specific shot compositions, editing techniques, costumes, settings, cinematography, lighting, and so on. The closing shots of *Ashik* and *Dove* are especially compelling, and they work well as bookends for structuring a discussion of the films, whether separately or together. I initially ask students what they make of the closing shots, fill in the contexts for the films, have students watch and discuss other scenes and characters, then revisit the closing shots.

Ashik concludes with a shot of a dove sitting atop a camera, in a metacinematic moment that reflexively concludes the intertwined wanderings of Ashik and the film itself. Mediation—whether through fairy tales, folk songs, language, music, or cinema—is foregrounded throughout the film, and most emphatically so in the closing shot. The film is further infused by mediations of genre: not only was the Oriental fairy tale a precedented, recognizable genre of Soviet cinema but *Ashik* was itself adapted from a Russian short story by Mikhail Lermontov that was framed as a transcription of a Turkish tale. I raise this to note the distinct valences of Russian Orientalism vis-à-vis Central Asian Turkic cultures, alongside the centrality of the *Nights* to the Oriental fairy tale genre of Soviet cinema.

The concluding shot of *Dove* is that of a calligraphic rendering of the Arabic letter *waw*, which Hasan's teacher describes as unique from all other letters, as both a letter of travelers and a letter whose complexity invokes God. *Dove*'s concluding shot also features a metacinematic convergence of the wanderings of the film and of the main character. Like cinema, calligraphy, particularly the letter *waw*, is simultaneously writing and image—that is, both symbol and icon, both literary and pictorial. Hassan's search for love and meaning in calligraphy, as a word as well as an image, captures the film's own formalist meanderings through a world of enchantment—that is, a world transformed by storytelling in the name of love, which is none other than the world of the *Nights*.

INTERTEXTS

Teaching the *Arabian Nights* through Graphic Novels

Shawkat M. Toorawa

Fifteen years ago, lamenting that relatively few students showed interest in courses in Arabic literature, I started teaching a course I titled The *Arabian Nights*: Then and Now. It attracted anywhere from thirty-five to sixty students. I am not (nor was I fifteen years ago) an expert on the *Arabian Nights* (hereafter, the *Nights*). Indeed, with a very small number of exceptions, Arabists in North America are not typically specialists in the *Nights*. But such courses have proliferated, no doubt because, just like me, others have found that teaching the *Nights* is a way of bringing students to Arabic literature, even if the importance of the *Nights*, as Geert Jan van Gelder notes when he explains why he excludes it from his 2012 anthology of translations from the premodern Arabic literary tradition, "is rather distorted by its fame in Western languages" (xvi). But once the students are through the door, as it were, I am in a position to introduce them to such wonderful Arabic works as *Arabian Nights and Days*, a novel by the 1988 Egyptian Nobel laureate Naguib Mahfouz.

The fact does remain, however, that the possibility of reading Mahfouz is not what typically attracts students to my course. Sometimes students are intrigued by the possibility of taking a university-level course about stories ("Aladdin," "Ali Baba," "Sindbad," etc.) that they read, or more likely had read to them, when they were young (I use Haddawy's translation in my course, in part because he describes first hearing stories from the *Nights* as a young child [*Arabian Nights* xi–xii]). Sometimes one is enchanted by the figure of Shahrazad. Sometimes a student is interested for the main reason I am myself attracted to the

Nights—namely, its adaptability, its adaptation, and its adaptations. The *Nights* have been endlessly adapted, modified, tailored, transformed, reshaped, rewritten, retold, reworked, and recreated. This versatility is acknowledged, and explicit, in my course description:

> The medieval Arabic cycle of stories known as the *Arabian Nights* or the *Thousand and One Nights* is a classic of world literature. The course is divided into two components: in one, we read the *Nights* and discuss both its dominant themes—inter alia deceit, love, sex, revenge, violence, and justice—and its storytelling contexts and antecedents (e.g., the Middle Persian *Tales of Bidpai*). And in the other, we explore the ways its themes and tales have been adapted and appropriated by later authors (e.g., John Barth, Neil Gaiman, and Edgar Allan Poe in English; Jorge Luis Borges in Spanish; Jan Potocki in French and Polish; and Naguib Mahfouz and Sadallah Wannous in Arabic) and by filmmakers such as Alexander Korda, Pier Paolo Pasolini and Steve Barron. (1)

It turns out, however, that one of the main reasons students are attracted to the class is the mention of Neil Gaiman—I know this is the case, as I always ask on the first day of class what piqued students' interest. The Neil Gaiman reading I assign is "Ramadan," part of his celebrated, award winning *Sandman* series of graphic novels. The term *graphic novel* (less commonly *comic book novel* and *sequential art*) refers to "a specialized use of the sequential art medium that consists of extended works in the form of books or albums" characterized by "higher production values and few of the restrictions on form and content that constrain most mass-market, commercial comics . . . in newspapers or in traditional comic books" (Tabachnik, Introduction 2).

Two questions arise: Why graphic novels? Which is to say, why do I (and others) teach them in a course on the *Nights*? And which graphic novels? That is, given limited time, which ones do I (and others) teach?

Why Graphic Novels?

There are several reasons why, among the most important of which are the following.

First, visual material and the *Nights* have a long history together, including illustrations in manuscripts; illustrations in printed books, notably woodcuts (see Irwin, *Visions*; Kobayashi; Unno); illustrated children's books; paintings; film; and animated film. It should come as no surprise, then, that the *Nights* has also found its way into the graphic novel. And it is no surprise either, given the lowbrow status of the *Nights* and its principally oral dissemination in its regions of origin, that this visual history is a largely Western one. The 1873 picture book *The Forty Thieves*, by Lucy Crane and Walter Crane, contains colored lithographs by Walter Crane; the book is set in China, and Walter Crane took his inspiration from ukiyo-e (Japanese woodcuts, especially those of Hiroshige), as did Edmund Dulac in the age of full color offset printing, though Dulac was also influenced by Persian and Mughal miniature painting (see Menges). Some contemporary artists channel the Orientalist visualization of their predecessors (an accusation leveled against the graphic novelist Craig Thompson in *Habibi*; see below), a vision that unapologetically characterizes countless graphic novels that capitalize on a taste for prurient visuals. To be fair, some European artists have departed from this visualization of the *Nights*, among them some of the great painters of the twentieth century: Marc Chagall, Paul Klee, and Henri Matisse.

Second, the *Nights* are considered lowbrow by scholars of the Arabic literary tradition and, indeed, by readers of Arabic literature generally. There are many reasons for this, among them that there is no stable text, the material is from the popular and semipopular tradition, there is a good deal of illicit activity in the *Nights*, and the frame tale is about serial rape and murder staved off by seduction and storytelling. Graphic novels are also perceived this way. But, as Cathy Thomas perceptively notes, "Graphic novels and comics are texts where we can observe the hybridization of ethnic, gender, and racial ideas; the study of them provides new perspectives to our scholarly inquiries. But there are those who still consider the medium low brow. Who then has the power to determine what is worth 'reading' as the most representative or central work for a period or people?" (1).

Third, the graphic novel has—one might even say forcefully—entered the mainstream. It is ubiquitous and is the basis, for example, for many of the most successful blockbuster films and TV shows. Even the Yale University Graduate School fall 2003 guide for new teaching assistants, *Tales from the Classroom*, was produced as a graphic novel [Cates and Wenthe]). Such uses are possible because "the abstraction and complexity of words combine with the eye-catching, immediate appeal of the images" (Tabachnik, Introduction 4; see also McCloud). Including them provides an opportunity to teach students about an artistic form with which they are very familiar—the graphic novel—but about which they have likely given very little thought. As Stephen Tabachnik notes, the "high literary and visual quality" of graphic novels provides a compelling reason for study and "fits students' sensibilities at a cognitive level," coinciding with today's hybrid reading experiences—split screen, rapid, even wordless ones; and nonlinear progression (Introduction 4). He notes also that "[i]n the present competition between the physical book and the electronic screen with its e-books and databases, the graphic novel, at least for now, signals the survival of the physical book.... Thus it can be used as a starting point for discussions about the history of the book" (5; see also Tabachnik "Comic Book World").

Fourth, the origin of the graphic novel is Belgian Frans Masereel's wordless woodcut novel from 1919, *Passionate Journey*, considered a counterpart of the silent film. In the early twentieth century both woodcuts (see above) and silent film are part of the story of the *Nights*. Two of the very earliest silent films ever made are based on the *Nights*: Raoul Walsh's 1924 *The Thief of Bagdad* and Lotte Reiniger's 1926 *Die Abenteuer des Prinzen Achmed* (*The Adventures of Prince Achmed*)—which is also the oldest surviving full-length animated feature film. Much is to be gained by pointing out to students the gains and losses of the various media through which one can access the *Nights*: by hearing them (no visuals, no text), reading them (neither sound nor visuals), watching silent films of them (no sound except music, some text), watching sound films of them (both sound and visuals, no text).

What is more, because so many graphic novels are adapted into films (something that has not yet occurred with any *Nights* graphic novels but seems inevitable, given the history of the adaptability and attraction to filmmakers of the *Nights* [see Irwin, "*A Thousand and One Nights* at the Movies"; Ouyang, "Metamorphoses of Scheherazade"]), it makes possible productive discussions of the relation between word and image, an important and misunderstood dimension of Arab and Arab Islamic culture generally. Much has in fact been made of the transfer of prose narratives into film media. As J. Caitlin Finlayson argues, however, "The common disparagement of graphic novels as reductive is . . . the very advantage they hold over films. The two-dimensional character in a graphic novel represents but does not embody the play text's persona—we are not distracted by the actor's breathing, idiosyncratic presence" (198). In this way, when teaching, we can direct attention back to the text and away from the inevitable influences exerted by a director's interpretations or by an actor's performance (198).

Jules Feiffer once described comics as "movies on paper" (qtd. in Rabkin 37), but in fact the differences are many and also significant. The reader controls time in the graphic novel and is not at the mercy of the rolling film; one can flip back and relive any sequence (see Rabkin). And the kinds of analyses available depend on different conceptions of layout: to use the terminology of Benoît Peeters, these conceptions are the "conventional," wherein visual aspects are independent of the narrative; the "rhetorical," wherein visual aspects are a function of the demands of the narrative; the "decorative," wherein visual design is discrete, and commands more attention than the narrative; and the "productive," wherein narrative is a product of the visual design (38–40; see also Eisner 38; Cohn; Rosen).

Fifth, as every instructor who includes graphic novels in their courses will confirm, you do not have to persuade students to read a graphic novel. In my personal experience, they usually devour any assigned graphic novel well before its assigned date in the syllabus.

And, finally, the only print resource about teaching the *Nights* of which I am aware (al-Musawi, "Teaching") does not address graphic novels.

Which Graphic Novels?

There are a great number of graphic novels and comic books that illustrate, feature, adapt, or derive inspiration from the *Nights*. I briefly discuss several I do not use before treating individually four I believe can profitably be used in a course on the *Nights*.

Two types of graphic novels and comic books I never use when teaching the *Nights* are those intended for the children's market, which are usually characterized by a great deal of sanitizing and typically omit the frame tale, and therefore Shahrazad, entirely; and those intended for the mature fantasy market, which are usually erotic or sexual, though typically with a great deal of attention paid to Shahrazad and her seductive storytelling. Although the writing is not noteworthy in these works, the art can sometimes be spectacular. In the juvenile category fall such works as Lillian Chestney's *Arabian Nights*, from the so-called golden age of comic books, and Carl Barks's Scrooge McDuck adventure *Cave of Ali Baba*. The mature category includes such works as *The Thousand and One Nights of Scheherazade*, by Eric Maltaite; "New Tales of the *Arabian Nights*," illustrated by the acclaimed Richard Corben, which first appeared in *Heavy Metal* in 1978–79 and was then collected as *The Last Voyage of Sindbad* (see Strnad); and Alfonso Azpiri's *Wet Dreams* series, which also first appeared in *Heavy Metal*. All of these routinely feature voluptuous, unclothed women. (Azpiri's cover for his volume *Reflections* is, incidentally, clearly the inspiration for the English artist Dave McKean's cover of Gaiman's *Fables and Reflections* volume of *The Sandman*.) Inevitably, given the subject matter and in particular the frame tale, the *Nights* has also generated a great deal of sexually explicit, usually pornographic, material: suffice it to mention here Loic Foxer's *Stella: A Thousand and One Nights*. I do include a *manhwa* title (*One Thousand and One Nights*, discussed below), but I do not use Shinobu Ohtaka's *Magi: Labyrinth of Magic*, a highly successful *shōnen* manga title—i.e., one aimed at audiences of boys between the ages of twelve and eighteen—that appeared in thirty-seven volumes between 2009 and 2017, although several of my colleagues do (see, e.g., Akasoy).

A work I have not yet used is *Habibi*. This tome of more than six hundred pages, which took several years to complete, is by the acclaimed graphic novelist Craig Thompson, whose 2003 *Blankets* was named the top comic of the year in one influential ranking (Arnold). *Habibi* tells the story of two children escaped from slavery, a young girl named Dodola and a young boy named Zam. *Habibi* does not tell *Nights* stories—if anything, the Quran is a more important Arabic source (e.g., 182, 202, 390). Meticulously and expertly illustrated, *Habibi* garnered a lot of attention, but the high praise it received has also been accompanied by a great deal of criticism for the way Thompson participates in an Orientalized, exoticized, and eroticized vision of women, womanhood, manhood, and gender relations (see Hatfield). Notably, Dodola's often sexually abused body, nature's various abortifacients, and Zam's castration—he becomes a eunuch—are all explicitly depicted and described (hence the work's channeling of the *Nights*). But, just as Alan Moore and Eddie Campbell's *From Hell* and Moore and Kevin O'Neill's *The League of Extraordinary Gentlemen* should not be viewed as "retro-Victorian reveries or inauthentic or low representations of a real and hence documentable era," neither should works such as *Habibi* be viewed (solely) as "retro[-medieval-]Islamic" (Ferguson 202). *Habibi* can fruitfully be used in the classroom for a discussion of the "complex meditations on the politics and history of visual representation" of the *Nights*.

The four works I do include in my class engage with the *Nights* in four very different ways and are artistically distinct too. This makes it easy to teach them discretely or together. They are Jeon JinSeok and Han SeungHee's *One Thousand and One Nights* (originally in Korean), which is a retelling with a strong focus on the frame tale; Gaiman's "Ramadan," which is deeply evocative of and implicated in the world of the *Nights*; Bill Willingham's *Fables: A Thousand and One Nights of Snowfall*, which adapts the Shahrazad tale; and Sergio Toppi's *Sharaz-De* (originally in Italian), which re-creates the *Nights*.

One Thousand and One Nights

Jeon and Han's *One Thousand and One Nights* is a *manhwa* work. *Manhwa* is the Korean term for *manga*, from *man* ("whimsical" or "impromptu") and *ga* ("pictures"), a particularly styled Japanese comic, which appears in paperback and usually runs thousands of pages. The name betrays the fact that initially— and in some quarters, still—sequential art forms are thought of as unserious and intended for children. In the United States, this can be explained by the fact that many early popular comics were Grub Street publications, printed on cheap paper and ink, homogenized, and produced for children, such as Wilhelm Busch's 1874 *Max and Maurice*, and Rudolf Dirks's 1897 *Katzenjammer Kids*. There are echoes here, of course, of the ways in which the *Nights* circulate in the Arabophone world (see Miquel).

I assign only the first of the series' ten volumes in my class, but I have found that students will often read the rest on their own initiative and their own time. The premise of the first volume (and the series) is as follows: The sultan is killing women every night after having discovered his wife's treachery. Sehara—a man, drawn androgynously in characteristic manga/*manhwa* style—in order to save his sister Dunya, dresses up as her and takes her place. The sultan discovers the subterfuge and insists on hearing Sehara's story. With such elements as the recasting of Shahrazad as a man, Dunya's incestuous love for her brother, and several scenes of nonconsensual sex, both male-female and male-male, this work can be very productively used for discussions of the role and importance of siblings in the *Nights*, of gender, of consensual and nonconsensual sex, and of transgressive love. One of the embedded tales is the story of Turandot, the inclusion of which allows for a deeper discussion of the nature of embedded tales and their functions. At one point, Sehara is put in prison, where he meets Jaafar, who has been imprisoned because the sultan believes Jaafar was involved with his wife. It is after reading this title that I introduce the story of Jaafar the

Barmakid's fall from (Harun al-Rashid's) grace because of the allegations about Jaafar and Harun's sister ʿAbbasa.

The Sandman: Fables and Reflections: "Ramadan"

Part of the *Sandman* series, Gaiman's story "Ramadan" melds the real Baghdad in its medieval heyday with an imagined Baghdad of the *Arabian Nights*. Harun is the hero of the tale. He rules over a glorious city, but after pondering at length, he comes to the realization that Baghdad will not and cannot last forever. He takes Morpheus all over his lands, and in the course of their travels tales are evoked, including many from the *Nights*; indeed, the artwork is also very reminiscent of illustrations from the *Nights*. At the end of the journey, Harun strikes a bargain with Morpheus: "I propose to give you this city. *My* city. I submit that you *purchase* it from me. Take it into dreams." "And in exchange?" asks Morpheus. "In exchange I want it *never* to *die*. To live forever. Can you do this thing?" And Morpheus replies, "After a fashion I can." All Harun has to do is tell his people and it will be. Harun falls asleep. When he awakens he has no recollection of the bargain and tries to buy a bottle in which Morpheus is carrying what appears to be a golden city, but Morpheus says it is not for sale. The story then cuts to modern-day Baghdad, and an old man (a storyteller) is telling a young boy about golden Baghdad. The city now (only) perdures in legend, and that legend is preserved in the *Nights*. The story and the art are in fact full of references and allusions to the *Nights* (e.g., the mechanical horse, the story of the fishermen, and so on). The figure in a dark gray embroidered cloak, with an oversized head in the shape of a crescent moon, on the cover of the volume evokes both Harun and his former glory and Morpheus (fig. 1). "Ramadan" allows the instructor to explore with students the nature of storytelling as a way of avoiding extinction—Shahrazad, but also Harun in the work, and of course Gaiman himself—and of preserving memory and also the motifs of sleep and dreams in the *Nights* and in the literary and cultural record generally. At thirty-four (full color) pages, it is a short piece that is not explicitly about the *Nights*, even though the implication is that the *Nights* is one of the few places that properly preserves the legendary glory of Baghdad, but its meta take on Harun, the so-called golden age of Baghdad, and the *Nights* works very well with students.

Fables: A Thousand and One Nights of Snowfall and *Arabian Nights (and Days)*

Willingham's *Fables* is an award-winning series in 150 issues (2002–15). The premise is that various characters (called "Fables") from fable and fairy tale have been driven out of their homelands by the Adversary and must now make common cause in exile in Fabletown (within New York City). Characters include Prince Charming, who by the time of *Arabian Nights (and Days)* is mayor (his predecessor was King Cole); Beauty, the deputy mayor, married to Beast, the

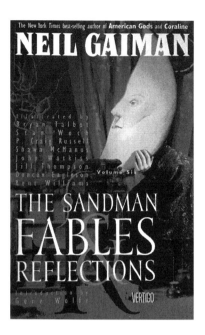

Figure 1. Cover of *The Sandman: Fables and Reflections*, written by Neil Gaiman and illustrated by P. Craig Russell et al., 1993. Photo credit: Asiya Toorawa.

current sheriff (his predecessor was Bigby Wolf); and Rose Red (Snow White's sister), who runs an annex called the Farm, where nonhuman-looking Fables have to live. Absent from the *Arabian Nights (and Days)* sequence of issues, which appeared as a separate graphic novel, but very important to the series, are Snow White and Bigby Wolf (who have six cubs together).

I assign *Arabian Nights (and Days)* so that students develop a proper understanding of the world of Fables and Fabletown, the better to be able then to introduce *Snowfall*. In *Arabian Nights (and Days)*, a delegation from the Arabian Homelands arrives in Fabletown seeking an alliance against encroachment by the Adversary and his allies. The encounter between the Arabian Fables and the Western Fables provides an ideal opportunity for characters from each side to learn about the other (e.g., about jinn, different types of magic, and courtly and cultural practices) and ideal material for classroom discussion about students' own learning about the other. As might be expected, Willingham also uses the visit of the Arabian Fables to embed tales.

In *Snowfall*, set in the early days of Fabletown (it is a spin-off prequel to the *Fables* series), Snow White is sent as an emissary from Fabletown to the Arabian Homelands to seek an alliance with Sultan Shahryar. She is exquisitely depicted in the cover art (fig. 2), a standing figure enveloped in a cape, her right hand touching a wall to steady her. Behind her are the heads of three wolves, representing the menace she faces. The vizier presents her not as an envoy but as the next woman to be married and killed, in order to delay his own daughter

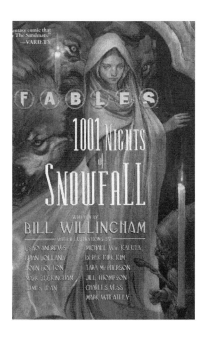

Figure 2. Cover of *Fables: A Thousand and One Nights of Snowfall*, written by Bill Willingham and illustrated by Esao Andrews et al., 2006. Photo credit: Asiya Toorawa.

Scheherazade from being so presented. When Snow White is in the sultan's presence, he ignores her explanation that she has been sent on a mission, tells her his story and why he is killing a new wife every night, and sets about to do so. "Not just yet, O King of the Age," responds Snow. "And it's here that she summoned all her wit and subtlety, artifice and subterfuge. . . . 'It's not fit that you've entertained me with a tale of your past, but received no such gift in return. It's not so late . . . and I have my own small tale of revenge and terrible lessons. Would you like to hear it?'" (21). The sultan agrees, and there follow nine stories describing the backstories to the run-ins many well-known characters have with the Adversary. None are *Nights*-esque, but on the thousandth night, Snow is out of stories. The sultan has fallen for her and lets her go, and it is now Scheherazade's turn: she asks Snow for advice on how to stay the ruler's hand, to which she replies, "He likes stories" (140). I have found it useful to juxtapose this graphic novel with the Barron film, and John Barth's *Dunyazadiad*, for discussions of the power of storytelling and the love that develops in the sultan for the storyteller.

One advantage of teaching revisionist comics and graphic material is that it allows the exploration "of the vast and varied world of seriality, multiple versions, and versionings . . . and intertextual references" (Taylor 172), a feature of the *Nights* and the way they have been elaborated within their origin traditions and beyond. As Laurie N. Taylor goes on to say, studying them "in light of their intertextual framework illuminates individual comics, the stories they revise, the cultural context for both originals and revisions, and the connections between the many versions and the many media in which those versions appear" (177; see also Bacchilega).

Sharaz-De: Tales from the Arabian Nights

In many ways Toppi's *Sharaz-De* is the graphic novel closest to the *Nights* in sensibility. It begins with a very slightly tweaked frame tale: the discovery by Shahzaman of his wife's infidelity and the failure of his brother Shahriyar to provide solace, until Shahzaman discovers Shahriyar's wife's is unfaithful too, something he reluctantly communicates to his brother. The enraged Shahriyar then decides to marry and execute a woman every night. Enter Sharaz-De, the daughter of a lord in a distant land who comes to her father and says, "Father, listen: I ask that you take me to the king, even if it causes you great pain." The father resists: "Your words are folly. If you go to him, he will take your beauty and then kill you." But she replies, "Perhaps that is not what will come to pass, father. Grant my request, I beg of you," which he does with a heavy heart (22). Once in the king's company, Sharaz-De asks for only one thing, that "[t]o brighten the hours ahead"—that is, the hours before her death—"I might recount stories ancient and rare till the new day robs me of speech and being," which the king grants (25). There follow ten tales, none from the *Nights*. Each features a character in difficulty, usually a person of power, who faces some difficulty for which a magical solution presents itself. But inevitably, there is a change in destiny, and the protagonist must face an unhappy fate. Of special interest is the fact that we are not returned to the frame tale: we are simply treated to these ten tales.

Toppi's graphic novel is wonderful to use in class. Discussion can center on his choice to have Shahrazad be from elsewhere, the choice to use non-*Nights* tales, the need for an ending, the absence of a Dunyazad figure, and much else besides. But it is also sumptuously drawn, as the filigree on the woman's burqa and the contrast of the shading with the ornate armor show (see figs. 3 and 4). Even the instructor who is not an expert in art will find much to talk with students about regarding Toppi's artistry and artistic choices, most of which are obvious to the untrained eye: the use of lines and vertical space, use of negative space, overlapping of images, interaction of panels, unusual placement of word bubbles, innovative use of gutters, use of color and black and white together in the same frame, single-page compositions (he also produced single-shot works), and outstanding draftsmanship. As the influential critic Paul Gravett notes in a piece titled "Sergio Toppi: Master of the Impossible,"

> In a perfect world, Sergio Toppi would be a household name in English-speaking comics circles. For starters, the look of modern American comic books, from Frank Miller, Walt Simonson and Bill Sienkiewicz to Denys Cowan, R. M. Guera and Sean Murphy, would not be the same without his massive, unmistakeable inspiration. And yet Toppi's own work remains

largely unknown beyond a coterie of admirers. There is a sad irony that his first ever graphic novel to be finally put into English this year —*Sharaz-de: Tales from the* Arabian Nights . . . out this week in the shops from Archaia—did not see print before his death on August 21st 2012, less than two months before his 80th birthday.

The *Nights* found their way into translation more rapidly than almost anything else in Arabic literature. May graphic novel iterations and incarnations find their way into syllabi and classrooms with similar speed and success.

Figure 3. Sergio Toppi, *Sharaz-De: Tales from the* Arabian Nights, 2013, p. 85. © Éditions Mosquito / Eredi Toppi. Reproduced with permission.

Figure 4. Cover of Sergio Toppi, *Sharaz-De: Tales from the* Arabian Nights, 2013. © Éditions Mosquito / Eredi Toppi. Reproduced with permission.

The *Thousand and One Nights* in American Film and Fiction

Margaret Litvin

Like "that other great collection of oriental tales, the Bible" (Irwin, Arabian Nights 237), the *Thousand and One Nights* warns strongly against curiosity. Meddling in others' business, asking about their customs, can lead only to trouble. "Whoever speaks of what concerns him not hears what pleases him not," reads the gold lettering over the door in "The Story of the Porter and the Three Women" (Haddawy, *Arabian Nights* 66). Or, in the earliest English version, translated from Antoine Galland's 1704 French text, "If you ask questions about that which does not belong to you, you may come to know that which will be no way pleasing to you." (Mack 70). Yet of course this playful paradox invites subversion at every turn. Curiosity drives the plot and many subplots of the *Nights*—without it there would be no story. Only when the Porter's fellow males ask the forbidden question (and "seven black men, with drawn swords in their hands" leap with nightmare precision from the floorboards) can the rest of the story's long, exciting thread of substories begin to unspool (Haddawy, *Arabian Nights* 85). Most of these, too, turn on the theme of forbidden knowledge. "We would be sitting pretty but for our curiosity," goes the refrain (Haddawy, *Arabian Nights* 124, 125, 132 [cf. 11, 13]), itself a "story tag" (as my class took to calling it) that invites an inquiring pull. Readers of the *Nights* learn, with gratitude, that if we watch *someone else* ask about other people's habits, we can hear things that please us very much indeed.

For American students studying the *Nights* (or any other Middle Eastern literary text), both curiosity and pleasure can be fraught. Today's undergraduates, the first generation with no conscious memories before 9/11, know mainly the hypermasculinized Orient of terror, not the feminized Orient of pleasure—explosions and beheadings, not odalisques and hammams. They need to notice the half-dormant clichés of Oriental luxury in their environment (Camel cigarettes, hookah lounges, harem-panted Halloween costumes) before they can even understand Edward Said's 1978 critique. Yet by the time they get to a college course focused on the Middle East, many of them have already absorbed some elements of postcolonial criticism. They may carry not only anxiety about Arabs or Islam but also a fear of stereotyping these. Some (including students of Arab or Muslim heritage) carry guilt about what they have repeatedly been told is their ignorance of the region. This fear and guilt can breed not openhearted curiosity but diffidence, fear of asking the wrong question and being thought a racist or a fool. Explicitly or implicitly, the syllabus and instructor set the ground rules. May students ask about cultural features that seem exotic? Must one automatically disapprove of all hybrid (interculturally appropriated) cultural products and look for original and authentic Arab texts—and if so, where in the *Nights* could those possibly be found? And what about pleasure? Is Orientalist kitsch only for dissection, or are we allowed to enjoy it?

Fortunately, the tradition of the *Thousand and One Nights* is large and contains multitudes. It quickly shows cultural essentialism to be both useful and absurd: on the one hand, the magisterial Baghdad-centric contributions of the editor Muhsin Mahdi and the translator Husain Haddawy; on the other, that the three *Nights* tales best known worldwide—those featuring Aladdin, Ali Baba, and Sindbad—were not part of the so-called original Arabic *Nights* at all. The *Nights* tradition exposes every possible authorship claim—that the *Nights* is at heart an Indian book, a Persian book, an Arab book, a French book—as both somehow true and obviously incomplete. Elements of globalization and exoticization within the text itself (the Porter's import-heavy shopping list, the Hunchback's location in China) quickly prove that looking east for color is no mere European fetish but the story's very essence. The text's carefree distortions—just for a start, the Sasanian-era Shahrazad tells stories about the Muslim caliph Harun al-Rashid, who lived at least 150 years later—show that historical accuracy is not the point. The explicit and at times satirical portrayal of identity politics (for instance, the way a wounded Shahriyar chooses gender over species, identifying with a horrible male jinni rather than the jinni's unfaithful but human wife [Haddawy, *Arabian Nights* 8–9]) suggest both that identities can be multiple and that every category of belonging can be taken too far. All this complexity can help a diverse class both to focus and to relax.

But it is when the stories ripple out into the world literary imagination that the fun really starts. The *Nights* tradition meets everyone where they are. It reaches into many languages and virtually every artistic genre, so whatever a student is interested in—from poetry to graphic novels, from folktales to film to ballet to modernist fiction to theater to anime—the *Nights* has been there too. This makes it easy to find high-quality adaptations of the *Nights* relevant to any given seminar group and a research paper topic to excite every individual student (Michael Lundell provides many opening suggestions in his *Journal of the Thousand and One Nights* at journalofthenights.blogspot.com). Here the question, "What features of the original text does this adaptation capture and emphasize?" is only the beginning. Even more important, how are characters, plots, settings, or nested story structures from the *Nights* deployed to stretch or enrich their receiving genres? What does adapting the *Nights* let a writer or artist do that would have been more difficult by other means? What audiences do the *Nights* help one reach, what censors do they help one elude, what formal experiments do they allow?

Reading the Nights *as a Tradition*

Particularly fruitful for teaching in universities in the United States are contemporary Anglo-American literary adaptations, those written since roughly

1990. New examples appear every year: such texts as Salman Rushdie's *Haroun and the Sea of Stories*, Neil Gaiman's "Ramadan," A. S. Byatt's *The Djinn in the Nightingale's Eye*, or, more recently, Mohja Kahf's *Emails from Scheherazad*, Rabih Alameddine's *The Hakawati*, P. B. Kerr's *Children of the Lamp* series, and Rushdie's *Two Years Eight Months and Twenty-Eight Nights*. Most of these are hybrid texts, rooted in postcolonial or globalized aesthetic worlds and referring to elements of popular culture and world politics in which many students have a prior interest. Yet they also reach back into the older tradition of the *Thousand and One Nights*, and students can be lured there too.

For example, Disney's 1992 and 2019 *Aladdin* films, which students may know from childhood, depend heavily on two earlier *Thief of Bagdad* films. The politics of the tale's evolution are obvious: Douglas Fairbanks's nimble 1924 *Thief* bifurcates by 1940 into a dreamy romantic lead and an infantilized South Asian sidekick (played by a former elephant driver, Sabu), whom the evil vizier bewitches and turns into a dog; Disney's 1992 animated film completes the animalization, recasting Sabu's character as Abu the adorable monkey. But deeper, less bilateral strands of allusion matter too. The 1924 American film, built from the so-called orphan tale "Prince Ahmad and the Fairy Banu," lifts techniques from German expressionism and Ballets Russes' *Scheherazade*, which in 1910 had wowed Parisians with the Orientalizing Russian music of Nikolai Rimsky-Korsakov and the avant-garde visual art of Léon Bakst. Tracing the motives behind such borrowings disassembles the so-called West (is Russia part of Europe or not?) and builds students' sense of competence navigating a complex cultural tradition.[1]

Films of the *Nights* teach yet another double lesson. As Robert Irwin has noted, they focus centrally on technology, the magic of our day:

> Very often the quest is designed as a structure that will serve as a showcase for special effects. . . . Technology has customarily been the prime mover in cinema's handling of material from the *Arabian Nights*. . . . [T]he medium is the message—this sort of film work is, in effect, using magic to create stories that are about magic.   *("Thousand and One Nights")*

But there is a powerful countercurrent: to confirm their human relatability and render their awe-inspiring new technologies safe and palatable for American families, filmmakers such as Raoul Walsh, Alexander Korda, and the Disney company also include a dose of technophobic moralizing. Thus, "Happiness must be earned" (*Thief* [1924]). The high-tech All-Seeing Eye is useless, but friendship and loyalty save the day (*Thief* [1940]). In the end it is not the blue genie's dancing elephants and magic palaces that win the princess but having the nerve to "tell her the truth" and "be yourself" (*Aladdin* [1992]).

The analytical approach just applied in capsule form to the American film tradition of the *Nights*—tracing intertextual relations, then exploring social, political, and artistic contexts and explaining subtexts meant for particular audiences—can also be fruitful for teaching contemporary literature. The rest of this essay will apply the same approach to one highly teachable twenty-first-century novel, G. Willow Wilson's novel *Alif the Unseen*.

Seeing Alif: *Intertexts, Contexts, Subtexts*

G. Willow Wilson is an American comic book writer whose oeuvre includes the series *Vixen*, *Ms. Marvel*, and *Invisible Kingdom* and the graphic novel *Cairo*, and the nongraphic novels *Alif the Unseen* and *The Bird King*. As she relates in her memoir *The Butterfly Mosque*, she is also a convert to Islam. Published in 2012, *Alif the Unseen* was her first nongraphic novel. Set in a fictional Gulf Arab principality modeled on the United Arab Emirates, it features two young people: the half-Indian computer encryption specialist nicknamed Alif and his girl next door, the Egyptian-born, niqab-wearing Dina.

Written just as the 2011 Arab uprisings were coming to a boil, *Alif* teems with tangled contacts between the human and spirit worlds. Alif, jilted by an Emirati girlfriend he met online, writes some spying software to track her and block her messages. But through Dina, the woman sends him a mysterious manuscript, at least seven hundred years old and preserved with a sinister, stinky resin. In their quest to understand the manuscript while eluding the State Security manhunt it has provoked, Alif and Dina seek help from a terrifying jinni. Their escape takes them to the Empty Quarter, here reimagined as the realm of the jinn (a typical sci-fi or fantasy parallel world—later, after being sprung from a disgusting prison, Alif flees to a jinn tavern that recalls the Star Wars cantina). Meanwhile Alif's code helps crash the State Security servers. The book's supervillain, an intelligence official, turns out to be literally in league with diabolical powers.

Alif has it all: a quest-and-escape plot, an eighteenth-century French forgery, computer hacking, hijab debates, theories of metaphor, brutal authoritarianism, Emirati ethnic prejudice, the furry but dangerous jinni Vikram the Vampire, and even the Arab Spring. Unpacking some of its intertexts, contexts, and subtexts offers a roadmap for teaching this witty page-turner. More generally, I hope to show how intertexts and contexts can act as story tags for students, offering keys to interpretation even for those entering with no background knowledge. With regard to intertexts, I ask, Which works (from the *Nights* tradition and elsewhere) does the novel intertextualize, and how are these allusions deployed?

Alif's plot turns on a relatively obscure piece of the *Nights* tradition. The foul-smelling manuscript (titled *Alf yeom wa yeom*, preserved with human amniotic fluid) turns out to be an Arabic version of *Les mille et un jours*, François Pétis de La Croix's eighteenth-century collection of tales published soon after Galland's *Nights*. Here, counterfactually, La Croix's pseudo-Oriental forgery is understood to be a real and potentially very dangerous text stolen by humans from the world of the jinn (cf. Marzolph and van Leeuwen 2: 720–21).

The novel's many other intertexts are prominent as well, and each plays an important role. Some intertexts—Egyptian popular music, the 1975 Amitabh Bachchan film *Sholay*—add color to the cultural background. Others advance the novel's argument about the insufficiency of human reason: Philip Pullman's *The Golden Compass*, the Qur'an (whose *muqaṭaʿāt* letters *alif—lam—mim* one character reads as "one-digit symbol substitutions . . . the first line of code ever written" [Wilson 77]), and Douglas Hofstadter's infinite-recursion joke about "God over Djinn" (Wilson 112; cf. Hofstadter). The Pullman intertext, for instance, stages Alif and Dina's discussion of metaphor early in the novel:

> Dina reached into her robe and drew out a battered copy of *The Golden Compass*.
> "Aren't you going to ask me what I thought?" she demanded.
> "I don't care. The English was probably too difficult for you."
> "It was no such thing. I understood every word. This book"—she waved it in the air—"is full of pagan images. It's dangerous."
> "Don't be ignorant. They're metaphors. I told you you wouldn't understand."
> "Metaphors are dangerous. Calling something by a false name changes it, and metaphor is just a fancy way of calling something by a false name."
> Alif snatched the book from her hand. There was a hiss of fabric as Dina tucked her chin, eyes disappearing beneath her lashes. Though he had not seen her face in nearly ten years, Alif knew she was pouting.
> "I'm sorry," he said, pressing the book to his chest. "I'm not feeling well today." (Wilson 20)

Later references to *The Golden Compass* track both Dina's softening toward the figurative world and Alif's new openness to the spiritual: "Dina stopped walking and stared at him with knitted brows. 'I can't believe this. You read all those kuffar fantasy novels and yet you deny something straight out of a holy book. . . . Remember: 'And the jinn We created in the Foretime from a smokeless fire'" (102).

Depending on the class's level and speed, intertexts can be explored in various ways. A speedier strategy is to assign one pair of students to prepare a presentation on all the intertexts and contexts (see below) relevant to the novel, perhaps using a background article if one exists. A different pair of students can tackle each text on the syllabus. A slower and more flexible method, if time and class size permit, is to have each student choose one particular intertext (perhaps from a menu compiled by the instructor) and share or present a short write-up on its general cultural significance and its particular significance in *Alif*.[2]

With regard to contexts, I ask, In what literary traditions does *Alif the Unseen* participate? In what social debates does it intervene? How can we guide students to make sense of the novel's complex and contradictory representations of

Muslims (including converts), Arab politics, and relations between the Middle East and the West?

Alif's literary contexts include the growing mainstream status of fantasy fiction since about 1997 (Alif received reviews in the *New York Times* and the London *Guardian*) and Anglo-American readers' fascination with Islam since 2001. One confluence is the recent spate of Muslim comic superheroes, including Wilson's own *Ms. Marvel* series, which has worked to both normalize and glorify Muslim lives in public discourse in the United States (Lewis and Lund).

Alif also comments on many social contexts: the world of gray-hat hackers, the rights and status of immigrants in Gulf Arab states, and, most important, the debates between adherents of Sufism and Salafism over proper Islamic faith and ritual. These references invite student micro-research projects.

Alif addresses two groups Wilson sees as uncomfortably similar: overly legalistic neofundamentalist Muslims, and Westerners in denial of their spirituality. This delicate self-positioning is fascinating to trace. Wilson's many interviews and public writings offer further clues, but a careful reader can also understand the debates from internal evidence.

For instance, the invisibility trope announced in the title ("the Unseen") ramifies through the book: the hacker Alif (whose real name is Muhammad) not only hides behind his handle and encryption strategies but also has his software spy on his ex-girlfriend, Intisar, in order to conceal him from her. He refers to the program as a hijab, signaling that veils, too, interest Wilson because they let women see without being seen. Meanwhile, the hidden surveillance state tracks every keystroke of Alif and his associates. Finally, there are the real unseen powers, the so-called hidden folk from the parallel jinn world. Throughout the novel, humans are mocked as literalist and narrow-minded for failing to see and accept them. (In a wink at readers who know Wilson's public persona, one such character is an annoying but endearing American Muslim convert studying in the Gulf. She starts out denying the existence of jinn and ends up married to one.)

With regard to subtexts, I ask: How does the book position itself for various audiences, and what messages does it send them?

The novel's most magical moment has no element of the supernatural. Instead, it focuses, like the cinematic *Nights* tradition sketched earlier, on the humbling of hubris and the empowerment of human moral resources. This scene occurs at a moment of despair. Hiding in the back of a mosque, using the imam's old computer, Alif has somehow used *Alf yeom wa yeom* to code a program that can think metaphorically to track and crash the State Security servers:

> He worked steadily. His fingers knew what he needed to do before his mind did. Pieces of the fragmented Hollywood hypervisor were still useable; he plugged lines of the familiar code into the sheikh's machine, watching with satisfaction as algorithmic towers grew before his eyes. Every so often he paused to reread a portion of the *Alf Yeom*, separating the frame story into

> two threads of code: Farukhuaz, the dark princess, became a set of Boolean algorithms: the nurse, her irrational counterpart, non-Boolean expressions. There was nothing he could not interpret numerically. The numbers themselves, like stories, were merely representative, stand-ins for meaning that lay deeper, embedded in pulses of electricity within the computer, the firing of neurons in Alif's mind, events whose defining elements blurred and merged as he worked. (Wilson 240)

The State Security servers' antivirus software has fought back, prompting a high-adrenaline comic-bookish computer duel like the classic shape-changing battle between the jinni and the girl in the "Second Dervish's Tale" from the *Nights* (Haddawy 110–11). Finally, Alif's translinguistic software tower (a hubristic human tower with its top in the heavens, like the Tower of Babel in Genesis 11.4) has crashed, melting the computer. State Security is breaking down the door. In a last minute alone with Dina, Alif asks her to comfort him. To readers' surprise, she takes him literally behind the veil, inside the robe that covers her face and body:

> Dina hesitated. Then she knelt in front of him, knee to knee, and threw her veil over his head.
>
> The darkness soothed Alif's dazzled eyes. After a moment his pupils adjusted, lessening the smarting pain in his head. *He could not have guessed the world she had created for herself.* Sewn into the underside of her long outer cloak were patches of bright silk: patterned, beaded, spangled with points of light; they hung above him like a tent, supported by her bare, bandaged arm. They lay on the floor facing one another. He rested his forehead in the curve of her neck, taking in the scent of her hair. She watched him. She was not beautiful, not by the measure of the magazines hidden beneath his bed at home. Not like Intisar. Her nose was as large as he remembered. She was unfashionably dark, leading Alif to guess she had never bothered with the skin-bleaching creams so many girls used to poison themselves. Of course she had not. She had pride.
>
> "What are you thinking?" she asked.
> "I'm thinking that you are all good things in one place," he said. (Wilson 244–45; emphasis added)

Looking deeply into Dina's eyes, Alif realizes "with something like humility that her most striking feature had always been visible to him" (245). Of course there is no kiss: Alif decides on a proper Muslim courtship, and his arrest separates our two heroes for nearly a hundred pages. But I would argue that this scene is the emotional climax of the novel. Like other American adaptations of the *Nights*, it demotes rational technological prowess, stressing human maturity and loyalty.

Yet this message is not Wilson's ultimate goal. Rather, by creating an elaborate fantasy world set in a Muslim context, and by inscribing herself deftly into the American tradition of *Nights*-based techno-skeptical discourse, Wilson auditions for a chance to join the cultural conversation on equal terms. In so doing she both earns and uses her position as a proud Muslim voice in American letters. One ambition is to set herself up as a fitting partner for, say, Pullman's *His Dark Materials* trilogy or even C. S. Lewis's religious allegory *The Chronicles of Narnia*. Whether or not you believe she succeeds, the quest is fascinating to watch.

NOTES

1. See Irwin, "*Thousand and One Nights*"; al-Taee; Cooperson.
2. In 1993 I was fortunate to take a college course with the modernism scholar Lawrence Rainey that did this allusion tracking with James Joyce's *Ulysses*.

The *Thousand and One Nights* and Mediterranean Framed Narrative Traditions

Karla Mallette

How can instructors help students appreciate the dazzling narrative invention and variety of the *Thousand and One Nights*—without succumbing to narrative fatigue?[1] In this essay, I propose using selected medieval framed narratives, along with judiciously chosen examples from modern fiction and film, to illustrate both narrative dynamics particular to the *Nights* and the big-picture history of storytelling before the advent of the printing press in general. *The Seven Sages of Rome* (known east of the Mediterranean as *The Book of Sindbad* [or *Sendebar* or *Syntipas*] *the Wise*) was an anonymous medieval framed narrative.[2] In this work, as in the *Nights*, storytelling ransoms lives. A young nobleman (the son of a king, caliph, or emperor) leaves home to finish his education. When he returns, his father's wife (his stepmother) falsely accuses him of attempting to rape her. An astrological reading has warned the boy against speaking in his own defense. The collection is an extended courtroom drama, in which a team of scholars tell stories defending the young man's innocence, and (in the Western versions) the wife tells stories illustrating his guilt. The collection was immensely popular. It appeared first in an Arabic version and would be translated into Greek, Latin, and the European vernaculars, attested by many manuscript and early print versions. In the *Decameron*, by Giovanni Boccaccio, a group of ten young noble men and ladies gather in Florence when the 1347 plague is at its height. To escape the death and mayhem of the city, they retreat to a villa outside town. There, to pass the time, they agree to tell stories to each other. The collection gathers ten stories told on ten days. Both the *Seven Sages* and the *Decameron* present tales as a diversion from or defense against death; in this, they resemble the *Nights*. In contrast, in the *Canterbury Tales*, by Geoffrey Chaucer, a series of tales are told to pass the time by a diverse group of pilgrims on their way to visit a shrine. Because it lacks an elaborate framing device that pits storytelling against death, the *Canterbury Tales* serves as a useful contrast to the narrative dynamic found in the *Nights*, the *Decameron*, and the *Seven Sages*.

Like medieval storytellers, modern movie and TV writers must produce endless narrative variations on set themes. When introducing the concept of the framed narrative, and narration as a way to distract the audience from imminent peril in particular, instructors may point out to students that (to quote "The Simpsons Already Did It," a *South Park* episode about narrative exhaustion) "*The Simpsons* did it." In the episode of *The Simpsons* called "The Seemingly Never-Ending Story," the characters relate a series of framed narratives that (like the *Nights*, the *Seven Sages*, and the *Decameron*) involve an audience in danger and entertained by a storyteller. The episode, written by Ian Maxtone-Graham and first broadcast on 12 March 2006, won *The Simpsons* an Emmy for Best

Animated Program. Scenes from this episode can be shown in class to illustrate how, still today, writers reuse narrative elements from deep literary history—including works like the one they are studying.

The discussion below is divided into three sections, each focusing on a specific characteristic of the *Nights* and comparing it to the *Seven Sages*, the *Decameron*, and the *Canterbury Tales*. Pedagogical exercises are proposed to help students think about the nature of narrative in general and how the *Nights* deploys narrative to a specific end. The goal is to encourage students to analyze the narratives gathered in the *Nights* in order to understand how they work—what makes them compelling narratives—and to appreciate why television script writers might still turn to them in the twenty-first century for inspiration.

Variations on a Theme

The *Nights* existed in multiple manuscript versions, and tales from the *Nights* were told and retold by professional and amateur storytellers. Details or whole tales may be adjusted or thoroughly transformed in the process. Students who are struggling to keep track of the variations within the text—especially in narrative sequences like "The Porter and the Three Women of Baghdad" or the Barber's tales—may lose sight of the appeal of narrative variation. The same was true of the *Seven Sages*—the extant manuscripts display myriad variations on basic narrative themes—and even an authored text like the *Decameron* (copyists might swap out their own story for one of Boccaccio's). Again, scripted television series can be used to illustrate the importance of variants. When shows like *The Simpsons* or *South Park* riff on recent movies (or each other), for instance, how do they transform narrative details familiar to their audience? How can a simple change in a plot setup or a character alter the dynamic and outcome of the narrative as a whole? The Halloween episodes of *The Simpsons*, which regularly take familiar horror films as models, are particularly good examples of this phenomenon.

In small-group discussion, guided paraphrase can allow students to play with narrative variation themselves. Story cycles like "The Merchant and the Jinni" or "The Porter and the Three Women of Baghdad" sort tales by narrative characteristics. The first features men who travel with animals, members of their family transformed by a spell as punishment for aggression against the protagonist. And in the second, we meet a series of men who enter underground spaces and there unwittingly bring doom on someone they love. After they analyze the similarities between the tales, ask students to generate a new story following the same narrative template. For instance, ask students to create a character traveling with an animal who represents a family member transformed, matching their narrative to the model presented by the tales in "The Merchant and the Jinni." They may even develop their tale variations together, as happens in Hollywood script rooms. Students are likely to come up with variations that are comic, tragic, and everything in between. Challenge them to think about the entertainment value of their stories: Are they likely to keep an audience amused? The instructor may require students to pitch their ideas to the class, which will put them in the position of the storyteller, and prove the mettle of their inventions. Call on students to explicate the moral of their tales: What is the takeaway for the audience? How do we engineer invented narrative to deliver a message? Ask them to relate the moral of their tale to the situation in which the model tale was narrated (in this example, "The Merchant and the Jinni") and then to the frame tale of the *Nights*. How does their invented narrative supplement—or undermine—the narrative model from the *Nights*? Do these tales encourage us to trust our intimate friends and relations, or do they counsel distrust? Do they encourage or discourage forgiveness toward those who betray us? This assignment requires students to analyze the tales closely and allows them to appreciate the narrative logic that holds together an extended work like the *Nights*.

Reading Frames against Embedded Tales

The world of the frame is differentiated from the world of the embedded tales in the *Nights*. Characters in the frame tale are elite, with the responsibilities and privileges of (imagined) aristocracy. Characters in the embedded tales—particularly at the beginning of the collection—live in a world more familiar to the audience and are more likely to deal with real-life problems. This is a quality the *Nights* shares with works like the *Seven Sages* and the *Decameron*. In the *Seven Sages*, the frame tale is set at the court of an emperor or caliph; the embedded tales involve much humbler characters—merchants, travelers, and the like. The frame tale of the *Decameron* is populated by elite characters who are not aristocrats yet are much more idealized and much less realistic than the characters we encounter in most of the embedded tales. In contrast, the frame of the *Canterbury Tales* features characters not much different from the ones we encounter in the embedded tales, such as a miller, a knight, a merchant, and members of religious orders. The disparity between frame and embedded tales in the case of the *Nights*, the *Decameron*, and the *Seven Sages* invites the reader to consider the dynamics and purpose of framing.

Students may be asked to read the framing narrative of the *Seven Sages* and the *Decameron*. Or the teacher may assign the *Seven Sages* to some students and the *Decameron* to others. The *Canterbury Tales* may be included in the exercise, in the original for more advanced classes or in an adaptation for high school or introductory university classes.[3] Students can be asked to fill out a matrix comparing the narrative elements of the frame tales, answering simple questions that compare the basic elements of the prologues in the works they are assigned: Who is speaking? Who is being addressed? How does the prologue describe the contents of the book? What is the point of the book, according to the prologue? The exercise may take the form of a jigsaw discussion. A class may be divided into groups, each completing the comparative exercise for a single work—comparing the *Thousand and One Nights* to the *Decameron*, for instance—then teaching the rest of the class how the *Nights* differs from the collection in question. Together, the class can assemble a master matrix comparing the framing narratives of each of these works. Or, in larger classes, the teacher may summarize the frame tales of the *Decameron*, the *Seven Sages*, and the *Canterbury Tales* and compare the works in a lecture.

The goal of this exercise is to help students understand the work done by the framing narrative. The setting, dramatis personae, and themes of framing and framed narratives need not align. An embedded narrative may contradict the stated intention, according to the framing narrative, for which it is related. Students can be encouraged to study the embedded frames in the same way, asking (for instance) how the motives for which tales are told within "The Merchant and the Jinni" or "The Porter and the Three Women of Baghdad" align with the messages embedded in those stories themselves. And the comparative exercise described in the previous paragraph may be adjusted to capture differences between frame and embedded narratives in discussions of those sections of the *Nights*. These exercises encourage fundamental critical reading skills: asking students to ask themselves whether the narratives they study are doing the work they tell us they are doing and, if not, what other purpose they advance.

The Stakes of Narration

The *Thousand and One Nights* directly connects storytelling to adjudicating or absolving the storyteller or someone close to the storyteller. This is true in the framing narrative and in the embedded frames and framed narratives that occur early in the book, up to and including the Hunchback cycle. The dark slapstick of the Barber's tales seems to bring this narrative dynamic to a close. Teachers can draw students' attention to the narrative insistence on this theme by assigning a simple structural analysis of the early tales in the collection. Give students a grid and ask them to describe characters, plot points, and morals of the frame tale, Yunan and Duban, and "The Tale of the Enchanted Prince." Each tale emphasizes trust, betrayal, and revenge. Again, this narrative strategy—using tales to assess fidelity, ransom lives, or distract from the presence of death—appears in the *Seven Sages* and in the *Decameron*, but not in the *Canterbury Tales*. Thanks to this thematic emphasis, the *Nights* (like the *Seven Sages* and the *Decameron*) functions as an extended meditation on the links between intimacy and betrayal on the one hand and storytelling and mortality on the other. This is one of the most compelling aspects of the *Nights*, and students should be challenged to think about the historical origins and the implications of this theme.

Instructors can lecture on the palace intrigues that cast a shadow over the rule of Harun al-Rashid, exaggerated popular versions of which may have inspired some of the toxic gender drama of the frame tale of the *Nights*. On the night of 28 January AD 803, Harun al-Rashid (for reasons that still puzzle historians) ordered the murder of the extended Barmakid clan—for generations, advisers to the caliph—including Jaafar, his bosom buddy. Arab historians tell us that his executioner, Masrur (who carouses with Harun and Jaafar in "The Porter and the Three Women of Baghdad"), refused to carry out Harun's command to murder Jaafar until Harun threatened to send another executioner after his head as well as Jaafar's. In their effort to understand Harun's massacre of the Barmakids, historians recounted a palace intrigue that involved Jaafar and Harun's sister.[4] These historical narratives certainly call into question the sunny image of Harun and Jaafar that emerges in "The Porter and the Three Women of Baghdad." And they change how we read Harun's courtroom challenges to the ladies at the end of that narrative, or the position of poor Jaafar in "The Three Apples." In "The Porter and the Three Women of Baghdad," three dervishes make their way to Harun to ask him to adjudicate their cases. Students can be asked to write their own ending to this tale before they read it (and before they know the dark stories about the historical Harun's injustice to the Barmakids). When composing their versions of the end, ask them to consider whether the dervishes deserve justice, as well as whether Harun is portrayed as a just king. The disparity between Harun's personality as portrayed in the *Nights* and in the historical accounts of his reign invites interesting classroom discussions of the political dimension of popular narrative and strategies that popular narrative may use to avoid politically risky material.

Finally, the political undercurrents—more obvious to earlier audiences of the work than they are to us—can be used to deepen the analysis of the tension between framing and framed narratives. The framing narrative of the *Nights* first punishes transgression and then uses narration to defer punishment. In a similar way, especially in the earlier embedded frames in the collection (through the Hunchback cycle), tales that end badly are contained within embedded frames that themselves end well. Throughout the collection, the happy ending of an embedded frame ransoms the tragic endings of the tales embedded within that frame, replicating the logic of the collection as a whole. Does the frame exist only to hold tales together in an extended narrative? What kind of hermeneutic or interpretive force does the frame exert on the tales embedded within it? Students can be asked to reflect on the tension between comic and tragic endings when considering the relation between framing and framed narratives.

A final modern example can illustrate the contemporary relevance of the narrative strategy of containing tragedy by embedding it within a comic narrative frame, as well as the theme of intimacy and betrayal, so central to the *Nights*. The short story "Lull," by the American author Kelly Link, begins with a series of palindromes, words and phrases that are spelled or sound the same backward and forward (like the title of the story, "lull"). This becomes a metaphor for the nested stories of a framed narrative, like the *Thousand and One Nights* or the story "Lull" itself. Framed narratives begin by narrating the act of storytelling, and works with multiple embedded frames end by backing out of each frame successively—a dynamic we find in the *Nights*, to a particularly heightened degree, at the end of "The Hunchback's Tale." And so the end of the tale must mirror its beginning, palindrome-style. Link introduces an intriguing variation on the framed narrative. In her version, the audience internal to her story issues a series of requirements that the tales told in the first embedded cycle must meet. The first of these rules: stories must go backward (271). They must start at the end and end at the beginning. One result of this reversed narrative structure is that, to quote her narrator, "It gets better" (282). Rather than exhibiting the entropy of normal human lives, ending in decline and death, the lives of the characters improve over time. Tragedy, backward, is comedy.

The *lull* of the title is the quiet time at night when we tell stories to each other. It refers to the fictions we create to fill those quiet times. And it embodies, in the palindromic form of the word, the structure of the framed narrative, which must close the circle of each narrative frame it opens. Link's story creates a dynamic that resembles the structure of the *Nights*, in which the dark matter of the tales is contained and ultimately reversed by the frame: children betray their parents, husbands and wives let each other down, yet the story ends on a note of hope. It is long and complex (and it contains explicit sexual material, so is inappropriate for high school courses). But highlights from the story may be shared with the class, and some are as delightful in their own right as the *Simpsons* episode described at the beginning of this essay. In the second level of embedded narration, a cheerleader narrates a tale to the Devil in a closet, following a drunken game of spin the bottle: a scene that is extremely weird, yet may be relatable for undergraduates today.

NOTES

1. In this essay I focus on the version of the *Nights* that I have taught most often, the Haddawy translation of the Mahdi edition.

2. For English translations of Eastern versions of this narrative, see Clouston and Epstein, respectively. Unfortunately, there is no Modern English translation of any of the many different Western versions (in Latin and the European vernaculars) of this work. There are, however, two modern editions of medieval English versions; see Brunner and Whitelock, respectively. Hans R. Runte has published online translations of many of the tales from French versions of the *Seven Sages*, but not, as far as I can tell, the frame tale. Runte's *Seven Sages* website no longer exists but has been archived by Dalhousie University (dalspace.library.dal.ca/handle/10222/49107).

3. The Coghill or Wright Modern English adaptations are recommended for classroom use.

4. For an account of the downfall of the Barmakids, see al-Tabari (201–30; see 201–02n297 for bibliographical references to other historians' accounts). Al-Tabari also relates tales about the affair between Jaafar and Harun's sister ʿAbbasa in particular (214–16; see 215n731 for bibliographic references to other historical sources and modern discussions). Hugh Kennedy gives an overview of historical explanations of Harun al-Rashid's massacre of the Barmakids (*Early Abbasid Caliphate* 127–29). On women and power in the caliphal family in Abbasid Baghdad as reflected in the historical accounts of the downfall of the Barmakids, see el-Hibri (42–44).

Intertextual Labyrinths: Borges and the *Nights*

Dominique Jullien

The *Thousand and One Nights* was a major intertext for the Argentine writer Jorge Luis Borges, who returned to it time and again throughout his long writing career. In addition to two long critical essays on the *Nights* ("The Translators of the *Thousand and One Nights*," first published in 1936, and "The *Thousand and One Nights*," collected in *Seven Nights* in 1980), Borges also made innumerable references, both explicit and implicit, to the *Nights* throughout his fiction and his poetry. In stories such as "Tlön, Uqbar, Orbis Tertius" (*Collected Fictions* 68–81), "The Garden of Forking Paths" (119–28), "The Zahir" (242–49), "Brodie's Report" (402–08), "The Book of Sand" (480–83), and others, the collection is mentioned by name; elsewhere, specific tales are rewritten ("The Story of the Two Dreamers" [56–57]) or invented tales are misattributed ("The Two Kings and the Two Labyrinths," falsely identified as a copyist's interpolation [263–64]). Given the centrality of both the *Nights* and Borges in world literature, students may want to understand the ramifications of Borges's interface with the book.

It is well known that Borges first read the *Nights* in English, in the nineteenth-century versions of Edward William Lane and Richard Francis Burton, both of which he discovered as a child in his father's library. Borges's version of the *Nights*, Robert Irwin states, "is an anglophone and anglophile one" (Irwin, Arabian Nights 282). More generally, Borges's reimagining of the *Nights* is often filtered through nineteenth-century English writers' dreams of the Orient, from Thomas De Quincey and Samuel Taylor Coleridge to Edward FitzGerald and Robert Louis Stevenson. Nevertheless, although his first contact with the book was through English, Borges would in time become familiar with many different versions, as well as keenly aware of the multilingual and translational nature of the *Nights*. In his influential essay "The Argentine Writer and Tradition," Borges makes a strong case for South American writers' right, indeed privilege, to be cosmopolitan: "I believe that our tradition is the whole of Western culture" (*Selected Non-Fictions* 426); this includes, of course, the *Thousand and One Nights*, the East's gift to the West. With its mix of Indian, Persian, and Arabic stories, set in places spanning the Mediterranean to China, the *Nights* is the ultimate cosmopolitan text, a text that entered Western culture through translation and changed it forever: incorporating into his own writing motifs from the *Nights* is an obvious way for an Argentine writer to claim his "universal birthright" (427). Borges's understanding of the *Nights* anticipates David Damrosch's definition of world literature as a mode of circulation (5). This essay focuses on three aspects of Borges's engagement with the *Nights* intertext: the question of creative translation and intermediality, seen through his appraisal of the

French translator Joseph-Charles Mardrus; the recreation of the *Nights* intertext as a so-called Oriental matter, with pronounced hybrid features; and the elaboration of a hypertextual Orient defined by orality, infinity, and anonymity.

Mardrus's "Creative Infidelity" and Cultural Modernity

Borges's early essay "The Translators of the *Thousand and One Nights*" demonstrates not only in-depth knowledge of the main translations available at the time but also a firm grasp of the theoretical issues involved in the translators' diverging choices. This makes the essay an ideal entry point into key questions of translation theory. I wish to highlight in particular the significance of one brief comment Borges made concerning Mardrus, which shows his sensitivity to the cultural backdrop of the French fin de siècle translation.

In his "Translators" essay, Borges departed significantly from established opinions. His was a poet's view, preferring Burton's flamboyant language and outrageous eroticism to Lane's more sober version and declining to praise Enno Littmann's recent German version despite its accuracy. What mattered to Borges was a translation's creative potential, its ability to generate and inspire new works. His essay consistently illustrates the idea that a diversity of translations can enrich both the original text and the host culture. One particularly vivid example is his assessment of the French translator Mardrus. Although he was quite aware that Mardrus's self-proclaimed literal translation was anything but, Borges celebrated its "happy and creative infidelity," suggesting that we should appreciate the visual potential of Mardrus's text, not focus on its infidelities. Mardrus, Borges stresses, translated not "the book's words but its scenes: a freedom denied to translators, but tolerated in illustrators" ("Translators" 106). Mardrus's translation is compared to a film adaptation (Borges mentions the lavish sets of director Cecil B. DeMille): the visual dimension becomes crucial. Borges's remarkably prescient intuition points to the issue of intermediality (in Jakobsonian terminology): the translation is seen not in textual isolation but in the rich context of early-twentieth-century artistic and material culture. For today's students, Borges's brief remark opens a treasure trove of cultural history. Mardrus's translation, which appeared from 1899 to 1904, coincided with the prewar golden age of illustrated editions, with such admirable book artists as Léon Carré, Mohammed Racim, Kees van Dongen, or François-Louis Schmied creating works of art for his text. Much of this work is readily available on the Internet, allowing the instructor to expose students to an exceptionally brilliant period in artists' books as well as provide a concrete starting point for a discussion about questions of translation, adaptation, and illustration.

The beginning of cinematography coincided precisely with Mardrus's heyday and also benefited from the popularity of the *Nights* in particular and Orientalism in general. It was Mardrus himself who introduced the young German film artist Lotte Reiniger to Parisian audiences: her shadow animation *Die Abenteuer des Prinzen Achmed* (*The Adventures of Prince Achmed*; 1926) was the first animated feature in history, long before Disney's *Snow White* (1937). Reiniger's classic film offers an excellent example of the creative blend of *Nights* stories and Orientalist iconographic borrowings. Mardrus (who himself went on to stage lavish multimedia *Nights*-inspired spectacles in Paris for the 1937 world's fair) was partly the source and partly the beneficiary of the second Orientalist wave, which saw the re-creation of the popular stories in the new cinematographic medium, from the legendary Georges Méliès's 1905 *Le palais des* Mille et une nuits (*The Palace of the* Thousand and One Nights, known as *The Palace of the* Arabian Nights) to Raoul Walsh's 1924 *The Thief of Bagdad*, so clearly indebted to German expressionism, and Alexander Korda's 1940 version of *Thief*, with award-winning special effects.

Borges's brief yet insightful appreciation of Mardrus as an illustrator is also worth developing in the context of the many cultural innovations of the prewar and immediate postwar years: the new translation coincided with the sensationally successful Ballets Russes, whose bright Orientalist decors and costumes, along with bold, athletic choreography, gave a whole new impetus to Orientalism. The ballet *Scheherazade*, set to a score by Nikolai Rimsky-Korsakov, took Paris and London by storm in 1910 and 1911 and sparked a new so-called Oriental fashion for women's clothes. The most successful of these new designers was a friend of Mardrus's, Paul Poiret, nicknamed "Poiret the Magnificent" after Suleiman the Magnificent. At Poiret's extravagant costumed ball, the "Thousand and Second Night" (24 June 1911) turbaned actors seated on Persian rugs read from Mardrus's translation to entertain guests dressed in so-called Oriental costumes of Poiret's design (Jullien, *Amoureux* 76–78). Most sensationally, Poiret's female guests (and customers) wore his innovative "harem pants": these scandalous gender-bending clothes would alarm traditionalists but delight women for the ease of movement they allowed. Together with the bicycle, popularized in the same years to the same polarized reception, the Oriental pants would facilitate an irreversible cultural change and play an important part in liberating Western women (early feminists often connected these two iconic images of the modern woman). Borges captured and understood Mardrus's significance for contemporary aesthetics, and his brief yet insightful remark on illustration is well worth unpacking in the classroom with visual aids.

Borges's appreciation of Mardrus suggests that for him, the *Thousand and One Nights* was less significant as a text than as Oriental matter. The same is true of his recreation of the *Nights* in his own writing, which weaves intertextual references into a variegated web of Oriental images.

Hybrid Orients

A poem like "The Orient" from *The Unending Rose* relies on the Borgesian technique of heterogeneous enumeration, calling forth Japanese haiku, genies trapped in bronze vessels, silk brought to Virgil by caravans, the Crucifixion story, the kabbalah, the mosques in Córdoba, or Kipling's novel *Kim* (Borges, *Obras* 3: 114). Borges's Orient and Borges's *Nights* are vividly composite. The *Thousand and One Nights* is primarily the result of hybridization, of the encounter between East and West: it is a contact zone between two different aesthetics. Not coincidentally, in the conclusion to his "Translators" essay, Borges muses on what might have resulted if Franz Kafka, rather than Littmann, had translated the *Nights*, if he had "remade it in line with the Germanic distortion, the *unheimlichkeit* of Germany" ("Translators" 109). The later essay, "The *Thousand and One Nights*," opens with a complementary statement: "A major event in the history of the West was the discovery of the East" (42). Borges consistently emphasized the benefits of cultural hybridity.

The same notion is also central to the long poem titled "Metaphors of the *Thousand and One Nights*," where Borges arranges images of the book around four master tropes. "The first metaphor is the river," the poem begins: the *Nights* is tied to an image of water flowing through lands, of navigation connecting distant cultures through trade, of voyagers (Sindbad, Ulysses), of global circulation of goods, ideas, and stories, dispensing to all "those miracles / which were Islam's, but now are / yours and mine" (36). This great unnamed river could be the Guadalquivir, the river flowing through the medieval kingdom of Al-Andalus and celebrated by the fictionalized Averroës and his friends in the story "Averroës' Search" (*Collected Fictions* 235–41). As a young aspiring writer Borges spent two years in Spain, from 1919 to 1921, forming a lasting friendship with an Andalusian writer, Rafael Cansinos Asséns: thus the river in the poem indirectly conjures up the memory of Cansinos, Borges's revered mentor. Through him, Al-Andalus, the Muslim past of Iberia, and Argentina, the distant Western outpost of the Spanish-speaking world, were connected. A prodigiously gifted polyglot and translator, Cansinos was for Borges a modern reincarnation of Spain's Muslim past, a time of religious tolerance and cultural prosperity. A convert to Judaism, Cansinos wrote Torah-inspired poems and translated the Koran, and he was the first to translate the *Nights* into Spanish directly from Arabic. In "The *Thousand and One Nights*," Borges states that Cansinos's translation is "perhaps the best of all the versions" (55); censored in Franco's Spain, it was published in 1955 in Mexico. Cansinos's generous celebration of a multicultural Orient, and his lifelong effort to bridge East and West, profoundly influenced Borges's own understanding of the *Nights*.

Dreams and Labyrinths

Another master trope in the poem "Metaphors of the *Thousand and One Nights*" is the dream, itself connected to the labyrinth and the book, all foundational metaphors of the Borges universe.

> The dream
> divides into another dream
> and then another, and so on,
> entwining in a static labyrinth.
> In this book is *the* Book.   (37)

"The Story of the Two Dreamers" (*Collected Fictions* 56–57), Borges's rewriting of the *Nights* tale "The Man Who Became Rich through a Dream" (which he could find in Burton), correlates the idea of dream and destiny, linking it metatextually to the idea of seeking abroad the key to one's own tradition that underlies both the fate of the Chinese spy in "The Garden of Forking Paths" (*Collected Fictions* 119–28) and the antinationalist argument put forth in the famous essay "The Argentine Writer and Tradition." In one of the most famous stories, "The South" (*Collected Fictions* 174–80), the protagonist, Juan Dahlmann, recovering from septicemia, reads a volume of the *Nights* as he journeys to his estate in the wild southern provinces of Argentina, where he will eventually meet his end: dream and destiny are once again intertwined here, as the Eastern story leads Dahlmann to his Western destiny, and also as the deadly knife fight may in fact be a figment of the delirious protagonist's imagination. The book-as-labyrinth image (materialized in the labyrinth printed on the frontispiece of every one of Burton's volumes) is also at the center of the "Parable of the Palace" (317–18). The paradigm of a book made infinite by embedding, recursion, and self-proliferation undergirds such beloved stories as "The Circular Ruins," in which the priest dreams a son only to realize he is himself the dream of another (96–100); "The Book of Sand," where the pages are innumerable as the sand (480–83); "Borges and I," where person and persona stand in an uneasy and infinite mirroring (324); and the mythical night 602, in which Shahrazad tells the king their own story; this last instance of *mise en abyme* is mentioned in connection with Yu Tsun's moment of self-revelation in "The Garden of Forking Paths." (Italo Calvino, who read the *Nights* as it were through Borges, was convinced that this circular night was a fiction invented by Borges: more recently, however, it has been traced back to a rare Burton edition in Borges's possession [Fishburn, "Readings" 39].) What Borges found in the *Nights* is what has come to define his own creative universe: "labyrinthine . . . paradoxes of circularity and infinity" (Irwin, Arabian Nights 283).

Hypertextual Web

The most important feature of the *Nights* according to Borges is the open-endedness, the infinity of stories. The very title to a Western reader suggests infinity: "The idea of infinity is consubstantial with *The Thousand and One Nights*" (Borges, "Thousand" 46). Borges, it appears, did not particularly highlight the themes that Eastern and Western readers have found most compelling—neither the political allegory, with its tales of resistance to a despot, of princely education (Ghazoul, *Nocturnal Poetics* 135; Jullien, *Borges* 27–38; Jullien, "Healing" 282–84), nor the feminist readings, which appropriate Shahrazad and a handful of other female characters (such as Tawaddud or Zumurrud) as feminist heroines. Instead, Borges preferred to focus on the hypertext, viewing the *Nights* as a transformative, traveling text made up of innumerable variants, constantly expanding by "inventive accretion" (P. Kennedy 201). In Borges's view, "The *1001 Nights* keeps growing or recreating itself" ("*Thousand*" 56).

This in turn supposes a reevaluation of the core Western notions of authorship and textuality, displaced by an Eastern model of literary composition characterized by anonymity and orality. "It is a book so vast that it is not necessary to have read it, for it is a part of our memory," Borges concludes (57). The essay evokes the legendary *confabulatores nocturni*, the storytellers of the night, in whose tales Alexander the Great is said to have taken pleasure (49). The Latin phrase is a quotation from Burton's "Terminal Essay" (included in the tenth volume of his translation of the *Nights* [10: 71]), itself borrowed from the German Orientalist Hammer Purgstall (greatly admired by Burton). Burton's essay is quoted once again in the prose poem "Someone" from *The History of Night*, which imagines the inventor of the *Nights* as a humble and anonymous storyteller in a nameless town, who will never know that he is our benefactor (Borges, *Obras* 3: 171). Borges's view of the *Nights* as a form of oral storytelling relying on memory, although it does not agree with historical evidence (see Bruce Fudge's essay in this volume on the written, rather than oral transmission of the *Nights*), aligns the Oriental storytellers with the Homeric rhapsodes and Celtic bards that populate his fictions (for example in "The Maker" [*Collected Fictions* 292–93] or "The Mirror and the Mask" [451–54]).

Borges's view of the *Nights*, which emphasizes orality, also adds a compelling autobiographical layer. After his blindness became almost complete in the fifties, Borges, who never learned Braille, turned to a semi-oral mode of composition, relying on memory, dictation, interviews, and readings. The mediation of the human voice between the text and the reader or writer conferred an anonymous and shared quality to his late work, something that perhaps—given Borges's early refutation of the idea of individual personality ("The Nothingness of Personality" was published as early as 1922)—had been its destiny from the beginning. Thus these "anonymous men of the night" ("*Thousand*" 49) are also self-portraits: the late essay on the *Nights* is included in *Seven Nights*, as is the essay on blindness.

Anticipating Roland Barthes (who famously proclaimed "the death of the author" in 1967) by almost a generation, Borges created the iconic figure of the author-as-nobody in one of his best-known fictions, "The Immortal": "I have been Homer; soon, like Ulysses, I shall be Nobody; soon, I shall be all men—I shall be dead" (Borges, *Collected Fictions* 194). Borges's Immortal, who has once been Homer, has also written the *Nights*, as the allusion to Bulaq, the district of Cairo where one of the major editions was produced in 1835, attests: "In the seventh century of the Hegira, on the outskirts of Bulaq, I transcribed with deliberate calligraphy, in a language I have forgotten, in an alphabet I know not, the seven voyages of Sindbad and the story of the City of Brass" (193). Now, left with only "words from other men" (195), he has forsaken all sense of individual self. In this allegory of literature as author-free, the storytelling paradigm serves to destabilize the certainties of authorship. Literary criticism in "Tlön, Uqbar, Orbis Tertius" takes matters to an even more fantastic extreme:

> It has been decided that all books are the work of a single author who is timeless and anonymous. Literary criticism often invents authors: it will take two dissimilar works—the *Tao Te Ching* and the *1001 Nights*, for instance—attribute them to a single author, and then in all good conscience determine the psychology of that most interesting *homme de lettres*."
> (*Collected Fictions* 77)

The *Thousand and One Nights*—a text without an urtext or a definitive version, a book in perpetual metamorphosis, where the author is lacking and substituted with an ever-growing number of readers, translators, rewriters—provided an apposite template for the Borgesian view of literature, characterized by infinity, fluidity, and anonymity. Against a proprietary view tethered to ideas of authorship and nationality, it proposed a dialogic model upholding antithetical parameters of gift, exchange, and global circulation.

CONTEXTS OF CIRCULATION

The *Thousand and One Nights* as Nigerian Literature

Abdalla Uba Adamu

The multiple translations of the *Thousand and One Nights* in various languages across the world ignore the existence of the *Nights* in African literature. Yet the easy mutability between the *Thousand and One Nights* and the oral literature of the Hausa of northern Nigeria prompts the question of whether the tales in the *Nights* were not Arabic but rather African literature; or, if a compromise is needed, suggests a new perception of the *Nights* as literature that reflects human societies, detached from a cartographic focal point, because it deals with universal human values. This is because of the adroit way selected tales from the *Nights* were not merely translated but transmuted into carefully adapted African literature, providing a distinct literary vantage point.

The *Thousand and One Nights* entered Hausa literary history in two forms, both printed during Nigeria's British colonial history, which lasted from 1901 to 1960, when Nigeria became independent. The first was a direct translation published in 1924 by Frank Edgar, a British colonial officer. Edgar relied on fragments of the Arabic copies of the tales he obtained from local Islamic clerics and scholars who helped him translate it into the Hausa language. The adult themes of some of the tales made the resultant book unsuitable for high school students, so this translation was not taught in schools.

The second appearance of the *Thousand and One Nights* in the Hausa language was in a collection of tales targeting high school students and published in 1937 (Imam). The collection was titled *Magana jari ce* (*Speech Is an Asset*). It contained about eighty-seven tales adapted from their original sources in German,

Dutch, Indian, and Middle Eastern literatures. These were not mere translations but reworkings of the original tales that, using devices from Hausa oral tradition, were passed on as Hausa tales, complete with illustrations by a Belgian artist, Jacqueline de Naeyer, who was then working for the company that published the volume. The illustrations added realism to the tales and further domesticated them to African contexts, despite their international origins.

In northern Nigerian classrooms of the 1930s, both the translated and adapted stories of *Thousand and One Nights* were taught not as Arabic literature but simply as Hausa tales. The adaptability of the *Nights* to Hausa literary structure was underscored by the oral nature of the *Nights*, whose development reflected the imprint of an oral storytelling culture. As Liz Gunner notes, "[T]he continent of Africa can be viewed as a site of enormous, long, and ongoing creativity in relation to orality as a vector for the production of social life, religious beliefs, and the constant constituting and reconstituting of society, ideology, and aesthetics" (1).

The responsiveness of the Nights to oral culture meshes perfectly with the oral nature of Hausa literature before 1910, when the British colonial administration introduced Western-type schools. The need for books in the Latin alphabet for use in the newly established schools necessitated the establishment of a Translation Bureau in 1929 in Zaria, northern Nigeria. It became the Literature Bureau in 1933. One of its functions was the translation of books from English and Arabic into Hausa for use in the schools. *Magana jari ce* was its most significant product. It was a frame novel, and the eighty-seven stories were narrated by two generations of parrots to a headstrong prince to prevent him from leaving the palace and getting assassinated while the monarch was away on a war expedition. This was adapted from the *Thousand and One Nights*, whose frame storyteller Shahrazad was forced to recite stories to a king to prevent her execution. Nine stories in the Hausa collection are from the *Thousand and One Nights*. These nine stories are more than mere translations of the Arabic *Thousand and One Nights*. They are literary transmutations that blur the narrative cartography of the so-called original texts.

This essay interrogates the pedagogy of the *Thousand and One Nights* as African literature in its translocated reimagining in African oral tradition and asks how American students can further appreciate the nature of African social systems through African literature from an emic perspective—that is, with reference not to outside criteria but to its own cultural mores. The main objective is to explore the didactic commonalities between Arabic and Hausa renditions of common human traits that are used as moral canvases in the tapestry of African cultural life. This will enable American students to understand the ecology of African cultural systems through folktales that are infused with moral lessons, even if the original substrata of these folktales are based on noncontiguous, but closely related, social systems. It may also suggest to teachers how to incorporate variations and adaptations from other traditions in their classrooms.

Thus, the essay is rooted in the traditional rendering of African literature that not only pays homage to an oral root, and thus communicates authenticity, but also provides an ethnographic account of a traditional African society. I based the essay on a single story from the *Thousand and One Nights*, "The Story of King Sindbad and His Falcon," which is adapted in the Hausa literature as "Saurin Fushi Shi Ka Kawo Da Na Sani" ("Quick Anger Leads to Regrets").

African Literature in the Cold

Mainstream narratives about African literature, principally fiction, taught in American colleges tend to be about the more accessible fiction written in English. The publication of Chinua Achebe's *Things Fall Apart* in 1958 not only drew universal attention to the contemporary African creative imagination but also established the art of the modern African novel. In 1986, Wole Soyinka became the first African to win the Nobel Prize for Literature and opened the gate for other African writers. By the close of the twentieth century, African literature had gained worldwide acceptance and legitimacy in the academy and was featured on the literature curriculum of schools and colleges across the globe. And of course in 2021 the Nobel Prize for Literature was awarded to Zanzibari novelist Abdulrazark Gurnah, who makes ample use of the structuring devices of the *Thousand and One Nights* in his fiction.

It must be acknowledged, however, that American teachers of African literature face the difficult choice of presenting a body of literature from a diverse source as if it is a single entity. This literature reflects the social, cultural, and political changes that have dynamically shaped the continent. Karin Barber argues that a clear division in African popular culture, including literature, exists between the "traditional"—understood as oral and "expressed exclusively in African languages"—and the "elite/modern/Westernized ... in a sense of inhabiting a world formed by higher education, full of mastery of European languages and representational conventions, defined by its cultural proximity to the metropolitan centres, and addressed to a minority but 'international' audience" (1). The latter tended to be seen as postcolonial in its critique of the colonial interregnum and its subsequent consequences on African societies.

Yet such a dichotomy tends to obscure the more traditional literature—whether oral or transcribed from oral traditions. African literature often acknowledges an endless conflict between the traditional and modern forms of its expression.

Desert Crossings: Baghdad in Africa

The American college student's imagination of the *Thousand and One Nights* has often been shaped by the film adaptations of the various tales. Whether on film or on the page, however, the archetypal perception of the Middle Eastern societies in the *Thousand and One Nights* creates a romantic vision of the land and its cultures—and seems so far away from African literature. Yet this is not so, because of the travels of the tales across the desert and their adaptation into local tales, complete with embellishments that hark back to the original.

"The Story of King Sindbad and His Falcon" appeared in the Macnaghten text that served as the basis for the translations by John Payne, Richard Francis Burton, and, more recently, Malcolm Lyons. The following is a synopsis of the story. The vizier of a Persian king, Sindbad, persuades the king to go on a hunt. The king agrees and sets off with his hunting pack and his trusted falcon, which has been trained as a hunter and never leaves his side. They eventually corner a gazelle, and the king proclaims death on any of his hunters who allows the gazelle to escape. The gazelle jumps at the gap where the king is and escapes. The hunting pack starts to nudge and wink at each other. On inquiring the reason, the king is reminded by the vizier of his promise to kill anyone who allows the gazelle to escape. The king then sets off after the gazelle. He eventually corners the animal and uses the falcon to pluck its eyes, incapacitating it, which gives the king an opportunity to cut off its head. Searching for water, he finds a nearby tree dripping liquid and decides to feed the falcon first. The bird knocks down the cup containing the liquid three times, and this annoys the king, so he cuts off its wing. The falcon communicates to the king to look up the tree dripping with the liquid. He sees a nest of vipers dripping poison, which he had mistaken for water. He takes the fatally injured falcon back to his camp and watches as the bird gives up its last breath and dies. He becomes remorseful for killing the bird that saved his life.

The story is replete with Middle Eastern (not necessarily Arabic) stock characters and traditions that American college students will easily discern from engagement with various forms of contemporary narratives about the Middle East. The tradition of hunting, for instance, is entrenched in the story, including the gory killing of the gazelle. American students attuned to animal rights may take issue with such a narrative, however. The vizier, whom American college students might imagine as a kind of prime minister, has occupied various stereotyped roles in Middle Eastern folklore, often emerging as a scheming, evil official—as for instance in *The Thief of Bagdad* (1940)—waiting to take over the throne when the king dies (and in some cases actually hastening the demise of the king to move things along). The vizier in this case seems eager to remind the king of the latter's pledge to kill anyone who lets the gazelle escape.

The most colorful stock character, however, would have to be the falcon, more easily understood as a duck hawk to North American students. As a bird of prey and used in hunting, it evokes the imagery of an avian killing machine, giving it a perfect maneuverability that makes its killing technique, although repellent to many, elegant to others attuned to similar scenes in films.

The same tale, "The Story of King Sindbad and His Falcon," was transmuted into the Hausa language in northern Nigeria as "Saurin Fushi Shi Ka Kawo Da Na Sani" ("Quick Anger Leads to Regrets"). The African version retains the fundamental premise of the original, such that American students of African languages can easily discern the differences between the two tales. A series of departures, however, reveal the orality of African literature, which college students might easily detect from their readings of more famous oral African literature, especially the accounts given in Ruth Finnegan's classic *Oral Literature in Africa*.

The Hausa title of the same tale, for instance, is a proverb whose fundamental premise is that individuals who lose their temper easily over an event will surely regret such a show of anger. American students may be interested in knowing that most African proverbs are used as bases of a moral tale that unfolds in narrative form. W. Jay Moon points out, "Like other oral literature, proverbs provide an aesthetic expression as an oral art form; therefore, the performance of the proverb, not just the words or logic of the utterance, also carries its meaning" (10). In this particular instance, the quick temper of the protagonist has led to a regrettable action. The use of African proverbs as part of narrative teaching is not peculiar to Africa. As Lewis Asimeng-Boahene indicates, the Nigerian Igbo proverb "It takes a whole village to raise a child" has to a large extent "been used to motivate communities throughout the U.S. to participate in the challenges of educating U.S. children" (118).

Next I offer a synopsis of the Hausa version of the Sindbad tale before analyzing it as African literature. A king and his courtiers were on a *kilisa* (a ride to exercise their horses). They came upon a malnourished, abandoned dog covered with ants. The king took pity on the dog and ordered it cleaned up and taken back to the palace and handed over to the *Sarkin Babanni* ("leader of eunuchs") to look after. In a few months the dog had recovered fully and had become a constant companion to the king, fiercely protecting him by not allowing anyone to come close to him in public. On one Eid al-Adha ("Sacrifice Feast") day, the king prevented the dog from following him to the praying grounds, instead commanding him to stay back at the palace in the king's chambers. While the dog waited for the king to return, a bowl of the fried meat from the traditional feast was taken to the king's chambers by a *Sadaka* ("concubine"). The bowl was left uncovered to cool, and the dog saw a *kumurci* ("black hooded cobra") dripping poison into the meat. The dog's warning howls were ignored. When the king returned to his chambers and tried to eat the meat, the dog also tried to prevent him by knocking his hand away from the bowl. This angered the king, and he started beating the dog. Despite the blows, the dog ate all the meat in the bowl, after which it lay down and died. It was then that the king got suspicious and ordered his security detail to behead the *Sadaka* on charges of attempting to poison him. As the *Sadaka* was about to be executed, the king smelled the odious smell of the cobra. On looking up to the rafters, he saw the coiled snake, its venom dripping directly where the bowl of meat was. It was then he realized that the dog had been trying to save him. He quickly rushed to the execution chamber and ordered the *Sadaka* freed. He created a mausoleum for the dog as a mark of honor for its devotion. He also warned his courtiers against making hasty judgments and being unkind to animals, for each one of us has our day.

The adapted tale teaches a lot of other things about Hausa society and its power relations—not often found in mainstream studies of African literature. For instance, power used to reside with the kings (or emirs, after the 1804 jihad), and it was absolute, for they could order the immediate execution of anyone who disobeyed their authority, or do the same out of anger, without any recourse to a justice system. Colonialism changed all that, of course, especially in northern Nigeria when the British ruled the populace through their native rulers, whose powers were decimated.

Despite retaining the general plot elements of the original, as American students would discern, the literary expansion of the Hausa version in many ways enhanced the original and Africanized it. In the process, the Hausa author provides American students with insights into the shape and social structure of Muslim palaces in northern Nigeria.

The Africanization of the tale from the *Thousand and One Nights* has its antecedents in Hausa oral tradition. The adaptation is replete with features of Hausa oral literature, which is didactic, and will educate American college students about precolonial African society, or rather the traditional society within the colonial regime, even though coloniality is never apparent in the tale. This is a departure from the African literature assigned more typically at American colleges, which usually celebrates Europhone postcolonial African writers whose focus is on relaying stories of the impact of colonialism on African societies.

Hausa oral tales often start with the "kingdom far, far away" template and feature unnamed rulers, who are referred to as kings. After the Islamic jihad of 1804 in northern Nigeria, the more Islamic title *emir* was adopted for the kings. The *kilisa*, an equestrian leisure pursuit of the royal and the noble, reveals the power structure of the society and shows a clear division between those in command and those who obey. In the adaptation, this equestrian pursuit sits better culturally than hunting—for Hausa kings do not go on hunting expeditions, since they consider the game killed in the process unclean.

Further, substituting a dog for the falcon creates a more realistic landscape in the African tradition, for falcons are not domesticated in Africa and are certainly not used for hunting. The king's friendship with a dog will strike a chord in American society, where the dog is considered "man's best friend."

The *Sarkin Babanni* ("leader of eunuchs") makes an appearance in the transmuted Hausa tale, even though he is not referred to in the tale from the *Thousand and One Nights*. This is a further literary expansion of the original. Whereas in the original tale the scenes took place during the hunt, in the African version we get a glimpse of the African palace's domestic ecology—thus giving readers not familiar with African palaces an idea of their mechanisms.

The role and function of the *Sarkin Babanni* in the palace give college students a direct ethnographic connection between Hausa and Middle Eastern societies. The *Sarkin Babanni*, a regular feature of Hausa palaces, is usually a eunuch. It is not clear how eunuchs came to be entrenched in Muslim Hausa palaces in northern Nigeria, but the practice must have crossed over from Byzantine and Ottoman histories.

Hausa eunuchs, usually belonging to the captive enslaved class, are appointed administrators in palaces and public affairs and are trusted with looking after the women in the king's harem under the assumption that the *Baba* ("eunuch") will not be tempted to have a sexual encounter with any of the women in the harem. That is, the eunuchs are preferred as keepers of the harem to avoid the so-called polluting of the lineage of the king with an unwanted pregnancy.

This harem structure, still a contemporary feature of many palaces in northern Nigeria, is usually associated with Middle Eastern cultures, as students may have observed from films such as *Harem*. Such traditional iconographies are rarely addressed in the more Europhone African literature in English of the type written by famous African postcolonial writers such as Chinua Achebe, Amadou Hampâté Bâ, Wole Soyinka, Ayi Kwei Armah, Ngũgĩ wa Thiong'o, and so on.

Another literary expansion in the African adaptation of the tale from the *Thousand and One Nights* is the introduction of the *Saɗaka*, the concubine. Both the *Saɗaka* and the *Baba* are still contemporary features of northern Nigerian ruling houses. Heidi J. Nast's extensive ethnographic study of concubines in Kano, northern Nigeria, attests to their presence, power, and sexual control of the palace domestic ecology. Concubines were usually prisoners of war or their descendants; concubine status, once assigned, was permanent. Considered as property, they could be inherited. There was a preference for daughters or wives of vanquished enemies because of such "women having expertise in running chiefly households" (Nast 96). They were also often given to kings as gifts and referred to as *Sa-ɗaka*—literally something to be stored away in the room for intimate use.

The concubine is disposable, as reflected in the fate of the *Saɗaka* in the Hausa adaptation of the tale. This is shown in the way the king ordered her head cut off on the assumption that she was trying to poison him, without diligence and investigation. This parallels the threat against the narrator of the *Thousand and One Nights*, who was herself slated for execution after being ravished. Shahrazad was saved only by her tales. In the Hausa versions of the *Thousand and One Nights*, the tales are narrated by a parrot, a metaphor for a woman deemed too loquacious according to local social mores. This will reveal to college students how traditional palaces in northern Nigeria treat women.

The Hausa version ends with an animal rights message in which the king urges kindness to animals, for one day they could be saviors. This reveals the gentle nature of the king who within the same narrative was ready to execute an enslaved woman on the basis of an assumption of guilt—thus revealing the moral of the story. As is typical of African oral literature, the tale must teach a lesson.

The correlation between the story in the *Thousand and One Nights* and Hausa literature came about due to the skillful adaptation rather than straightforward translation of the original story into a Hausa version. In the process of what can be described only as elegant literary onomatopoeic adaptation, the fundamental premise of the original is echoed in the target language but given both semantic and literary expansion to bring to the fore cultural features of the target language that enrich both the source and target stories.

Teaching both versions of the story will enhance learning for American students of the *Thousand and One Nights* by demonstrating the cultural dynamics of the same story in different social contexts. The didactic and moral ending of the Hausa version is a template that looks toward social reform rather than individual salvation. The king is remorseful that he almost ordered the execution of a valuable courtier, and the tale provides a message about being kind to animals.

The literary expansions of the original tale in Hausa illustrate that African literature is more than a diary of Europhone postcolonial narratives. It includes a vast amount of literature in indigenous languages that offers a realistic ethnographic picture of the dynamics of African societies. That the Sindbad story sits well in Africa also reflects a common template for human behavior, regardless of race—for the fundamental lessons delivered by the storytellers remain the same.

Orality and Performance of the *Thousand and One Nights*

Susan Slyomovics

For the Arabic-speaking world, what are the ways orality and performance interact with written literature? This question illuminates intricate relations between writing and orality, manuscripts and spoken narratives, classical Arabic and the varieties of vernacular speech. If there is a debt owed by the Arabic textual tradition of the *Thousand and One Nights* to oral traditions, at the very least this essay demonstrates that tales from the *Nights* are still performed. A living performance tradition and a rich oral-writing dynamic can present teachers with a means to consider the contemporary relevance and performance of the *Nights* in the Arab world. In addition, the nexus of performance, orality, and text lends itself to speculation about the probable origins of many tales and the ways a work of verbal art may also exist in multiple oral and written variants. Just as orality need not be in opposition to literacy, so too may storytellers inhabit a world of oral performances alongside written forms of the very tales they recount to audiences.

Despite a rich culture of oral performance, manuscript-based studies about the *Nights* predominate. Indeed, the wide-ranging linguistic and geographic variability in performances could be said to parallel or even complement the variety of recensions of the *Nights*. This is because the multiglossic range of what is termed "Arabic" broadly divides language and literature between the formal, written, literary, classical language that is no one's native speech (*fuṣḥā*) and the many varieties of spoken regional and national dialects. As the language of Qur'anic revelation, Arabic produced an idealized form deemed morally and grammatically purer to the extent that a long-standing bias continues to elevate a literate, written classical tradition of *fuṣḥā*. In contrast, Arabic vernaculars are frequently and mistakenly characterized as corrupt variants of Islamic high culture, language, and religion. A divinely inspired language stands in stark opposition to dialect origins attributed to the *Nights*.

Oral and vernacular provenance is assigned to the *Nights* according to etiological tales from within the Arabic literary tradition. As early as the tenth century, the Baghdad bookseller known as Ibn al-Nadīm famously insisted that because the *Nights* derived from folktales in dialect, it was vulgar and tasteless (*kitābun ġaṯṯun bāridu l-hadīth*; literally "a coarse book cold in the telling"). Ibn al-Nadīm provided two accounts of the *Night's* origins in his *Kitāb al-Fihrist*, his second stressing the formative role of a discerning editor:

> Abu Abdallah Muhammad b. Abdus al-Jahshiyari . . . gathered storytellers round him and took from them the best of what they knew and were able to tell, and he chose out of the fable and storybooks whatever pleased

him. He was a skillful craftsman, so he put together from this material 480 nights, each night an entire story of fifty pages, more or less, but death surprised him before he completed the thousand tales as he had intended.

(Fihrist of al-Nadīm 2: 713)

This partial edition belongs to the long line of literate compilers, copyists, and editors engaged in reworking a body of oral folk literature by adding or expurgating individual tales. Their editorial labors are associated with centuries of claims to uplift oral narrative through classicizing writing in conformity with standards set by *fuṣḥā*. Another episode typical of textual histories of the *Nights* is that Ibn al-Nadīm or al-Jahšiyārī's fragmentary manuscript was never found. Incomplete texts, a presumed missing original manuscript, and the role of the refining editor remain enduring features in the impossible quest for an original, authentic written work while producing a plethora of ever-changing, indeterminate versions, translations, and editions.

Thus far, descriptions of tale collecting and the ultimate loss of those very same collected tales survey the history of Arabic-language recensions. So too do disappearing original texts figure among Western translators-adapters and editors, especially the translation by Antoine Galland, introduced to Europe in 1704. Galland reproduced one Arabic tradition from the *Nights* of borrowing from the oral to supplement the written when he inserted tales not found in the oldest extant fifteenth-century Syrian manuscript (known as Bibliothèque Nationale 3609–3611). Instead, Galland owed many of the West's beloved tales to oral versions he learned from Ḥannā Diyāb, a visiting Syrian storyteller,

> On the morning of March 25 [1709] according to the entry in his *Journal* . . . he [Galland] went to call on Paul Lucas, the oriental traveler. Paul Lucas was going out, but Galland remained and talked with Hanna, a Maronite of Aleppo whom Lucas had brought with him from that town, and Hanna at once began to tell him stories in Arabic which Galland recognized as *fort beaux*. From Galland's *Journal* we learn that this went on at intervals up to June 2, and that he received in this way a large number of stories and held them either in his memory, aided by abstracts in his *Journal*, or in actual transcripts furnished to him by Hanna. (MacDonald 394)

Galland's fateful encounter in Paris with the verbal artistry of a living Arab storyteller mimics the plight of Shahrazad in the frame tale. Just as she must narrate each evening to avoid death at the hands of her king and husband, Galland was driven by exigent publishers to come up with the twelve-volume *Les* Mille et une nuits: Contes arabes traduits en français (*The* Thousand and One Nights: Arabic Tales Translated into French) between 1704 and 1717 in order to arrive at the literal number of 1,001 nights of tales from any available sources. The storytelling talents of Diyab, who arrived miraculously from the heartland of the Arab East, permitted Galland to satisfy the demands of Parisian publishers. He incorporated Diyab's oral renditions into his collection of stories hitherto largely reliant on the aforementioned Syrian manuscript. Diyab's versions written down for Galland were never found, other than the summaries recorded in Galland's diary. A pattern of translators and editors who bring their own adaptations of the *Nights* into existence fits Galland. In this case, however, Galland is clearly the creator of a composite *Arabian Nights*, not merely a translator, who seemingly drew directly from the oral storytelling tradition in addition to written texts.

The role of an individual editor or translator who relies heavily on the Arabic storyteller is not necessarily at odds with the notion of collective folk authorship based on the oral tradition. Widely known and beloved tales that circulate orally have long been subjected to so-called linguistic improvement and restructured to provide moral uplift. A belief in an individual Arab author for the *Nights* was also the central argument of Edward William Lane, the British lexicographer and translator of the *Arabian Nights' Entertainments*. Lane's conviction about the existence of a Cairene author who fashioned these texts need not undermine the ancillary role of translators. Lane also consistently remade the Arabic text according to selective perceptions about his nineteenth-century Victorian-era audiences, just as Galland's edition reflected his times. Lane's English translation is a compilation of several available Egyptian manuscripts, especially the Būlāq I edition of 1835 which he redated as an "individual work" of solo authorship to around 1500. He conjectured that the Būlāq author, most likely from Cairo, wrote down tales "doubtless of an older *origin* . . . remodelled, so as to become pictures of the state of manners which existed among the Arabs, and especially among those of Egypt." In turn, Lane suppressed hallmarks often associated with orality when he expurgated "tedious" poems, "objectionable" sexuality, and repetition found in the form of oral-formulaic passages or recurring tales (Thousand 1: xiii–xiv). How tales were told mattered less to him than their value as data about lost social worlds. Remodeling is hereby given a new justification. Lane viewed his work as an accurate ethnography of Egyptian manners and customs to reflect urban Cairo in the late fifteenth and early sixteenth centuries (Thousand 1: viii).

Copious notes accompany Lane's edition. He was an important chronicler of his contemporary scene, witnessing many vibrant public evening recitations by Cairene *mohadditeen* ("storytellers"). Despite anachronistic perspectives, Lane noted elements relevant to the oral/written dynamic in his comments about reciters in performance who relied on printed editions or manuscripts (*Account* 395). For example, he concluded that the exorbitant purchase price of manuscripts accounted for dwindling numbers of Cairene reciters specializing in the *Nights* (409). The mid-nineteenth-century Cairo practice of using texts in recitations was also witnessed by Remke Kruk in her 1997 account about a literate storyteller in Marrakesh. Kruk observes that although the Moroccan storyteller knows the text by heart, he draws from editions printed in Cairo "read out [in] classical (or rather post-classical) Arabic with more or less (according to their own level of education) strong overtones of dialect pronunciation" (194). Editions of the *Nights* printed in Cairo were exported throughout the Arabic-speaking world as far as Morocco. Lane's account, corroborated by Kruk a century later, indicates that reciters were often literate, and public recitations relied on available printed editions, often visibly held and consulted in public. Nor does Lane confirm if printed versions used by Cairene storytellers were transcribed from earlier performances transformed into texts or were shorter mnemonic redactions used as aide-mémoire. The presence of a book as a physical artifact underpins the authority of the tales even among illiterate reciters.

It is also possible that a printed book from the East possesses potent talismanic properties to represent tangible proof of authenticity while informing less about any given storyteller's level of literacy. This is the case for 'Awaḍ Allāh 'Abd al-Jalīl 'Alī, an illiterate Egyptian epic poet and reciter to whom I was introduced during my research and fieldwork in Egypt (1979–90). His oral performance of a tale from the *Nights* is my key example to compare a written tale with its orally performed version. 'Awaḍ Allāh bestowed divine and written origins to his storytelling, according to an etiological tale handed down to him from his grandfather 'Alī, who came upon a book in the desert. That night, sleeping in a cave, the Prophet al-Khiḍr came to 'Alī in a dream, saying, "Iqra'" ("recite," or possibly "read"). Because he was illiterate, 'Alī answered, "I cannot." Again al-Khiḍr commanded him by saying, "Iqra'," and again 'Alī replied, "I cannot." Yet a third time al-Khiḍr said, "Iqra'." This time, to his surprise, 'Alī could read what was written in the book, and he began to recite. 'Alī memorized this book and taught his son 'Abd al-Jalīl, who taught his son 'Awaḍ Allāh. After memorizing the book, Ali lost the ability to read and also lost the book (Slyomovics, *Merchant* 11–13).

'Awaḍ Allāh's belief in a divinely inspired written text derived through oral transmission recalls in certain ways the Prophet Muhammad's revelation. The parallel recedes as the pattern of the *Nights* recurs, one in which no book or text is to be found. This in turn resembles Galland's missing transcriptions of Diyāb's oral renditions or even al-Jahšiyārī's lost manuscript of collected oral tales despite attestations by the reliable Ibn al-Nadīm. All examples lend primacy to oral provenance, yet all remain faithful to the trace of a missing, but more authentic written rendition. They do so by according mystical powers to the material presence of a book or manuscript insofar as the artifact is on display during intimate face-to-face encounters between storytellers and audiences. If the oral is primary, the written form is necessary despite the lack of standardization to render oral performance from Arabic dialects into writing. Constrained by the limits of Arabic script to approximate fully the spoken varieties, a range of writing strategies has evolved, from imprecise transcription of the dialect to partial transformation into a so-called corrected literary language to direct translation from the language of the dialect into the language of classical (or Modern standard) Arabic.

The Argument for Oral Origins: Rethinking Folktale Classification Systems

Exceptions to the dichotomy of oral dialectal versus written classical Arabic abound in orally performed traditions throughout the Middle East and North Africa. There are Qur'anic recitations, religious praise songs, sermons, political speeches, and even formally prepared poetry recitations pronounced in classical or Modern standard Arabic. Nonetheless, for the *Nights*, the argument for oral origins makes two assumptions. First, individual tales once were and continue to be orally recited and performed throughout the Arabic-speaking world. Second, written editions are literary representations sourced from folktales, a claim that presupposes prior oral circulation at the time editions were produced (el-Shamy, *Motif Index* 1). Such are the views of folklorist Hasan M. el-Shamy, who designates many narratives in the *Nights* as products of "indigenous lore" still communicated to this day orally ("mouth-to-ear") in vernacular rather than written or spoken classical Arabic forms ("Oral Connections" 9 and 11). He models a widespread phenomenon of parallel linguistic and narrative worlds consisting of the oral and written: "Clearly, oral and written narratives belong to separate cognitive systems. Although the two systems do to some extent overlap and affect each other, the separation between the two systems is the dominant trend" (*Folktales* 1). El-Shamy includes folk-reported taxonomies that distinguish between stories read in books and those circulating in oral tradition; for example, during a session audiotaped in 1969, el-Shamy described an Upper Egyptian storyteller who discriminated between folk knowledge and book learning:

> When I told the narrator of "The Noble and the Vile" (tale no. 14) about the variant of his story that exists in *The Arabian Nights*, he responded, "Yes, it is the same, but still it is not the same. This one comes out of a book; that one is something we just know." Another informant who was mainly interested in songs said, "I don't know any *hawadeet* ["tales"], but I can tell you a *qissàh* ["story"] from *The Thousand [and One] Nights*." . . . In a number of cases, oral and printed versions of the same tale exist side by side in a community. They do not merge, nor does the bearer become fully aware of the duality of the tradition. (xlix)

To study what the folk know as opposed to what they believe comes from a book, international folkloristics scholarship comparatively organizes folktales into tale types and motifs based on the assumption that, despite the huge number of folktales recounted globally, most tales are variations on limited themes. Folktale classification systems were established over time, notably for anglophone scholars by Antti Aarne, Stith Thompson, and Hans-Jörg Uther, resulting in Aarne-Thompson's *Types of the Folktale* and Thompson's *Motif-Index*. For the purposes of cross-cultural comparison, they developed numbering systems down to the decimal point for both the larger narrative unit of the tale as well as the smaller narrative building block of the motif. Typologies of the *Nights* began with the French scholarly reference book by Victor Chauvin entitled *Bibliographie des ouvrages arabes ou relatifs aux Arabes publiés dans l'Europe chrétienne de 1810 à 1885* (*Bibliography of Arab or Arab-Related Works Published in Christian Europe from 1810 to 1885*), in which volumes 4 to 7 were dedicated to summarizing and annotating 450 individual tales from the *Arabian Nights*. Drawing on Chauvin, the Aarne-Thompson (AT) tale type classifications myopically integrated only sixty-four Chauvin-numbered tales (listed in el-Shamy's footnotes in *Motif Index*). There were two main negative outcomes from the AT Western-oriented folktale type index reliant on merely one-fifth of Chauvin's plots of the *Nights*: only those folktale narratives comparable to the largely Eurocentric pool were included, and, more objectionable, only those seventy tales from the *Nights* came to represent the Arab Islamic narrative to Westerners.

Although European indexes constitute a basic folktale tool kit for international comparative scholarly analyses, el-Shamy's magisterial *A Motif Index of the* Thousand and One Nights extended and challenged Eurocentric classifications by foregrounding distinctions between the oral and written. El-Shamy's contributions depart from a history of folktale classifications based on composite European texts of the *Nights* to include the oral. He chose an undated four-volume so-called indigenous Cairo edition as his foundational recension for analyzing motifs while remaining consistent with the standard AT folktale analytic frameworks. Repurposing classifications derived from narrow European notions of the *Nights*, el-Shamy addresses the vast corpus of hitherto uncategorized Arabic oral traditions by distinguishing between what he terms a European composite edition of the *Arabian Nights* produced by Western editors and his preferred native Arabic anthologies; instead, he relies on the *Makṭabat al-Jumhūriyyah* of the Cairo edition as an "authentic folk tradition" because of its "contents, printing techniques, raw materials, drawings, commercial outlets and readership (usually read to a throng of people)" (*Motif Index* 11). Thus el-Shamy's motif index remains the sole valuable guide to Egyptian-inflected oral materials of the *Nights*.

Comparing the Written and Oral Text: The "Tale of Anās al-Wujūd"

Folklorists have long drawn on oral folk collections, tales, and motifs inspired by the *Nights* to highlight textual, structural, and linguistic differences between oral performances and printed editions (Marzolph, Arabian Nights *in Transnational Perspective*). Examples are oral folktales by Sicilian storytellers, perhaps influenced by three centuries of Arab rule over Sicily (Corrao); nineteenth-century literary Persian translations compared by Margaret Mills to the 1975 oral performance she recorded in Dari-Afghan Persian of the "Tale of Jūdar" in Afghanistan; the work of Sabir Badalkhan, who relates Balochi oral renditions of "Aladdin" recounted by illiterate tellers in Pakistan to their relevant literary analogues; and Palestinian oral variants, such as the "Tale of Maʿruf the Cobbler" (Muhawi and Kanaana 307–18). Oral performances and printed versions based on orality share overlapping folk motifs and tale types, as the work of el-Shamy documents, at the level of the tale itself. Oral counterparts to the written *Nights* from Sicilian, Afghan, Balochi, and Palestinian examples arrive at similar conclusions: Texts deemed of oral provenance possess the characteristic linguistic features of deploying colloquial terms, idioms, verbal conjugations, and inconsistent orthography. Similarly, Arabic spoken performances and Arabic print materials based on oral versions in dialect eliminate grammatical case endings, with the latter requiring that the reader and text share the same dialect, hence pronunciation, since orthography reflects and adapts to the Arabic dialect because it rarely includes vowels.

At the level of phrases, repeated themes, and motifs, Milman Parry and Albert B. Lord proposed that evidence for a work's traditional oral provenance can be discerned through typical patterning they called formula. Repetitions occurring both in oral-formulaic phrases or epithet descriptions of main characters are among the characteristics that enable oral improvisation according to the Parry-Lord theory (see Lord). A prominent feature of Egyptian Arabic performance associated with telling a tale is the proliferation of punning techniques. Oral-formulaic phrases and punning in performance contribute to the possibility of an oral provenance for the *Nights* or at least describe the presence of oral versions that continue to be performed alongside written publications. It is noteworthy that Lane alerted his readers to the importance of puns in his translation by remarking on their absence in his translation because paronomasia or complex forms of punning found in oral performance in dialect were impossible for him to translate (Thousand xvii–xviii). Whereas an oral performance employs numerous puns, conventional transcriptions found in printed editions cannot accommodate them. That the oral text was meant to be sung and heard explains why paronomasia is so frequent a feature of performance in Egypt but is rarely reproduced in writing. The Arabic language is suited to punning techniques that rely on the triconsonantal root system into which vowels, hence meaning, are poured. Sound itself, because it provides multiple meanings through the use of vocalic infixes, separates the consonants into patterns that multiply endlessly to delight listeners by the interplay of condensation and ambiguity in puns. Arab audiences are familiar with such wordplay and enjoy the ways puns merge several meanings into a single item. The manipulation of potential connotations in language is particularly appropriate to oral texts.

My recording of an oral performance of the "Tale of Anās al-Wujūd" enables a comparison based on field recordings by a living Upper Egyptian storyteller. Taboo events and sexual innuendos appear in this rendition, which I audiotaped in 1983 from a performance by ʿAwaḍ Allāh ʿAbd al-Jalīl ʿAlī in Upper Egypt. The accompanying transcription of the storyteller's Ṣaʿīdī (or Upper Egyptian dialect) and English translation are maintained by the University of California, Los Angeles (see ʿAwaḍ Allāh ʿAbd al-Jalīl ʿAlī, "Tale of Anas" and "Merchant").

To begin with, the oral version of the recorded performance is brief. The principle of economy of narrative produces a seemingly truncated variant missing many adventures as well as various interlocutors noted in lengthy written versions summarized in Ulrich Marzolph and Richard van Leeuwen (2: 438) and Chauvin (6: 127–29; tale 282). The tale's hero, Anās al-Wujūd, and the heroine, al-Ward fī al-Akmām, each encounter beggars, princes, and talking animals along the route to their eventual reunion in prose and poetry. In contrast, ʿAwaḍ Allāh, the southern Egyptian storyteller, speaks and sings to his live audience entirely in verse, intentionally drawing on the richness of puns that point to several referents at the same time. In my interviews with the storyteller, even the heroine's name expresses more than one meaning, including female sexual desire. Al-Ward fī al-Akmām is literally a "rose in its calyx" or sleeve, or a rose springing from the clefts of its hood, a "rose in bud" or a "bud in the rose." English translations use "Rose," "Rosebud," or "Bud in the Rose," to which ʿAwaḍ Allāh also assigned a double meaning of "clitoris," which he explained to me was the most beautiful part of the female anatomy. Other punning examples at the level of narrative sequences encompass the theme of the lovers writing letters carried to each other. The lovers' epistolary exchanges, aided by a maidservant acting as messenger, are discovered during return delivery. They trigger the heroine's exile to a distant, forbidding castle. In ʿAwaḍ Allāh's oral version, mother defends daughter to halt her banishment and end the tale, whereas the written versions continue onward from the heroine's forced departure through numerous adventures in distant lands until they eventually reunite and return home to marry.

Foregrounded in letters exchanged between Rose and Anās is an erotic content specific to the style of orally sung performance. These occasions allow for a range of paronomastic devices characteristic of Egyptian folk narrative in the vernacular, devices that can convey both sexual and political double meanings (Slyomovics, "Arabic Folk Literature"). The voice of the storyteller ʿAwaḍ Allāh expresses the erotic play of meaning in the epistolary lyrics, rendered permissible and audible perhaps by their being uttered in the male voice. These lines follow the text and video recording, in which ʿAwaḍ Allāh sings Rose's letter to her absent lover (Slyomovics, "Performing" 405–19):

> ʾaskar ʾana w-inta ya ʾanas ilwujūd wa law ʾalf ʿām (line 197)
> Let us be intoxicated, you and I, O Anās al-Wujūd, for a thousand years!
>
> ʾaskar ana w-inta law ʾalfēn sana (line 198)
> Let us be intoxicated, you and I, two thousand years—
>
> kaʾinnahu (line 199)
> as if
>
> laḥẓa fī ḥuḍni ʾana (line 200)
> a moment in my embrace.

ma tunẓūr iššagēn (line 201)
look upon my cleavage

wi šayḫi 'ana (line 202)
I an "old man" ("sheikh" and its opposite "young girl")
    and my sash

'abyaḍ wi maḥtūṭ lu—lḥalag (line 203)
white and wearing an earring

wiyyah -lḫuzzām (line 204)
with a nose-ring

dagg ittiyūr (line 206)
delicate as a bird

The storyteller's puns, immediately apprehended by the Upper Egyptian hearer, required lengthy explanations for me to translate. In line 201, the word *iššagēn* is interpreted by the audience as a "cleft," an open interpretation applicable to the vulva, buttocks, or breasts and translated here as "cleavage." The first translation of line 202 for *šayḫ*, more familiarly the English "sheikh," means literally "old man." The poet's use of oppositional poetic substitution (termed *tabdīl*) poetically conveys its reverse, namely "young girl," leading to a simultaneous translation in which the words "and sheikh" are combined to mean a women's "sash" (*wišayḫ*), thereby refocusing the listener on to the female torso. Line 203, "white and wearing an earring," has the surface meaning of describing a pale-complexioned maiden wearing an earring and was also interpreted for me as the "nipple" or "clitoris," all double meanings cascading from the first interpretation of the "cleft" metaphor in line 201. Line 204, "with a nose-ring," repeats complex punning of the previous line to designate the areola of the nipple or the vaginal opening. Line 206 ends Rose's erotic self-description in the voice of an elderly male poet with a phrase to be understood as a metaphor comparing the folds of the genitals to delicate bird tracks. The word *dagg* may also mean "thinness," or "subtlety," that is, "thin or subtle as a bird."

The storyteller's tale continues with the nurse who conveys this letter from Rose to Anās, who replies with a letter of his own. This time the male letter writer in the tale and the male voice of the storyteller are matched by gender. He too describes Rose's beautiful body, beginning with her bow-shaped eyebrows and languorous eyes and traveling downward. After reaching her belly and navel, his verses pick up on and respond to Rose's erotic self-description of her genitals as a "sheikh" or "old man." Rose's use of "old man" for "young girl" is baffling until the lover's reply is heard. He compares the pleasures and dangers of sexual intercourse to the benefits and obligations of a religious pilgrimage at the shrine of the sheikh in which the vulva's rounded curves resemble the dome of a shrine:

> You look at her venerable sheikh, around him a shrine
> You look at a venerable sheikh, around him a mausoleum.
> The ill who visit him are sure to find rest.
> You deposit a pledge to the sheikh.
> You visit the mausoleum.
> Enter without permission, you will soon be harmed!   (lines 276–81)

Oral versions offer many contrasts to the written ones available in English translations. The "Tale of Anās al-Wujūd" is available in various translations of Galland into English, as well as versions from Richard Francis Burton, Lane, and Malcolm C. Lyons, but is not found in Mahdi's early-fourteenth-century Syrian manuscript. The written text recounts the multiple adventures and separations of two star-crossed lovers to occupy eleven of Shahrazad's thousand and one nights. In writing, the tale possesses a "once upon a time" beginning, middle, and ending, happily concluding with a marriage. These written texts are lengthy, with complicated plot twists alternating between prose narrative and dialogue in verses, during which a large cast of characters divert and complicate the plot by recounting their stories along the way, all of which has been analyzed as tales embedded in the Egyptian landscape and dialect (Garcin). Poetic verse in the written version occurs sparingly whenever characters address each other directly in speech or writing. The exceptions to these aforementioned Arabic texts and their translations is Mark Muehlhaeusler's remarkable project to analyze seven nineteenth-century European manuscript versions of this tale written entirely in verses of four-line stanzas, including two vocalized manuscripts. When comparing these manuscripts to my recording of an oral performance, Muehlhaeusler concludes that "some passages in the text remained remarkably stable over the intervening hundred and eighty years of transmission which must have been at least partly oral" (viii–ix).

In contrast, the oral performance appears as a briefer, truncated variant of the written, yet filled with glorious wordplay unavailable in any written version. A reading that acknowledges the several meanings evoked by a single word shows the extent to which the oral exploits paronomasia, language reversals shared among listeners, and the male storyteller's voice to express both feminine as well masculine sexuality that color his message with a variety of connotations. 'Awaḍ Allāh is a famous punster, deploying puns provoked by the mnemonic exigencies of oral performance, which in turn limit the potential cast of characters to merely Anās, Rose, their respective parents, and a maidservant. Written narrative imposes few constraints on the number of characters, allowing for the development of character through the representation of complicated dramatic situations. Puns in performance make up for this limitation by conveying characterological motivation through polysemic semantics. Paronomasia not only argues for rich and erotic experiences of oral performance but also argues against repeated condemnations about the "stylistic poverty" of the *Nights* in its written form (Borges, "Translators" 101). Consequently, I articulate a fundamental difference between oral and printed editions of the "Tale of Anās al-Wujūd": the oral characterizes through language and the printed through story.

Arguments against Orality and on Behalf of Literary Origins

The literary critic Peter D. Molan maintains that tales from the *Nights* were consciously molded by editors to mimic the prevailing style of oral storytellers even if they might have originated as written texts that found their way into oral tradition and would again be "polished up by their redactors upon being written down" (191). In this way, Molan argues against the orality of the *Nights* by returning to its very textual history that gave us so many examples, from al-Jahšiyārī to Galland by way of Lane and Burton, and that place the compiler-translator-editor at the heart of literary creativity. If there ever were a close relation to an assumed oral tradition, Molan selects other features to attest to the increasing distance between text and orality with each subsequent redaction and translation. As an example, he cites the prevalence of prose narrative as the hallmark of writing that replaces oral poetry. Other features are the removal of repetition and formulas of orality (cf. Pineault). Molan notes the disappearing and extrinsic use of oral speech in the phrases *qāla* ("he said") or *qāla al-rāwī* ("the poet said"), which either hearken back to oral origins or can also be understood as written interpolations to simulate the oral (195).

The analysis of Fedwa Malti-Douglas against orality emanates from feminist-inflected readings of the work's famous structuring framework. Shahrazad embodies female orality and storytelling, whereas the king, largely the silent listener throughout the thousand and one nights, represents male domination. He controls the storyteller's fate but also that of her tales because he orders them to become widely disseminated as written texts:

> Her world is the evanescent one of oral performance—both measured by and linked to time: a thousand and one nights. To the males is the authority and permanence of written literature. . . . Shahrazâd's extraordinary role is a temporary one. . . . The "nights" are like dreams that end with the rise of the literary sun of vision, reality, and male preeminence. (11–28)

The oral female storyteller recedes in the face of a redactor-in-chief, emblematically the despotic head of state, whether Alexander the Great or Shahriyar. Malti-Douglas's insight about male editorial control through writing holds true for transformations by legions of translators. Unusually, the Lyons translation of 2008 acknowledges that orality's losses are writing's gain:

> What has been sacrificed is the decorative elaboration of the original, as well as the extra dimension of allusiveness it provides. In the latter case, it is not merely that one incident will recall another, either within the *Nights* themselves or, more widely, in the huge corpus of Arabic popular literature, but a single phrase, one description or one line of poetry must have served to call other contexts to the mind of the original audience. To explore these intricacies, however, is the task of a commentary rather than of a translation. (Lyons, Arabian Nights, 1: xx–xxi)

Such is the fate of versions performed in dialect. The tale recounted by the illiterate Upper Egyptian storyteller requires extensive commentary about multiple punned meanings in English translation. The advent of recordings, films, and hypertext permits oral enactments to live on and illuminate the aural marvels of written and transcribed texts through sensory experiences of hearing and seeing a live performance.

The "Thousand and Second Night" Motif
Evanghelia Stead

Teachers today may expect the *Thousand and One Nights*, considered one of the more influential works in comparative and world literature, to have a magnetic appeal for students. Nonetheless, when I started teaching the subject in 2010, it was not without hesitation. How, I wondered, might I impart the work's intricate historical transmission from ancient Indian languages and Persian to Arabic adaptations; its subsequent translation into French and other modern languages; the many readings across versions it implies; its numerous complex issues regarding authorship, language, and diffusion; and the vastness of its critical checklist in twelve one-hour classroom lectures to undergraduates generally unfamiliar with the text's narrative practices, followed by as many ninety-minute sessions for students to present their work to their fellows during the term? The time allotted hardly sufficed to explore such a wealth of knowledge, transformations, variations, and invention. Here I share ways to convert these challenges into dynamic course matter.

The experience related is based on a second-year undergraduate course and a master's seminar, both in comparative literature. I show how this discipline supplies students with a broad variety of skills, how such experience may apply to other curricula, and how the *Thousand and One Nights* is fundamental in grasping the workings of world literature. I focus particularly on reading the *Thousand and One Nights* through the "Thousand and Second Night" motif. The theme, primarily noticeable through its recurring title, regularly raises the question of whether and how Shahrazad's narration continues, directly inviting narrative trends to convene, diverge, or contrast. Handled in a wide spectrum of literatures and a variety of languages, the motif involves all genres in West and East, short stories and novels being the most numerous in the syllabus, given the weight on narrative of the Arabic masterpiece. The motif is also manifest in poetry, drama, essays, and a narrative device specific to modern literature, the "critical story."

The "Thousand and Second Night" motif seems to originate in Western literature roughly one century after the eighteenth-century resurgence of the *Nights* in translation, once the Oriental craze provoked by Antoine Galland's version had subsided. Given the nineteenth century's media-driven sophistication and narrative awareness, Western literature proves to be the first hotbed of the "Thousand and Second Night." Arabic literature then turns to the "Thousand and Second Night" in the twentieth century. Chronological distance from the return of the *Nights* in the West (eighteenth century) and in the East (nineteenth century) seems indeed necessary for the "Thousand and Second Night" to assimilate the Arabic opus, acclimatize it within national trends, and engage with it critically and creatively. The "Thousand and Second Night" is still active and ingeniously resourceful in present-day literature, each year introducing a few new texts to confirm its fecundity. Both well- and lesser-known writers have taken up the challenge. The motif also extends to fashion, cinema, advertisement, even smart parties, such as the "Thousand and Second" gala night in Oriental costume for the Parisian elite, planned by fashion designer Paul Poiret and held at the especially decorated gardens of his Parisian residence on 24 June 1911, with the help of Raoul Dufy and other artists. Indeed, the newly eroticized and strongly visual *Nights* version by Joseph-Charles Mardrus had prompted new enthusiasm for the work.

The "Thousand and Second Night" motif has two advantages over other approaches to the influence of the *Thousand and One Nights* on literature: its panoramic view embracing the Arabic model as a whole, and its immediacy. Closely following the final tale in the *Thousand and One Nights*, and occurring literally on the morrow of its finale, the first question the "Thousand and Second Night" raises is how precisely the original ends. This question is anything but simple, involves far-reaching comparisons between the surviving endings, and prompts discussion of their implications. Why and how is Shahrazad granted life? What makes Shahriyar unbind himself from the cruel oath he has sworn and reconcile himself to existence and women? Each extant denouement engages with interpretations of the meaning of the cycle itself, of the work as a whole, and assesses Shahrazad's part as a storyteller in a different way.

The most widely familiar end, introducing children (up to three), brings to the fore a motherly and dependent Shahrazad, imploring the sultan for pity on their behalf. In strong contrast, culminations celebrating her narrative capacity, recognized by Shahriyar, point to its curative power. As for conclusions that involve Shahrazad's veiled telling of the very frame tale of the king and the unfaithful queen, they strongly allude to the story's complex tale-within-a-tale-within-a-tale structure and to the multifaceted implications of similar compositions. Heinz Grotzfeld's well-known essay, "Neglected Conclusions of the *Arabian Nights*: Gleanings in Forgotten and Overlooked Recensions," is here particularly helpful, as it stresses that the most customary end (that of the mother), prominent in later Egyptian manuscripts, may well not be the oldest. By comparing these conclusions, and by observing their playing of the mother against the storyteller, students get to grasp the purport of the overall narrative of the *Nights* and its embedded tales as well as the vital importance of Shahrazad's device. They also discover that the *Nights* is an open-ended masterpiece encouraging continuation or divergence: whatever the termination, the work beckons and appeals. Writers respond accordingly. Additionally, the panoramic view of the "Thousand and Second Night" offers authors a broad variety of choices: they may engage with the end, with the cycle or story they like best, or with several of them. Last, as the "Thousand and Second Night" draws on the labyrinthine structure of the *Nights*, the task grows remarkably intricate, mainly in short genres—that is, poems, short stories, novellas, or even novels.

Second-Year Undergraduate Course

Such a course may involve less experienced students, whose idea of the *Nights* could be very sketchy, based on hearsay, children's books, Disney, Hollywood, comics, and so on. ("There must be a princess somewhere," an anonymous student responded trustingly or humorously to an initial quiz on the three ideas the *Nights* spontaneously bring to mind.) Classes need to furnish and broaden a clear knowledge base and develop and shape the students' culture and awareness, helping them improve the quality of their inquiry. In my experience, two consecutive terms—the first on the tales of the *Nights* themselves and the questions they raise; the second on comparing the *Nights* with the "Thousand and Second Night" theme in several languages and traditions—are an ideal formula for undergraduates. The first term may thus be based on the intricate history of the collection, its travels and transformations from the first known version (the Nabia Abbott fragment) up to the Galland edition and the eighteenth-century Oriental craze.

The second term can move on to comparison with the "Thousand and Second Night" motif, students having by then acquired historical understanding of and analytical reading skills needed for the *Nights*. I have taught this motif in a number of ways, starting with the three tales that sparked my first exploration, published with commentaries as *Contes de la mille et deuxième nuit (Tales of the Thousand and Second Night)*. In this, two better-known "Thousand and Second Night" texts, one by the French writer Théophile Gautier and the other by the American writer Edgar Allan Poe, meet a less well known Romanian "Thousand and Second Night" counterpoint tale by Nicolae Davidescu, "O mie de nopți și a doua noapte: Povestire critică" ("The Thousand and Second Night: A Critical Story"), that brings all three narratives into subtle dialogue. The volume offers both the originals and their translations into French on the facing page. Poe's translation is given twice, in a modern literary version by Claude Richard and Jean-Marie Maguin and in a reprint of the expanded nineteenth-century version by "Le Grand Jacques" (identified as Richard Lesclide), ingeniously illustrated by André Gill. Students thus work on comparisons based on both original and translation, compare the two Poe translations, and develop skills in reading with images.

This grouping trains students in both inter- and intratextual reading. Intertextual reading allows them to read each story against the background of the *Thousand and One Nights*, whereas intratextual reading helps them refine textual analysis by comparing the three stories in the book with one another against the backdrop of the *Thousand and One Nights*. As a matter of fact, Davidescu (who had translated tales by Gautier and Poe into Romanian in his youth) borrows his title from Gautier and summons Poe himself as a mythical persona within his "critical story," along with his most famous poem, "The Raven." He also reissues Gautier's own critical Shahrazad as a creative reviewer and evaluator of Arabic and Western literatures, since she compares Poe's "The Raven" (rehearsed in Romanian by Dunyazad) to a few of her own tales in the *Nights*.

In intertextual reading, the class compares each tale with the *Nights* as a whole or in parts. Students familiarize themselves with several versions of the *Nights*, as each modern text refers to a different cultural reception of the *Nights*. Thanks to the stories' intricate relation to the original, students learn to better define tale construction and to weigh narratives from East and West. Their critical assessment of literary heritage changes significantly in their study through Gautier and Poe, as the comparative approach makes a strong claim at reevaluation. In fact, Poe's story, with its quadruple framing and extra-rich footnotes, can lead to perplexity for readers and critics. It is esteemed for diverse reasons and belittled by some. Gautier's has been much neglected, dismissed as Orientalist pasticcio or poor imitation. As both Poe and Gautier's tales end with Shahrazad's death, the latter, taken at face value, may become proof of the modern story's inability to equal the model. Conversely, in close comparative analysis, as students bring these tales into dialogue with the *Nights*, they come to perceive their irony and value them as subtle tours de force, transferring or discussing several key features of the *Nights* in contemporary writing.

When Gautier pictures Shahrazad knocking at his door in nineteenth-century Paris, anxiously begging for a story from him or (in a later summary) from the celebrated novelists of the day, the amusing situation is a clever parallel triggering analogies between medieval storytelling, regularly broken off at dawn, and serial modern narrative in press installments (feuilletons). Gautier discusses his own work and fate, his production as a feuilleton writer being far superior to his output as a writer of stories and novels or as a poet, while drawing on an inefficient *Nights* tale. Poe's situation is analogous and even more intricate. Students thus discover that debate on how modern writers produce an efficient tale dates from the nineteenth century, well before John Barth's often-discussed inventions on the theme. Last but not least, the class is introduced to one of the hallmarks of the "Thousand and Second Night," its critical and metaliterary aspect, evident in Davidescu's subtitle, "A Critical Story." In this hybrid genre, fiction meets critical thought and draws nearer the essay. In present-day literature, Abdelfattah Kilito's *Dites-moi le songe* (*Tell Me the Dream*), a modular novel in four variants as well as an essay with questions on the *Nights* immersed in fiction, attests its importance.

Intratextual reading, on the other hand, looks at combined readings of two or all three cited short stories. It also guides students toward closer insights about the authors' aesthetic values, prompts questions of poetic authority and inspiration, alludes to important debates in literature, and shows how texts broadly interlink. At this stage, other texts may be added to the three cited as valuable extras.

The class explores how Davidescu reads Poe's "The Raven" alongside his "Philosophy of Composition," a complex piece, gauging Poe's motivations regarding his critics. Charles Baudelaire's French translation and elaboration of the "Philosophy" essay and Stéphane Mallarmé's enlightening commentary in his own translation of Poe's poems provide extra insight. Intratextual reading thus opens vistas for students into authors' habits of tricking and playing with audiences and critics. Students discover that, in Davidescu's story, the conclusive tale by King Shahriyar, on a dreamer and a cherry stone, is none other than "Historia de los dos que soñaron" ("The Story of the Two Dreamers"), one of the two stories borrowed from the *Nights* by Jorge Luis Borges, translated, and appended to his own *Historia universal de la infamia* (*A Universal History of Infamy*). This in turn sparks further readings and enlightening comparisons for students. When they compare the many versions of the two dreamers' story (Richard Francis Burton, Borges, Davidescu, Jamel Eddine Bencheikh and André Miquel's recent French translation, up to "A Fortune Regained" in Marina Warner's *Stranger Magic*), they realize that, although the story structure is always the same, the wording, details, and final meaning differ considerably. World literature's agency is in this very reworking, and a lively discussion on retelling and creation can occur in class. Further, the connection to Borges points to readings of his own fiction and nonfiction, particularly his two essays on the *Thousand and One Nights*, as foundational texts of world literature. Indeed, his fiction and poetry can be readily compared to "Thousand and Second Night" tales.

While training students in basic comparative literature exercises, such as comparative essays and comments, such a course introduces them to a broad variety of interlinked texts; enhances their historical awareness and literary knowledge; improves their critical thinking, insight, and proficiency as readers; and allows them to develop a nuanced knowledge of extra-European literature. Such a syllabus is adaptable to teaching world or European literature, the reception of important texts, and cross-cultural transpositions. This course fully exemplifies how Eastern and Western traditions meet and trade while contesting the merely colonialist or domineering Western approach, a definite hindrance to how we conceive world literature.

Graduate Seminar

The comparative literature master's seminar involved much more experienced fourth- or fifth-year graduate students from three departments (Literature, Languages, and History) with a variety of language skills, including Arabic. Since both students of Maghreb origin and those familiar with various aspects of Eastern or Muslim cultures were enrolled, three two-hour sessions on the history, transmission, adaptations, and characteristic features of the *Thousand and One Nights*, including an annotated selected bibliography, supplied the tools necessary to tackle a specific topic: reading twentieth-century history through the "Thousand and Second Night" motif.

The syllabus combined six long texts chosen for their mix of distinct features, languages, cultural areas, and historical moments. The suggestions offered here are not intended fully to reflect the texts' subtlety and intricacy but rather to focus on the outcome of such a teaching experience. I also identify a few essays that could be of help. *Den tusen och andra natten: En arabesk* (*The Thousand and Second Night: An Arabesque*), a novel published in Swedish by Frank Heller (pen name of Martin Gunnar Serner), was read by students in Edwin Bjorkman's American English translation (*The Thousand and Second Night: An Arabesque*). The novel infuses two hackneyed themes (a magic carpet and a treasure) with new vigor as it reads post–First World War Europe seen from Tunisia through the quests and ventures of two colorful trios of adventurers, alluding to British, French, German, and Swedish attitudes during the war. An acknowledged contribution to the evolution of the contemporary Syrian novel, *Alf lāila wa lailatān* (*A Thousand and Two Nights*), an Arabic *Thousand and Second Night* by Hāni al-Rāhib, read in Arabic, combines the *Thousand and One Nights* with the traumatic experience of the Arab-Israeli Six-Day War of June 1967. Several French texts follow, beginning with a long poem by the Moroccan poet Mostafa Nissaboury, *La mille et deuxième nuit* (*The Thousand and Second Night*), inspired by the violently repressed Casablanca uprising in 1965, in the poet's spirit also linked to the historical defeat of the Arab world in 1967. Given its wealth of sensual tales exemplifying ample Eastern influence (from Greece to Japan), Alain Nueil's novel of the same title, set in a defiant and averse harem, appears at first reading to mirror the eroticism of the *Nights*. It quickly develops into a somber rumination on sexual violence, however, reflecting on disaster and reparation, reliant on the Isis myth. *La mille et deuxième nuit: Conte* (*The Thousand and Second Night: A Tale*), by Tahar Mazouz, a writer of Algerian origin living in France, recounts the falling away of a young man from his traditional tribal and Muslim kinship. It combines sexual initiation, books, and a military engagement among the *harkis* (Algerian paramilitary troops siding with the French army who fought their own nationals during the Algerian War of Independence [1954–62]) and reflects the writer's father's personal experience. Last, Kilito's *Dites-moi le songe*, the only text not to directly engage with the proposed topic, was added as an initiation, both in form and meaning, to the intricate questions that inspiration from the *Thousand and One Nights* stirs in modern literature.

Each of the above was given a special introduction, along with historical and contextual reminders, to put students at ease with references; point out the symbolic, allegorical, metaphorical, and mythical patterns involved; and propose restricted themes for discussion in class. Students familiarized themselves with all the readings, directly (in the original) or indirectly (through translation or detailed commentary). They each presented oral work on one text only, considering each text in its own specificity and right as researcher or audience while gradually delving into the complexities of the *Thousand and One Nights* and the overall thorny topic of history. For a more comparative approach, students were invited to choose three texts from the syllabus as the basis of a written essay on the overall topic, to be submitted three weeks after the seminar. Subjects and foci were suggested to help them better orient their work and raise issues, which did not hinder them from developing their own personal investigation or interest in a direction they found striking.

The treatment of violence and revolt in relation to the *Thousand and One Nights* will not come as a surprise. The frame tale readily lends itself to the issue, and Shahrazad can be read as a symbol of resistance to political tyranny. Indeed, Muhsin Mahdi has commented on politics and religion in the *Nights* ("Religion"). Depending on given writers' resourcefulness, imagination, and skills, what the "Thousand and Second Night" theme invites more particularly is a range of questions that regularly challenge stereotypes and offer a nuanced view of Orientalism and postcolonialism. They variously bear on the way the *Nights* are considered, imagination and use of myth, narrative structures and treatment, and language.

As modern historic upheavals, particularly war, are reflected in twentieth-century plots, several "Thousand and Second Nights" challenge the perception of the *Nights* as an innocuous collection of Orientalist marvelous tales with the intensity of historic, ethical, and political questions spawned by continuing conflicts in both the East and West. In al-Rāhib's novel, the *Thousand and One Nights* epitomizes the persistent night of apathy and compliancy in which the Arab world is plunged, the 1967 war having been a cruel awakening. Conceived in independent Morocco and attuned to the violence of the sixties, Nissaboury's poetry is a complex gesture against colonial culture and language, explicitly dismantling the marvels of the *Nights*. His Shahrazad is a shadow and a beggar, hobbling on a crutch in the medina, surrounded by other once grand heroes of the *Nights* who are now destitute, abused, or alienated by violence and madness. Mazouz's tale turns to the mythical figure of Kahina, Berber queen and ferocious opponent of the eighth-century Arab conquest in North Africa, often mentioned in colonial and postcolonial memories or history-inspired accounts (Hannoum). Heller devises a tale based on a woven Kandahar carpet and three covetous brothers, cleverly structuring his novel through the weaving metaphor, interlacing narrative voices and modes, and reflecting on the havoc brought by war. Students discover in these works a strong tendency to rip open the myth of the *Nights*, that is, that of a text buried under cheap Orientalist paraphernalia, as part of Edward Said's *Orientalism*. But they also perceive that reducing the texts to simplified readings would be unfair, since the texts generally also take on the challenge of the *Nights* in structure, style, and language choices.

Structurally, Heller, Nueil, and Kilito are the craftiest, each in his own way. Heller and Nueil play (differently) with both embedding and embedded devices, Nueil capsizing his novel's structure at the very end. Kilito unfurls a series of questions on the *Nights* through a limited variety of situations and swappable identities, questioning anonymity, story structure, meaning itself, and stratagems such as the clichéd "unknown manuscript" trick. As the seminar turns to tone, style, and language issues, students see the "Thousand and Second Night" taking on vibrant questions in modern creation. Nissaboury, for instance, whose poem is a "contest with language," (Nissaboury, "Prise de position liminaire") introduces them to the *melhoun* culture he admires, a term referring not so much to "melody" as to "barbarism," a lingo specific to the defeated, implanting into French (the colonialist language) hybrid expressions or images. In Heller's novel, students discover how two narrative voices already compete: that of Aouina, close to natural elements (wind, spring water), extensively narrating the key tale of the carpet, and the hybrid voice of an alienated narrator who boasts of being a reincarnation of major Arabic poetic figures but only rattles away in long episodes. Such attempts permeate the "Thousand and Second Night" narrative with linguistic and stylistic experiments that strongly remind students of some of the reasons the medieval *Thousand and One Nights* was excluded from the classical Arabic canon: hybrid language and average literature. Heller's novel is indeed average in plot, execution, style, even language—but not necessarily a failure.

Such challenging reading assignments allow students to learn what to make of inter- and intratextual allusions, to compare narrative frames with their contents, and to confront the narrative traditions of East and West. They develop a capacity to link thematic approaches with poetic devices and issues (such as narrative scope, irony, metafiction, picturing of the poetic self, etc.) and value literature's sensitive echo of history in modern times.

If we consider the *Thousand and One Nights* as a corpus of interrelated (mostly anonymous) literary texts across time, whose adaptation, translation, and transmission contributed to shaping the very idea of world literature, teaching the *Nights* from the "Thousand and Second Night" perspective strongly emphasizes the remarkable extent to which modern texts by different (named) writers interconnect and interrelate. World literature no longer appears as a historicized series of major chapters, shaped around each country's claims to international celebrity, nor as an endless series of famous authors with individual works, but rather as a web of interconnections and incessant alterations. As words interlock and join to make texts, as languages meet and exchange in translation, so texts interweave to create world literature. The *Thousand and One Nights* and the "Thousand and Second Night" tradition allow us to observe these phenomena as they are being shaped. These texts make world literature as much as they exemplify its very agency.

NOTES ON CONTRIBUTORS

Abdalla Uba Adamu teaches information and media studies at Bayero University Kano. His research focuses on how Arabian, Persian, and Indian folklore are transmuted into Hausa popular culture, an exploration he calls "imperialism from below" that counters the emphasis of cultural transmission from the West to Africa. He is the author of *Transglobal Media Flows and African Popular Culture: Revolution and Reaction in Muslim Hausa Popular Culture* (2007).

Roger Allen is a leading translator of Arabic literature, including a number of fictional works by modern Arab writers, such as Naguib Mahfouz, Jabra Ibrahim Jabra, Yusuf Idris, 'Abd al-rahman Munif, Mayy Telmissany, Ben Salim Himmich, Ahmad al-Tawfiq, and Hana al-Shaykh. Among his published studies on Arabic literature are *The Arabic Novel: An Historical and Critical Introduction* (1982) and *The Arabic Literary Heritage* (1998).

Bruce Fudge is professor of Arabic at the University of Geneva. He is the author of numerous articles and two books: *Qur'anic Hermeneutics: Al-Tabrisi and the Craft of Commentary* (2011) and *A Hundred and One Nights / Kitāb mi'at laylah wa-laylah* (2016), for which he edited the Arabic text and completed the English translation.

Suzanne Gauch's research and teaching interests include film, gender, and postcolonial studies. She is the author of *Maghrebs in Motion: North African Cinema in Nine Movements* (2016), which analyzes innovations in Algerian, Moroccan, and Tunisian filmmaking in the late twentieth and early twenty-first centuries, and of *Liberating Shahrazad: Feminism, Postcolonialism, and Islam* (2007).

Paulo Lemos Horta is associate professor of literature and creative writing at New York University, Abu Dhabi. He is the author of *Marvellous Thieves: Secret Authors of the Arabian Nights* (2017), editor of *The Annotated* Arabian Nights (2021) and *Aladdin: A New Translation* (2018), and coeditor, with Bruce Robbins, of *Cosmopolitanisms* (2017).

Dominique Jullien is professor of comparative literature and French studies at the University of California, Santa Barbara. She is the author of *Proust et ses modèles: Les Mille et une nuits et les Mémoires de Saint-Simon* (1989), *Les amoureux de Schéhérazade: Variations modernes sur les Mille et une nuits* (2009), and *Borges, Buddhism and World Literature: A Morphology of Renunciation Tales* (2019). She teaches the *Nights* in various contexts, most recently in upper-division courses on Europe's view of the Orient and in graduate seminars on the *Nights* in and as world literature.

Margaret Litvin is associate professor of Arabic and comparative literature at Boston University (BU) and author of *Hamlet's Arab Journey: Shakespeare's Prince and Nasser's Ghost* (2011). At BU she founded the Middle East and North Africa Studies Program and regularly teaches courses on literary translation, global Shakespeares, and the *Thousand and One Nights* in the world literary imagination. Her essay in this volume is dedicated to the memory of Maria Rosa Menocal (1953–2012).

Karla Mallette is a scholar of medieval Mediterranean literature, primarily in Italian and Arabic. She has written two books, coedited one, and written a number of articles on medieval literature and on Mediterranean studies. She wrote about the *Thousand and One Nights* in *European Modernity and the Arab Mediterranean* (2010) and has taught the *Nights* in great books courses at the American University of Beirut, Northwestern University, and the University of Michigan. She is professor of Italian and Middle East studies at the University of Michigan and currently serves as chair of Michigan's Department of Middle East Studies.

Ulrich Marzolph served as a senior member of the editorial committee of the *Enzyklopädie des Märchens* (1986–2015) and as adjunct professor of Islamic studies at the University of Göttingen. His field of expertise is the narrative culture of the Muslim world. In addition to numerous essays and encyclopedic articles in the field, he has published *The Arabian Nights Encyclopedia* (2004; together with Richard van Leeuwen) and the edited volumes *The Arabian Nights Reader* (2006) and *The Arabian Nights in Transnational Perspective* (2007). Most recently, he is the author of *Relief after Hardship: The Ottoman Turkish Model for The Thousand and One Days* (2017) and *101 Middle Eastern Tales and Their Impact on Western Oral Tradition* (2020).

Wen-chin Ouyang (歐陽文津) is professor of Arabic and comparative literature at SOAS, University of London. She is the author of *Literary Criticism in Medieval Arabic-Islamic Culture: The Making of a Tradition* (1997), *Poetics of Love in the Arabic Novel* (2012), and *Politics of Nostalgia in the Arabic Novel* (2013). She has also published widely on the *Thousand and One Nights*, often in comparison with classical and modern Arabic narrative traditions, European and Hollywood cinema, magic realism, and Chinese storytelling.

Maurice Pomerantz, associate professor of literature at New York University, Abu Dhabi, is a scholar of Arabic literature of the premodern period. His interests include Arabic belles-lettres poetry and prose. He is the author of *Licit Magic: The Life and Letters of al-Ṣāḥib b. ʿAbbād* (2016) and coauthor, with Bilal Orfali, of *The Maqāmāt of al-Hamadhānī: Authorship, Texts, and Contexts* (2022).

Nadine Roth teaches history at New York University, Abu Dhabi. A historian of modern Europe, she is currently working on a book manuscript on Hanna Diyab and the tales he contributed to the *Thousand and One Nights* as the production of cultural exchange in the Mediterranean.

Rachel Schine is assistant professor of Arabic and religious studies at the University of Maryland. Her work focuses on orality, storytelling practices, gender, sexuality, race, and race-making in premodern Muslim literatures and social history. Her current book project assesses the racialization of Black protagonists in the popular *sīrahs*, and she has published on a range of related topics in Arabophone premodernity.

Susan Slyomovics is distinguished professor of anthropology and Near Eastern languages and cultures at the University of California, Los Angeles, where she teaches an undergraduate class on the *Thousand and One Nights*. She is the editor of *The Walled Arab City in Literature, Architecture and History: The Living Medina in the Maghrib* (2001) and *Clifford Geertz in Morocco* (2010) and author of *The Merchant of Art: An Egyptian Hilali Epic Poet in Performance* (1987), *The Object of Memory: Arab and Jew Narrate the Palestinian Village* (1998, awarded the 1999 Albert Hourani book prize), *The Performance of Human Rights in Morocco* (2005), and *How to Accept German Reparations* (2015).

Evanghelia Stead, honorary fellow of the Institut Universitaire de France (2016–21), is comparative literature and print culture professor at UVSQ-Paris Saclay, a linguist, and a literary translator. She has run the TIGRE seminar on print and media culture at the École Normale Supérieure, Paris, since 2004 and has published extensively on print culture, iconography, reception of key texts, myth, the fin de siècle, Goethe's *Faust*, and the "Thousand and Second Night" literary tradition. She has frequently taught on the *Nights* from a comparative point of view.

Samhita Sunya is assistant professor of cinema in the Department of Middle Eastern and South Asian Languages and Cultures at the University of Virginia. She is the author of *Sirens of Modernity: World Cinema via Bombay* (2022) and guest coeditor of *South by South/West Asia*, a special issue of *Film History* (2020). Her published work on Hindi cinema includes contributions to *Positions, Jump Cut, Film History*, and *Jadaliyya*.

Shawkat M. Toorawa is chair of the Department of Near Eastern Languages and Civilizations at Yale University, where he is professor of Arabic literature and of comparative literature. His interests include the Qur'an, the literary and writerly culture of Abbasid Baghdad, the Waqwaq Tree and islands, modern poetry, Indian Ocean studies, and science fiction film and literature. He has published *Ibn Abī Ṭāhir Ṭayfūr: A Ninth-Century Bookman in Baghdad* (2004), translated Gregor Schoeler's *The Aural and the Read: The Genesis of Literature in Islam* (2009), and edited and collaboratively translated Ibn al-Sāʿi's *Consorts of the Caliphs: Women and the Court of Baghdad* (2015). He is an executive editor of the Library of Arabic Literature.

Parisa Vaziri is assistant professor of comparative literature and Near Eastern studies at Cornell University. Her work engages legacies of Indian Ocean world slavery in the *longue durée* through prisms of visual media. Her research overlaps interests in critical theory, Black studies, Middle Eastern cultural production, and film and media studies. Her current book project, *Racial Blackness and Indian Ocean Slavery: Iran's Media Archive*, is forthcoming from University of Minnesota Press.

WORKS CITED

Aarne, Antti, and Stith Thompson. *The Types of the Folktale*. Suomalainen Tiedeakatemia, 1961. FF Communications 184.

Abbott, Nabia. "A Ninth-Century Fragment of the 'Thousand Nights': New Light on the Early History of the *Arabian Nights*." *Journal of Near Eastern Studies*, vol. 8, 1949, pp. 129–64.

Abdel-Halim, Mohamed. *Antoine Galland: Sa vie et son oeuvre*. A. G. Nizet, 1964.

Die Abenteuer des Prinzen Achmed. Directed by Lotte Reiniger, Comenius-Film GmbH, 1926.

Ahmed, Sara. "A Phenomenology of Whiteness." *Feminist Theory*, vol. 8, 2007, pp. 149–68.

Akasoy, Anna. Syllabus for *Arabian Nights*: East and West. Spring 2017, Hunter College, City University of New York.

Akel, Ibrahim. "Liste des manuscrits arabes des *Nuits*." Chraïbi, *Arabic Manuscripts*, pp. 65–114.

———. "Quelques remarques sur la bibliothèque d'Antoine Galland et l'arrivée des *Mille et une nuits* en Occident." *Antoine Galland et l'Orient des savants*, edited by Pierre-Sylvain Filliozat and Michel Zink, Académie des Inscriptions et Belles-Lettres, 2017, pp. 197–215.

Aladdin. Directed by Ron Clements and John Musker, Walt Disney Pictures, 1992.

Aladdin. Directed by Guy Ritchie, Walt Disney Pictures, 2019.

Alameddine, Rabih. *The Hakawati*. Alfred A. Knopf, 2008.

Ali, Kecia. *Marriage and Slavery in Early Islam*. Harvard UP, 2010.

Alibaba aur chalis chor. Directed by Homi Wadia, Basant Pictures, 1954.

Ali Baba et les quarante voleurs. Directed by Ferdinand Zecca, Pathé, 1902.

Allen, Roger. "An Analysis of the 'Tale of the Three Apples' from the *Thousand and One Nights*." *Logos Islamikos: Festschrift for Professor G. M. Wickens*, Pontifical Institute of Mediaeval Studies, 1984, pp. 51–60.

Allen, Roger, and D. S. Richards, editors. *Arabic Literature in the Post-classical Period*. Cambridge UP, 2006. Cambridge History of Arabic Literature.

Antrim, Zayde. "Qamarayn: The Erotics of Sameness in the *Thousand and One Nights*." *Al-ʿUṣūr al-Wusṭā*, vol. 28, 2020, pp. 1–44.

Appiah, Kwame Anthony. *Cosmopolitanism: Ethics in a World of Strangers*. W. W. Norton, 2006.

Apter, Emily. *The Translation Zone*. Princeton UP, 2011.

Arabian Nights. Hallmark Entertainment, 2000.

Arabian Nights. Directed by John Rawlins, Universal Pictures, 1942.

Armes, Roy. "The Poetic Vision of Nacer Khemir." *Third Text*, vol. 24, no. 1, 2010, pp. 69–82.

Arnold, Andrew. "Top 10 Everything 2003: Comics." *Time*, 18 Dec. 2003, web.archive.org/web/20110120173855/http://www.time.com/time/specials/packages/article/0,28804,2001842_2001833_2002066,00.html.

Ashcroft, Bill. *The Empire Writes Back: Theory and Practice in Post-colonial Literatures*. Routledge, 2002.

Ashik Kerib. Directed by Sergei Parajanov and Dodo Abashidze, Kartuli Pilmi, 1989.

Asimeng-Boahene, Lewis. "*Mirror of a People*: The Pedagogical Value of African Proverbs as Cultural Resource Tools in Content Area in Social Studies Classrooms." *African Traditional and Oral Literature as Pedagogical Tools in Content Area Classrooms: K–12*, edited by Asimeng-Boahene and Michael Baffoe, Information Age Publishing, 2014, pp. 111–28.

Atwood, Margaret. *Stone Mattress: Nine Wicked Tales*. Anchor, 2015.

ʿAwaḍ Allāh ʿAbd al-Jalīl ʿAlī. "The Merchant of Art." 1986. *UCLA Center for Near Eastern Studies*, 2009, www.international.ucla.edu/cnes/article/108092.

———. "The 'Tale of Anas al-Wujūd and al-Ward fi-l-Akmām': An Oral Performance." Photographed, translated, and transliterated by Susan Slyomovics, multimedia by Rahul Bhushan, produced for the web by Scott Gruber, 2009, *UCLA Center for Near Eastern Studies*, www.international.ucla.edu/cnes/video/108046.

Azpiri, Alfonso. *Reflections*. Heavy Metal, 2001.

———. *Wet Dreams*. Heavy Metal, 2000.

Babaie, Sussan, et al. *Slaves of the Shah: New Elites of Safavid Iran*. I. B. Tauris, 2004.

Bacchilega, Cristina. *Fairy Tales Transformed? Twenty-First-Century Adaptations and the Politics of Wonder*. Wayne State UP, 2013.

Badalkhan, Sabir. "The Tale of 'Aladdin and the Magic Lamp' in Balochi." Marzolph, *Arabian Nights in Transnational Perspective*, pp. 331–46.

Baghoolizadeh, Beeta. "The Myths of Haji Firuz: The Racist Contours of the Iranian Minstrel." *Lateral: Journal of the Cultural Studies Association*, vol. 10, no. 1, 2021, https://doi.org/10.25158/L10.1.12.

Barber, Karin. *Readings in African Popular Culture*. Indiana UP, 1997.

Barks, Carl. *Cave of Ali Baba*. *Uncle Scrooge Adventures*, vol. 37, 1962.

Barth, John. *Dunyazadiad*. *Chimera*, by Barth, Random House, 1972, pp. 1–56.

Barthes, Roland. "The Death of the Author." Translated by Richard Howard, *Aspen*, nos. 5–6, 1967.

Baudelaire, Charles. "La genèse d'un poëme." *Œuvres en prose*, by Edgar Allan Poe, translated by Baudelaire, edited by Yves-Gérard Le Dantec, Gallimard, 1952, pp. 979–97.

Beaumont, Daniel. *Slave of Desire: Sex, Love, and Death in the* Thousand and One Nights. Fairleigh Dickinson UP, 2002.

Bencheikh, Jamel-Eddine. *Les* Mille et une nuits, *ou, La parole prisonnière*. Gallimard, 1988.

———, and André Miquel, translators. *Les mille et une nuits*. Gallimard, 2005. 3 vols.

——— et al. *Mille et un contes de la nuit*. Gallimard, 1991.

Bin Ḥasan, al-Munsif. *Al-'Abīd wa-al-jawārī fī ḥikāyāt* Alf laylah wa-laylah. Sirās lil-Nashr, 1994.

Boccaccio, Giovanni. *The Decameron*. Translated by Mark Musa, Signet Classics, 2010.

Borges, Jorge Luis. "The Argentine Writer and Tradition." Borges, *Selected Non-fictions*, pp. 420–27.

———. *Collected Fictions*. Translated by Andrew Hurley, Penguin Books, 1998.

———. "Metaphors of the *Thousand and One Nights*." 1977. Translated by Jack Ross, *Magazine*, vol. 1, 2003, pp. 36–38.

———. "The Nothingness of Personality." Borges, *Selected Non-fictions*, pp. 3–9.

———. *Obras completas*. Emecé, 1989. 3 vols.

———. *Selected Non-fictions*. Edited by Eliot Weinberger, translated by Esther Allen et al., Penguin Books, 1999.

———. *Seven Nights*. Translated by Eliot Weinberger, New Directions, 1980.

———. "The *Thousand and One Nights*." Borges, *Seven Nights*, pp. 42–57.

———. "The Translators of the *Thousand and One Nights*." Borges, *Selected Non-fictions*, pp. 92–109.

Bottigheimer, Ruth B. "The Case of the Ebony Horse: Part 1." *Gramarye*, vol. 5, 2014, pp. 9–20.

Bray, Julia. "A Caliph and His Public Relations." *Middle Eastern Literatures*, vol. 7, no. 2, 2004, pp. 159–70.

———. "Men, Women and Slaves in Abbasid Society." Brubaker and Smith, pp. 121–46.

Brubaker, Leslie, and Julia M. H. Smith. *Gender in the Early Medieval World: East and West, 300–900*. Cambridge UP, 2004.

Brunner, Karl, editor. *The* Seven Sages of Rome *(Southern Version)*. Kraus Reprint, 1988.

Burton, Richard Francis, translator. *The Book of the Thousand Nights and a Night*. London, 1885–86. 10 vols.

Busch, Wilhelm. *Max and Maurice: A Juvenile History in Seven Tricks*. Translated by Charles T. Brooks, Rupert Brothers, 1874.

Byatt, A. S. *The Djinn in the Nightingale's Eye: Five Fairy Stories*. Random House, 1997.

Calvino, Italo. *Invisible Cities*. Translated by William Weaver, Harcourt, 1978.

Caracciolo, Peter. "The House of Fiction and *le Jardin Anglo-Chinois*." *Middle Eastern Literatures*, vol. 7, no. 2, 2004, pp. 199–211.

Carter, Angela. *"The Bloody Chamber" and Other Stories*. Vintage Classics, 2016.

Casanova, Pascale. *The World Republic of Letters*. Translated by Malcolm DeBevoise, Harvard UP, 2004.

Caswell, Fuad Matthew. *The Slave Girls of Baghdad: The* Qiyān *in the Early Abbasid Era*. I. B. Tauris, 2011.

Cates, Isaac, and Mike Wenthe. *Tales from the Classroom*. Yale U Graduate School, 2003.

Chaucer, Geoffrey. *Canterbury Tales*. Edited by A. C. Cawley, Alfred A. Knopf, 1992.

Chauvin, Victor. *Bibliographie des ouvrages arabes ou relatifs aux Arabes publiés dans l'Europe chrétienne de 1810 à 1885: Les* Mille et une nuits. Vaillant-Carmanne, 1892–1905. 12 vols.

Chawaf, Chantal. *Le corps et le verbe: La langue en sens inverse*. Presses de la Renaissance, 1992.

Chestney, Lillian, illustrator. *Arabian Nights*. Lettering by Fred Eng, Gilberton Corporation, 1943. Classics Illustrated 8.

Chiang, Ted. "The Merchant and the Alchemist's Gate." *Exhalation*, by Chiang, Alfred A. Knopf, 2019, pp. 3–36.

Chraïbi, Aboubakr, editor. *Arabic Manuscripts of the Thousand and One Nights*. Espaces et Signes, 2016.

———. *Classer les récits: Théories et pratiques*. Harmattan, 2007.

———. *Les Mille et une nuits: Histoire du texte et classification des contes*. Harmattan, 2008.

———. "Situation, Motivation, and Action in the Arabian Nights." Marzolph and van Leeuwen, pp. 5–9.

Chu Chin Chow. Directed by Walter Forde, Gainsborough Pictures, 1934.

Chu Chin Chow. Directed by Herbert Wilcox, Metro Goldwyn Mayer, 1925.

Cixous, Hélène. "The Laugh of the Medusa." Translated by Keith Cohen and Paula Cohen, *Signs*, vol. 1, no. 4, 1976, pp. 875–93.

Clouston, W. A. *The Book of Sindibād; or, The Story of the King, His Son, the Damsel, and the Seven Vazīrs, from the Persian and Arabic*. J. Cameron, 1884.

Cohn, Jesse. "Mise-en-Page: A Vocabulary for Page Layouts." Tabachnik, *Teaching*, pp. 44–57.

Cooperson, Michael. "The Monstruous Births of 'Aladdin.'" Marzolph, *Arabian Nights Reader*, pp. 265–82.

Corrao, Francesca Maria. "The *Arabian Nights* in Sicily." *Fabula*, vol. 45, nos. 3–4, 2004, pp. 237–45.

Crane, Lucy, and Walter Crane. *The Forty Thieves*. Illustrated by Walter Crane, George Routledge and Sons, 1873.

Damrosch, David. *What Is World Literature?* Princeton UP, 2003.

Dirks, Rudolph. *The Katzenjammer Kids: A Series of Comic Pictures*. 1897. *New York American and Journal*, 1902.

Diyab, Hanna. *The Book of Travels*. Edited by Johannes Stephan, translated by Elias Muhanna, New York UP, 2021.

———. *D'Alep à Paris: Les pérégrinations d'un jeune Syrien au temps de Louis XIV*. Edited by Paule Fahmé-Thiéry et al., Actes Sud, 2015.

———. *The Man Who Wrote Aladdin: The Life and Times of Hanna Diyab*. Translated by Paul Lunde, Zeticula, 2020.

Djebar, Assia. *A Sister to Scheherazade*. Translated by Dorothy S. Blair, Heinemann, 1993.

Dobie, Madeleine. "Translation in the Contact Zone: Antoine Galland's Mille et une nuits: Contes arabes." Makdisi and Nussbaum, pp. 25–49.

The Dove's Lost Necklace. Written and directed by Nacer Khemir, Carthago Films, 1992.

Duggan, Anne E., and Don Haase, editors. *Folktales and Fairy Tales: Traditions and Texts from around the World*. 2nd ed., ABC-CLIO, 2016.

Dutchman. Written by Amiri Baraka, directed by Anthony Harvey, Kaitlin Productions / Dutchman Film Company, 1967.

Edgar, Frank. *Dare dubu da daya: Littafi na biyu*. C.M.S. Bookshop, 1924.

Edward Said on Orientalism. Directed by Sut Jhally, Media Education Foundation, 1998.

Eğri, Sadettin, editor. *Elfü Leyletin ve Leyle Hikâyetleri: Binbir Gece Masalları: Bursa Nüshası*. Bursa Büyükşehir Belediyesi Kitaplığı, 2016.

Ehki, ya Shahrazade. Directed by Yousry Nasrallah, Misr Cinema, 2009.

Eisner, Will. *Comics and Sequential Art*. Poorhouse, 1985.

El Hamel, Chouki. *Black Morocco: A History of Slavery, Race, and Islam*. Cambridge UP, 2014.

Epstein, Morris. *Tales of Sendebar [Mishle Sendabar]: An Edition and Translation of the Hebrew Version of the Seven Sages, Based on Unpublished Manuscripts*. Jewish Publication Society of America, 1967.

Fanon, Frantz. *Black Skin, White Masks*. Translated by Richard Philcox, Grove Press, 2008.

Ferguson, Christine. "Steam Punk and the Visualization of the Victorian: Alan Moore's *The League of Extraordinary Gentlemen* and *From Hell*." Tabachnik, *Teaching*, pp. 200–07.

Finlayson, J. Caitlin. "The Boundaries of Genre: Translating Shakespeare in Antony Johnston and Brett Weldele's *Julius*." Tabachnik, *Teaching*, pp. 188–199.

Finnegan, Ruth. *Oral Literature in Africa*. Open Book Publishers, 2012.

Il fiore delle Mille e una notte. Directed by Pier Paolo Pasolini, produced by Alberto Grimaldi, 1974.

Fishbein, Michael, editor. *Kalīlah and Dimnah: Fables of Virtue and Vice*. Translated by Fishbein and James E. Montgomery, Library of Arabic Literature, New York UP, 2021.

Fishburn, Evelyn. "Readings and Rereadings of Night 602." *Variaciones Borges*, vol. 18, 2004, pp. 35–42.

Foxer, Loic. *Stella: A Thousand and One Nights*. Translated by Halibut, fantasycomix.com. Accessed 31 Dec. 2017.

Fudge, Bruce, editor and translator. *A Hundred and One Nights / Kitāb miʾat laylah wa-laylah*. New York UP, 2016. Library of Arabic Literature.

———. "More Translators of the *Thousand and One Nights*." *Journal of the American Oriental Society*, vol. 136, 2016, pp. 135–46.

———. "Signs of Scripture in 'The City of Brass.'" *Journal of Qurʾānic Studies*, vol. 8, no. 1, 2006, pp. 88–118.

———. "Underworlds and Otherworlds in the *Thousand and One Nights*." *Utopias and Dystopias in Arabic Writings*, edited by Wen-chin Ouyang, special issue of *Middle Eastern Literature*, vol. 15, no. 3, 2012, pp. 257–72.

Gabrieli, Francesco, editor. Le mille e una notte: *Prima versione integrale dall'arabo*. Einaudi, 1972.

Gaiman, Neil. "Ramadan." *The Sandman: Fables and Reflections*, illustrated by P. Craig Russell et al., cover art by Dave McKean, colored by Digital Chameleon, Vertigo / DC Comics, 1993. Vol. 6 of *The Sandman*.

Gaiser, Adam. "Slaves and Silver across the Strait of Gibraltar: Politics and Trade between Umayyad Iberia and Khārijite North Africa." *Medieval Encounters*, vol. 19, nos. 1–2, 2013, pp. 41–70.

Galland, Antoine. *Le journal d'Antoine Galland, 1646–1715: La période parisienne*. Edited by Frédéric Bauden and Richard Waller, vol. 1, Peeters, 2011.

———. *Les* Mille et une nuits: *Contes arabes traduits en français*. Paris, 1704–17. 12 vols.

———. *Les* Mille et une nuits: *Contes arabes traduits en français*. Edited by Jean-Paul Sermain, Gallimard, 2004. 3 vols.

Garcin, Jean-Claude. *Pour une lecture historique des* Mille et une nuits. Actes Sud, 2013.

Gelder, Geert Jan van, editor and translator. *Classical Arabic Literature: A Library of Arabic Literature Anthology*. New York UP, 2012.

Genette, Gerard. *Narrative Discourse: An Essay in Method*. Translated by Jane E. Lewin, Cornell UP, 1980.

Gerhardt, Mia. *The Art of Story-telling: A Literary Study of the* Thousand and One Nights. Brill, 1963.

Gérôme, Jean-Léon. *The Bath*. 1880. *Fine Arts Museum of San Francisco*, art.famsf.org/jean-léon-gérôme/bath-196129.

———. *Moorish Bath*. 1870. *Museum of Fine Arts Boston*, collections.mfa.org/objects/32124.

Ghazoul, Ferial J. *The* Arabian Nights: *A Structural Analysis*. Cairo Associated Institution for the Study and Presentation of Arab Cultural Values, 1980.

———. *Nocturnal Poetics: The* Arabian Nights *in Comparative Context*. American U in Cairo P, 1996.

Gibb, H. A. R. *Arabic Literature*. Clarendon Press, 1963.

Gissing, George. *Charles Dickens: A Critical Study*. Dodd, Mead, 1898.

Goitein, Solomon D. "The Oldest Documentary Evidence for the Title *Alf laila wa-laila*." *Journal of the American Oriental Society*, vol. 78, 1958, pp. 301–02.

Gomez, Michael. *African Dominion: A New History of Empire in Early and Medieval West Africa*. Princeton UP, 2018.

Gordon, Matthew, and Kathryn A. Hain, editors. *Concubines and Courtesans: Women and Slavery in Islamic History*. Oxford UP, 2017.

Granara, William, and Ibrahim Akel. *The* Thousand and One Nights: *Sources, Transformations, and Relationship with Literature, the Arts and the Sciences*. Brill, 2020.

Gravett, Paul. "Sergio Toppi: Master of the Impossible." *Paul Gravett*, 22 Dec. 2012, www.paulgravett.com/articles/article/sergio_toppi.

Grotzfeld, Heinz. "The Age of the Galland Manuscript of the *Nights*: Numismatic Evidence for Dating a Manuscript?" *Journal of Arabic and Islamic Studies*, vol. 1, 1966–67, pp. 50–64.

———. "Neglected Conclusions of the *Arabian Nights*: Gleanings in Forgotten and Overlooked Recensions." *Journal of Arabic Literature*, vol. 16, 1985, pp. 73–87.

Gunner, Liz. "Africa and Orality." *The Cambridge History of African and Caribbean Literature*, edited by Simon Gikandi and Irele Abiola, vol. 1, Cambridge UP, 2004, pp. 1–18.

Gutas, Dmitri. *Greek Thought, Arabic Culture*. Routledge, 1998.

Haddawy, Husain, translator. *The Arabian Nights*. W. W. Norton, 1990.

———, translator. *"Sindbad" and Other Popular Stories from the* Arabian Nights. W. W. Norton, 1996.

Ḥakīm, Tawfīq al-. *Shahrazād*. Dār Miṣr, 1934.

Ḥakīm, Tawfīq al-, and Tāhā Ḥusayn. *Al-Qaṣr al-mashūr*. Dār al-Nashr al-Ḥadīth, 1936.

Hamid, Mohsin. *Exit West*. Penguin, 2018.

Hamori, Andras. "A Comic Romance from the *Thousand and One Nights*: The 'Tale of Two Viziers.'" *Arabica*, vol. 30, 1983, pp. 38–56.

———. *On the Art of Medieval Arabic Literature*. Princeton UP, 1974.

Hannoum, Abdelmajid. *Colonial Histories, Post-colonial Memories: The Legend of the Kahina, a North African Heroine*. Heinemann, 2001.

Harem. Directed by Arthur Joffe, Union Generale Cinematographique, 1985.

Harris, Carissa M. *Obscene Pedagogies: Transgressive Talk and Sexual Education in Late Medieval Britain*. Cornell UP, 2018.

Hatfield, Charles. "A *Habibi* Roundtable." *The Comics Journal*, 27 Oct. 2011, www.tcj.com/a-habibi-roundtable/.

Heath, Peter. *The Thirsty Sword: Sırat ʿAntar and the Arabic Popular Epic*. U of Utah P, 1996.

Hees, Syrinx von. "The Astonishing: A Critique and Re-reading of ʿAǧāʾib Literature." *Middle Eastern Literatures*, vol. 8, no. 2, 2005, pp. 101–20.

Heinrichs, Wolfhart P. "The Function(s) of Poetry in the *Arabian Nights*." *O Ye Gentlemen: Arabic Studies on Science and Literary Culture in Honour of Remke Kruk*, edited by Arnoud Vrolijk and Jan Hogendijk, Brill, 2007, pp. 353–62.

Hellboy 2: The Golden Army. Directed by Guillermo del Toro, Universal Pictures, 2008.

Heller, Frank. *The Thousand and Second Night: An Arabesque*. Translated by Edwin Bjorkman, Thomas Y. Crowell, 1925.

———. *Den tusen och andra natten: En arabesk*. Albert Bonniers Förlag, 1923.

Heller-Roazen, Daniel, and Muhsin Mahdi, editors. *The Arabian Nights*. Translated by Husain Haddawy, Norton Critical Edition, W. W. Norton, 2010.

Hennig, Richard. *Terrae incognitae: Eine Zusammenstellung und kritische Bewertung der wichtigsten vorcolumbischen Entdeckungsreisen an Hand der darüber vorliegenden Originalberichte*. Brill, 1944.

Hibri, Tayeb el-. *Reinterpreting Islamic Historiography*. Cambridge UP, 1999.

Hofstadter, Douglas. *Gödel, Escher, Bach: An Eternal Golden Braid*. Basic Books, 1979.

Hole, Richard. *Remarks on the* Arabian Nights' Entertainments: *In Which the Origin of Sindbad's Voyages, and Other Oriental Fictions, Is Particularly Considered*. London, 1797.

Hopkinson, Nalo. *Skin Folk: Stories*. Open Road Media, 2018.

Horta, Paulo Lemos. "Beyond the Palace: Transnational Itineraries of the City in the *Arabian Nights*." *PMLA*, vol. 131, no. 2, Mar. 2016, pp. 487–96.

———. "Cosmopolitan Prejudice." *Cosmopolitanisms*, edited by Bruce Robbins and Horta, New York UP, 2017, pp. 153–68.

———. *Marvellous Thieves: Secret Authors of the* Arabian Nights. Harvard UP, 2017.

Hovannisian, Richard C., and Georges Sabagh, editors. *The* Thousand and One Nights *in Arabic Literature and Society.* Cambridge UP, 1997.

Hunwick, John O. "A Region of the Mind: Medieval Arab Views of African Geography and Ethnography and Their Legacy." *Sudanic Africa*, vol. 16, 2005, pp. 103–36.

Ḥusayn, Ṭāhā. *Aḥlām Shahrazād.* Dār al-Maʿārif, 1943.

Ibn Battūta. *The Travels of Ibn Battutah.* Edited by Tim Mackintosh-Smith, Picador, 2003.

Ibn al-Jawzī, ʿAbd al-Raḥmān ibn ʿAlī. *Dhamm al-hawā.* Dār al-Kutub al-Ḥadītha, 1962.

Ibn Kathīr. *Al-Bidāyah wa-l-nihāyah.* Edited by Muḥammad Ḥassān ʿUbayd, vol. 9, Dār Ibn Kathīr, 2007.

Ibn al-Nadīm. *Al-Fihrist.* Edited by Riḍā al-Mazandarānī, Dār al-Masīra, 1988.

———. *Al-Fihrist.* Edited by R. Tajaddod, Marvi Offset Printing, 1973.

———. *The* Fihrist *of al-Nadīm: A Tenth-Century Survey of Islamic Culture.* Translated by Bayard Dodge, Columbia UP, 1970. 2 vols.

Ibn Rusta, Umar Abū Alī. *Kitāb al-alāq al-nafīsa.* Dār ādir, 1990.

Ibn al-Sāʿī, ʿAlī ibn Anjab. *Consorts of the Caliphs: Women and the Court of Baghdad.* Edited by Shawkat M. Toorawa, New York UP, 2015.

Imam, Abubakar. *Magana jari ce.* Northern Nigeria Publishing Company, 1937.

Irigaray, Luce. *Speculum of the Other Woman.* Translated by Gillian C. Gill, Cornell UP, 1985.

Irwin, Robert. Afterword. Seale, *Annotated* Arabian Nights, pp. 701–09.

———. *The* Arabian Nights*: A Companion.* Allen Lane, 1994.

———. "The *Arabian Nights* and the Origins of the Western Novel." Kennedy and Warner, pp. 143–53.

———. "The *Arabian Nights* in Film Adaptation." Marzolph and van Leeuwen, pp. 21–25.

———. *Ibn Khaldun: An Intellectual Biography.* Princeton UP, 2018.

———. Preface. *The* Arabian Nights*: A Companion*, by Irwin, 2nd ed., I. B. Tauris, 2003.

———. "A Thousand and One Nights at the Movies." *Middle Eastern Literatures*, vol. 7, July 2004, pp. 223–33.

———. *Visions of the Jinn: Illustrators of the* Arabian Nights. Arcadian Library / Oxford UP, 2010.

Jeon JinSeok. *One Thousand and One Nights.* Illustrated by Han SeungHee, translated by HyeYoung Im and J. Torres, Yen Press, 2008. 10 vols.

Jullien, Dominique. *Les amoureux de Schéhérazade: Variations modernes sur les* Mille et une nuits. Droz, 2009.

———. *Borges, Buddhism and World Literature: A Morphology of Renunciation Tales.* Palgrave Macmillan, 2019.

———. "Healing by Exempla: Political Therapy in the *Nights*' Hypertext." Granara and Akel, pp. 280–95.

Kahf, Mohja. *Emails from Scheherazad.* UP of Florida, 2003.

Kennedy, Hugh. *The Early Abbasid Caliphate: A Political History*. Croom Helm, 1981.

Kennedy, Philip F. "Borges and the Missing Pages of the *Nights*." Kennedy and Warner, pp. 195–217.

Kennedy, Philip F., and Marina Warner, editors. *Scheherazade's Children: Global Encounters with the* Arabian Nights. New York UP, 2013.

Kia, Mana. *Persianate Selves*. Stanford UP, 2020.

Kilito, Abdelfattah ['Abd al-Fattāḥ Kīlīṭū]. *Al-Adab wal-irtiyāb*. Dār Tūqbāl, 2007.

———. *Les Arabes et l'art du récit*. Actes Sud, 2009.

———. *Arabs and the Art of Storytelling*. Translated by Mbarek Sryfi and Eric Sellin. Syracuse UP, 2014.

———. *Dites-moi le songe*. Actes Sud, 2010.

Kobayashi, Kazue. "The Evolution of the *Arabian Nights* Illustrations: An Art-Historical Review." Yamanaka and Nishio, pp. 171–93.

Kruk, Remke. "'In the Popular Manner': Sira-Recitation in Marrakesh Anno 1997." *Edebiyât: Journal of Near Eastern Literatures*, new series, vol. 10, no. 2, 1999, pp. 183–97.

Kueny, Kathryn. *Conceiving Identities: Maternity in Medieval Muslim Discourse*. State U of New York P, 2013.

Lane, Edward William. *An Account of the Manners and Customs of the Modern Egyptians*. 1836. East-West Publications, 1978.

———. *An Arabic-English Lexicon*. London, 1863.

———. *The* Thousand and One Nights, *Commonly Called, in England, the* Arabian Nights' Entertainments. Illustrated by William Harvey, London, 1840. 3 vols.

Larzul, Sylvette. "Further Considerations on Galland's *Mille et une nuits*: A Study of the Tales Told by Hanna." *The Arabian Nights, Past and Present*, special issue of *Marvels and Tales*, edited by Ulrich Marzolph, vol. 18, no. 2, Jan. 2004, pp. 258–71.

Leeuwen, Richard van. "Space as Metaphor in *Alf laylah wa-laylah*: The Archetypal City." Neuwirth et al., pp. 493–505.

Lewis, A. David, and Martin Lund, editors. *Muslim Superheroes: Comics, Islam, and Representation*. Harvard UP, 2017.

Link, Kelly. "Lull." *Magic for Beginners*, by Link, Harcourt Books, 2005, pp. 259–97.

Lord, Albert B. *The Singer of Tales*. Harvard UP, 1960.

The Lord of the Rings: The Return of the King. Directed by Peter Jackson, New Line Cinema, 2003.

Lovejoy, Paul E. *Transformations in Slavery: A History of Slavery in Africa*. Cambridge UP, 2012.

Lyons, Malcolm C., translator. *The* Arabian Nights: *Tales of the* Thousand and One Nights. With Ursula Lyons, introduction by Robert Irwin, Penguin Books, 2008. 3 vols.

———. *Tales of the Marvellous and News of the Strange*. Penguin, 2014.

MacDonald, Duncan Black. "A Bibliographical and Literary Study of the First Appearance of the *Arabian Nights* in Europe." *Library Quarterly*, vol. 2, 1932, pp. 387–420.

Mack, Robert L., editor. *Arabian Nights' Entertainments*. Oxford UP, 1995.
Mackley, J. S. *The Legend of St Brendan: A Comparative Study of the Latin and Anglo-Norman Versions*. Brill, 2008.
Mahdi, Muhsin. "From History to Fiction: The Tale Told by the King's Steward." Mahdi, *Thousand*, vol. 3, pp. 164–80.
———. "Religion and Politics in the *Nights*." Mahdi, *Thousand*, vol. 3, pp. 127–39.
———. *The Thousand and One Nights*. Brill, 1995.
———, editor. *The Thousand and One Nights (Alf layla wa-layla)*. Brill, 2013. 2 vols.
———, editor. *The* Thousand and One Nights (Alf layla wa-layla)*: From the Earliest Known Sources* [*Kitāb* Alf layla wa-layla*: Min uṣūlihi al-'Arabiyyah al-ūlā*]. Brill, 1984–94. 3 vols.
Mahfouz, Naguib [Najib Mahfuz]. *Arabian Nights and Days*. 1979. Translated by Denys Johnson-Davies, Anchor, 1995.
———. *The Harafish*. 1977. Translated by Catherine Cobham, Anchor, 1997.
———. *Midaq Alley*. 1947. Translated by Trevor Le Gassick, Anchor, 1992.
———. *The Shaitan Speaks*. Unpublished collective translation. New York University, Abu Dhabi, 2014.
Makdisi, Saree, and Felicity Nussbaum, editors. *The* Arabian Nights *in Historical Context: Between East and West*. Oxford UP, 2008.
Mallarmé, Stéphane, translator. *Les Poèmes d'Edgar Poe*. Librairie Gallimard / Éditions de la Nouvelle Revue Française, 1928.
Maltaite, Eric. *The Thousand and One Nights of Scheherazade*. Translated by Joe Johnson, Eurotica, 2001.
Malti-Douglas, Fedwa. *Woman's Body, Woman's Word: Gender and Discourse in Arabo-Islamic Writing*. Princeton UP, 1991.
Mardrus, J. C., translator. *The Book of the* Thousand Nights and One Night. Edited by Mardrus and E. P. Mathers, Routledge, 1986. 4 vols.
Marmon, Shaun Elizabeth. *Eunuchs and Sacred Boundaries in Islamic Society*. Oxford UP, 1995.
Marzolph, Ulrich. "Aladdin Almighty: Middle Eastern Magic in the Service of Western Consumer Culture." *Journal of American Folklore*, vol. 132, no. 525, 2019, pp. 275–90.
———. "Das Aladdin-Syndrom: Zur Phänomenologie des narrativen Orientalismus." *Hören, Sagen, Lesen, Lernen: Bausteine zu einer Geschichte der kommunikativen Kultur. Festschrift Rudolf Schenda*, edited by Ursula Brunold-Bigler and Hermann Bausinger, Lang, 1995, pp. 449–62.
———, editor. *The* Arabian Nights *Bibliography. Ulrich Marzolph: Exploring the Narrative Culture of the Muslim World*, 2023, wwwuser.gwdg.de~umarzol/arabiannights.html.
———. "The *Arabian Nights* in Comparative Folk Narrative Research." Yamanaka and Nishio, pp. 3–24.
———, editor. *The* Arabian Nights *in Transnational Perspective*. Wayne State UP, 2007.
———, editor. *The* Arabian Nights *Reader*. Wayne State UP, 2006.

———. "An Early Persian Precursor to the Tales of Sindbād the Seafaring Merchant." *Zeitschrift der Deutschen Morgenländischen Gesellschaft*, vol. 167, no. 1, 2017, pp. 127–41.

———. "The Man Who Made the *Nights* Immortal: The Tales of the Syrian Maronite Storyteller Ḥannā Diyāb." *Marvels and Tales*, vol. 32, no. 1, 2018, pp. 114–29.

———. *Relief after Hardship: The Ottoman Turkish Model for the* Thousand and One Days. Wayne State UP, 2017.

———. "A Scholar in the Making: Antoine Galland's Early Travel Diaries in the Light of Comparative Folk Narrative Research." *Middle Eastern Literatures*, vol. 18, no. 3, 2015, pp. 283–300.

Marzolph, Ulrich, and Richard van Leeuwen, editors. *The* Arabian Nights *Encyclopedia*. ABC-CLIO, 2004. 2 vols.

Masereel, Frans. *Passionate Journey: A Vision in Woodcuts*. Dover, 2007.

Masʿūdī, al-. *Murūj al-dhahab*. Edited by Charles Pellat, PU Libanaise, 1966.

Mazouz, Tahar. *La mille et deuxième nuit: Conte*. Édilivre Aparis, 2010.

McBrayer, Mary Kay. "Should We Be Okay with the New *Aladdin*?" *Book Riot*, 8 July 2019, bookriot.com/should-we-be-okay-with-the-new-aladdin.

McCloud, Scott. *Understanding Comics: The Invisible Art*. Tundra, 1993.

Menges, Jeff. Arabian Nights *Illustrated: Art of Dulac, Folkard, Parris and Others*. Dover, 2011.

Mernissi, Fatima. *Dreams of Trespass: Tales of a Harem Girlhood*. Basic Books, 2008.

Mills, Margaret A. "*Alf Laylah Fārsi* in Performance: Afghanistan 1975." *Fabula*, vol. 45, nos. 3–4, 2004, pp. 294–310.

Miquel, André. "The *Thousand and One Nights* in Arabic Literature and Society." Hovannisian and Sabagh, pp. 6–13.

Molan, Peter D. "*The* Arabian Nights: The Oral Connection." *Edebiyât: Journal of Near Eastern Literatures*, new series, vol. 2, 1988, pp. 191–204.

Montgomery, James E. "Al-Sindībad and Polyphemus: Reflections on the Genesis of an Archetype." Neuwirth et al., pp. 437–66.

———. "Ibn Rusta's Lack of 'Eloquence,' the Rus, and Samanid Cosmography." *Edebiyât: Journal of Near Eastern Literatures*, vol. 12, no. 1, 2001, pp. 73–93.

Moon, W. Jay. *African Proverbs Reveal Christianity in Culture: A Narrative Portrayal of Builsa Proverbs Contextualizing Christianity in Ghana*. Pickwick Publications, 2009.

Moretti, Franco, editor. *The Novel*. Princeton UP, 2007. 2 vols.

Morrison, Toni. *Playing in the Dark: Whiteness and the Literary Imagination*. Vintage Books, 1992.

Mottahedeh, Roy. "'Ajāʾib in the *Thousand and One Nights*." Hovannisian and Sabagh, pp. 29–39.

Der müde Tod. Directed by Fritz Lang, Decla-Bioscop AG, 1921.

Muehlhaeusler, Mark, editor. *The Story of Anas al-Wujūd: Nineteenth-Century Verse Recensions of an* Arabian Nights *Tale in Egyptian Colloquial Arabic*. Faenum Publishing, 2016, www.faenumpublishing.com/anas.html.

Muhawi, Ibrahim, and Sharif Kanaana. *Speak, Bird, Speak Again: Palestinian Arab Folktales.* U of California P, 1989.

Musallam, Basim. *Sex and Society in Islam: Birth Control before the Nineteenth Century.* Cambridge UP, 1983.

Musawi, Muhsin J. al-. *The Arabian Nights in Contemporary World Cultures.* Cambridge UP, 2021.

———. *The Islamic Context of the* Thousand and One Nights. Columbia UP, 2009.

——— [published as Muhsin Jassim Ali]. *Scheherazade in England: A Study of Nineteenth-Century English Criticism of the* Arabian Nights. Three Continents Press, 1981.

———. "Teaching the *Arabian Nights.*" *Arabic Literature for the Classroom: Teaching Methods, Theories, Themes and Texts,* edited by al-Musawi, Routledge, 2016, pp. 287–311.

Myrne, Pernialla. "A Jariya's Prospects in Abbasid Baghdad." *Concubines and Courtesans: Women and Slavery in Islamic History,* edited by Matthew S. Gordon and Kathryn A. Hain, Oxford UP, 2017, pp. 52–74.

Nadaff, Sandra. *Arabesque: Narrative Structure and the Aesthetics of Repetition in the* Thousand and One Nights. Northwestern UP, 1991.

Najmabadi, Afsaneh. "Reading 'Wiles of Women' Stories as Fictions of Masculinity." *Imagined Masculinities: Male Identity and Culture in the Modern Middle East,* edited by Mai Ghoussoub and Emma Sinclair-Webb, Saqi Books, 2000.

Nast, Heidi J. *Concubines and Power: Five Hundred Years in a Northern Nigerian Palace.* U of Minnesota P, 2005.

Neuwirth, Angelika, et al., editors. *Myths, Historical Archetypes and Symbolic Figures in Arabic Literature.* Deutsche Morgenländische Gesellschaft, 1999.

Nissaboury, Mostafa. *La mille et deuxième nuit: Poème.* Schoof, 1975.

———. "Prise de position liminaire." *La mémoire future: Anthologie de la nouvelle poésie du Maroc,* edited by Tahar Ben Jelloun, François Maspéro, 1976, pp. 159–60.

Nueil, Alain. *La mille et deuxième nuit.* Mercure de France, 1997.

Oehlenschläger, Adam. *Aladdin; or, The Wonderful Lamp: A Dramatic Poem in Two Parts.* Translated by Theodore Martin, London, 1857.

Ohtaka, Shinobu. *Magi: Labyrinth of Magic.* Shogakukan, 2009–17. 37 vols.

Orfali, Bilal W., and Maurice A. Pomerantz. *The Maqāmāt of al-Hamadhānī: Authorship, Texts, and Contexts.* Reichert Verlag, 2022.

Ouyang, Wen-chin, editor. *The Arabian Nights.* Tales selected by Ouyang and Paulo Lemos Horta, Everyman's Library Classics, 2014.

———. "Metamorphoses of Scheherazade in Literature and Film." *Bulletin of the School of Oriental and African Studies,* vol. 66, no. 3, 2003, pp. 402–18.

———. "Whose Story Is It? Sindbad the Sailor in Literature and Film." *Middle Eastern Literatures,* vol. 7, no. 2, 2004, pp. 133–47.

Ouyang, Wen-chin, and Geert Jan van Gelder. *New Perspectives on* Arabian Nights: *Ideological Variations and Narrative Horizons.* Routledge, 2005.

Oyeyemi, Helen. *What Is Yours Is Not Yours: Stories.* Riverhead Books, 2016.

Le palais des Mille et une nuits. Directed by Georges Méliès, Star-Film, 1905.
Pannewick, Friedericke. "Performativity and Mobility: Middle Eastern Traditions on the Move." *Cultural Mobility: A Manifesto*, edited by Stephen Greenblatt, Cambridge UP, 2010, pp. 215–49.
Payne, John, translator. *The Portable Arabian Nights*. Edited by Joseph Campbell, Viking Press, 1952.
Peeters, Benoît. *Case, planche, récit: Lire la bande dessinée*. Casterman, 1998.
Pinault, David. *Story-telling Techniques in the* Arabian Nights. Brill, 1992.
Piñon, Nélida. *Voices of the Desert*. Translated by Clifford E. Landers, Alfred A. Knopf, 2009.
Piper, Adrian. "Passing for White, Passing for Black." *Transition*, no. 58, 1992, pp. 4–32.
Poe, Edgar Allan. "The Thousand-and-Second Tale of Scheherazade." *Complete Tales and Poems*, by Poe, Castle Books, 2003, pp. 107–16.
Pohádky Tisíce a jedné noci. Directed by Karel Zeman, Filmové Studio Gottwaldov, 1974.
Polaschegg, Andrea. *Der andere Orientalismus: Regeln deutsch-morgenländischer Imagination im 19. Jahrhundert*. Walter de Gruyter, 2005.
Pomerantz, Maurice A. "Tales from the Crypt: On Some Uncharted Voyages of Sindbad the Sailor." *Narrative Culture*, vol. 2, no. 2, 2015, pp. 250–69.
Prabhala, Anupama [*published as* Anupama Kapse]. "Around the World in Eighty Minutes: Douglas Fairbanks and the Indian Stunt Film." *Silent Cinema and the Politics of Space*, edited by Jennifer Bean et al., Indiana UP, 2014, pp. 210–34.
Proverbio, Delio Vania. "The *Arabian Nights* through Some Ancient-Osmanlı Translations." Chraïbi, *Arabic Manuscripts*, pp. 367–429.
Pullman, Philip. *Aladdin and the Enchanted Lamp*. Scholastic, 2013.
Qalamāwī, Suhayr al-. *Alf layla wa-layla*. Dār al-Maʿārif, 1976.
Rabkin, Eric S. "Reading Time in Graphic Narrative." Tabachnik, *Teaching*, pp. 36–43.
Rāhib, Hāni al-. *Alf lāʾila wa lailatān*. Al-muʾassasa al-ʿarabiyya al-ʿāmma li-l-taʾlîf wa-l-nashr, 1977.
Raiders of the Lost Ark. Directed by Steven Spielberg, Lucasfilm, 1981.
Rastegar, Kamran. *Literary Modernity between the Middle East and Europe: Textual Transactions in Nineteenth-Century Arabic, English, and Persian Literatures*. Routledge, 2010.
Reel Bad Arabs: How Hollywood Vilifies a People. Directed by Sut Jhally, Media Education Foundation, 2006.
Reynolds, Dwight. "Popular Prose in the Post-Classical Period." Allen and Richards, pp. 245–69.
———. "*A Thousand and One Nights*: A History of the Text and Its Reception." Allen and Richards, pp. 270–91.
Ringrose, Kathryn M. *The Perfect Servant: Eunuchs and the Social Construction of Gender in Byzantium*. U of Chicago P, 2003.
Rosen, Elizabeth. "The Narrative Intersection of Image and Text: Teaching Panel Frames in Comics." Tabachnik, *Teaching*, pp. 58–66.

Ruiz, Juan. *The Book of Good Love*. Orion Publishing, 1999.
Rushdie, Salman. *Haroun and the Sea of Stories*. Granta, 1990.
———. *Two Years Eight Months and Twenty-Eight Nights*. Random House, 2015.
Sadan, Joseph. "Hārūn al-Rashīd and the Brewer: Preliminary Remarks on the *Adab* of the Elite versus the *Ḥikāyāt*." *Studies in Canonical and Popular Arabic Literature*, edited by Shimon Ballas and Reuven Snir, York Press, 1998, pp. 1–22.
Said, Edward. *Orientalism*. Pantheon Books, 1978.
Saleh, Tayeb [Ṣāliḥ, al-Ṭayyib]. *Season of Migration to the North*. Translated by Denys Johnson-Davies, Heinemann, 1966.
Samatar, Sofia. "Spectacle of the Other: Recreating *A Thousand and One Nights* in Film." *Fairy-Tale Films beyond Disney: International Perspectives*, edited by Jack Zipes et al., Routledge, 2015, pp. 34–47.
Savage, Elizabeth. "Berbers and Blacks: Ibadi Slave Traffic in Eighth-Century North Africa." *Journal of African History*, vol. 33, no. 3, 1992, pp. 351–68.
Schwab, Raymond. *The Oriental Renaissance: Europe's Rediscovery of India and the East, 1680–1880*. Translated by Gene Patterson-King and Victor Reinking, Columbia UP, 1984.
Seale, Yasmine, translator. Aladdin: *A New Translation*. Edited by Paulo Lemos Horta, Liveright, 2018.
———, translator. *The Annotated* Arabian Nights. Edited by Paulo Lemos Horta, W. W. Norton, 2021.
"The Seemingly Never-Ending Story." *The Simpsons*, season 17, episode 13, Fox, 12 Mar. 2006.
Senya ichiya monogatari. Directed by Eiichi Yamamoto, Mushi Productions, 1969.
"Sevdaliza—Shahmaran." *YouTube*, uploaded by Sevdaliza, 31 July 2018, www.youtube.com/watch?v=2uMsLPlPfJo.
The Seventh Voyage of Sinbad. Animation by Ray Harryhausen, Columbia Pictures, 1958.
Sexton, Anne. *Transformations: Poems*. Mariner Books, 2001.
Shab-e-Ghuzi. Directed and produced by Farrokh Ghaffari, Iran Nama, 1965.
Shaheen, Jack. "Dr Jack Shaheen: 'More Leadership Needed on Park 51 Conversation.'" Interview by Christian Avard, *HuffPost*, 29 Aug. 2010, updated 6 Dec. 2017, huffpost.com/entry/dr-jack-shaheen-more-lead_b_698469. The Blog.
Shamma, Tarek. *Translation and the Manipulation of Difference: Arabic Literature in Nineteenth-Century England*. St. Jerome Publishing, 2009.
Shamy, Hasan M. el-. *Folktales of Egypt*. U of Chicago P, 1980.
———. "A Motif Index of *Alf laylah wa laylah*: Its Relevance to the Study of Culture, Society, the Individual, and Character Transmutation." *Journal of Arabic Literature*, vol. 36, 2005, pp. 235–68.
———. *A Motif Index of the* Thousand and One Nights. Indiana UP, 2006.
———. "The Oral Connections of *Alf laylah wa laylah*." Marzolph and van Leeuwen, vol. 1, pp. 9–12.
Shaykh, Hanan al-. One Thousand and One Nights: *A Retelling*. Anchor, 2014.

Silvestre de Sacy, [Antoine-Isaac]. "Mémoire sur l'origine du recueil de contes intitulé les *Mille et une nuits*." *Mémoires de l'Institut Royal de France, Académie des Inscriptions et Belles-lettres*, vol. 10, 1833, pp. 30–64.

"The Simpsons Already Did It." *South Park*, season 6, episode 7, Comedy Central, 26 June 2002.

Sinbad: Legend of the Seven Seas. DreamWorks, 2003.

Sīrāfī, Abū Zayd al-. *Accounts of China and India*. Translated by Tim Mackintosh-Smith. New York UP, 2017.

Sīrat al-Amīrah Dhāt al-himmah wa-waladi-hā ʿAbd al-Wahhāb. Vol. 1, Al-Maktabah al-thaqāfiyyah, 1980.

Slyomovics, Susan. "Arabic Folk Literature and Political Expression." *Arab Studies Quarterly*, vol. 8, no. 2, 1986, pp. 178–85.

———. *The Merchant of Art: An Egyptian Hilali Oral Epic Poet in Performance*. U of California P, 1987.

———. "Performing *A Thousand and One Nights* in Egypt." *Oral Tradition*, vol. 9, no. 2, 1994, pp. 390–419.

Spillers, Hortense. "Mama's Baby, Papa's Maybe: An American Grammar Book." *Diacritics*, vol. 17, no. 2, 1987, pp. 65–81.

Star Wars. Directed by George Lucas, Lucasfilm, 1977.

Stead, Evanghelia. *Contes de la mille et deuxième nuit: Théophile Gautier, Edgar Allan Poe, Nicolae Davidescu, Richard Lesclide et André Gill*. Jérôme Millon, 2011.

Stringer, Julian. "Global Cities and the International Film Festival Economy." *Cinema and the City: Film and Urban Societies in a Global Context*, edited by Mark Shiel and Tony Fitzmaurice, Blackwell, 2001, pp. 134–44.

Strnad, Jan. *The Last Voyage of Sindbad*. Illustrated by Richard Corben, 2nd ed., Catalan Communications, 1988. Originally published as "New Tales of the *Arabian Nights*" in *Heavy Metal*, vols. 15–28, 1978–79.

Sumurun. Directed by Ernst Lubitsch, 1920.

Supple, Timothy. Personal communication with Paulo Horta. June 2022.

Tabachnik, Stephen E. "A Comic Book World." *World Literature Today*, vol. 81, no. 2, 2007, pp. 24–28.

———. Introduction. Tabachnik, *Teaching*, pp. 1–15.

———, editor. *Teaching the Graphic Novel*. Modern Language Association of America, 2009.

Ṭabarī, Abū Jaʿfar Jarīr ibn Muḥammad al-. *The ʿAbbasid Caliphate in Equilibrium*. Translated by C. E. Bosworth, State U of New York P, 1989. Vol. 30 of *The History of al-Ṭabarī*.

Taee, Nasser al-. "Under the Spell of Magic: The Oriental Tale in Rimsky-Korsakov's *Scheherazade*." Makdisi and Nussbaum, pp. 265–95.

Tāj, ʿAbd Allāh. *Maṣādir "Alf layla wa-layla" al-ʿarabiyya*. Dār al-Mīzān, 2006.

Tanūkhī, Abū ʿAlī al-Muḥassin ibn ʿAlī al-. *Al-Faraj baʿd al-shidda*. Edited by ʿAbbūd al-Shāljī. Dār Ṣādir, 1978. 4 vols.

Taylor, Laurie N. "Snow White in the City: Teaching Fables, Nursery Rhymes, and Revisions in Graphic Novels." Tabachnik, *Teaching*, pp. 172–78.

Thaʿlabī, Aḥmad ibn Muḥammad. *ʿArāʾis al-majālis fī qiṣaṣ al-anbitāʾ; or, Lives of the Prophets*. Translated by William B. Brinner, Brill, 2002.

———. *Qiṣaṣ al-anbiyāʾ*. Dār al-Fikr, 1989.

The Thief of Bagdad. Produced by Alexander Korda, London Films, 1940.

The Thief of Bagdad. Directed by Raoul Walsh, Douglas Fairbanks Pictures, 1924.

Thomann, Johannes. "Die frühesten türkischen Übersetzungen von *Tausendundeiner Nacht* und deren Bedeutung für die arabische Textgeschichte." *Asiatische Studien*, vol. 70, no. 1, 2016, pp. 171–219.

Thomas, Cathy. Syllabus for Introduction to a Literary Topic: Graphic Novels and Comics. Summer 2014, U of California, Santa Cruz, summer.ucsc.edu/courses/course-syllabi/2014/lit-61f-syllabus-summer-2014.pdf.

Thomas, Rosie. *Bombay before Bollywood: Film City Fantasies*. State U of New York P, 2013.

Thompson, Craig. *Habibi*. Pantheon Books, 2011.

Thompson, Stith. *Motif-Index of Folk-Literature: A Classification of Narrative Elements in Folktales, Ballads, Myths, Fables, Mediaeval Romances, Exempla, Fabliaux, Jest-Books, and Local Legends*. Rosenkilde and Bagger, 1955–58. 6 vols.

Todorov, Tzvetan. *The Poetics of Prose*. Translated by Richard Howard, Blackwell, 2006.

Toorawa, Shawkat M. Syllabus for *Arabian Nights*, Then and Now. Spring 2017, Yale U, New Haven.

Toppi, Sergio. *Sharaz-De: Tales from the* Arabian Nights. Translated by Edward Gauvin, lettered by Deron Bennett, Archaia, 2013.

Torrens, Henry Whitelock, translator. *The Book of the Thousand Nights and One Night*. Calcutta, London, 1838.

Tougher, Shaun. *The Eunuch in Byzantine History and Society*. Routledge, 2008.

Tuczay, Christa A. "Motifs in 'The Arabian Nights' and in Ancient and Medieval European Literature: A Comparison." *Folklore*, vol. 116, no. 3, 2005, pp. 272–91.

Unno, Hiroshi. A Thousand and One Nights: *The Art of Folklore, Poetry, Fashion and Book Design of the Islamic World*. PIE Books, 2017.

Vaziri, Parisa. "On 'Saidiya': Indian Ocean World Slavery and Blackness beyond Horizon." *Qui Parle*, vol. 28, no. 2, 2019, pp. 241–80.

Venuti, Lawrence. *The Translator's Invisibility: A History of Translation*. 2nd ed., Routledge, 2008.

Das Wachsfigurenkabinett. Directed by Paul Leni, Neptune-Film A.G., 1921.

Warner, Marina. *Stranger Magic: Charmed States and the* Arabian Nights. Chatto and Windus, 2011.

Wehr, Hans, editor. *Al-Ḥikāyāt al-ʿajībah wal-akhbār al-gharībah*. Franz Steiner, 1956.

White, Hayden. *The Content of the Form: Narrative Discourse and Historical Representation*. Johns Hopkins UP, 1990.

Whitelock, Jill. *The* Seven Sages of Rome *(Midland Version)*. Oxford UP, 2005.

Willingham, Bill. *Fables: Arabian Nights (and Days)*. Illustrated by Mark Buckingham et al., DC Comics, 2006. Nos. 42–47 of *Fables*.

———. *Fables: A Thousand and One Nights of Snowfall*. Illustrated by Esao Andrews et al., DC Comics, 2006.

Wilson, G. Willow. *Alif the Unseen*. Grove Press, 2012.

Wright, John. *The Trans-Saharan Slave Trade*. Routledge, 2007.

Yamanaka, Yuriko, and Tetsuo Nishio, editors. *The* Arabian Nights *and Orientalism: Perspectives from East and West*. I. B. Tauris, 2005.

Ziolkowski, Jan M. *Fairy Tales from before Fairy Tales: The Medieval Latin Past of Wonderful Lies*. U of Michigan P, 2009.

Zipes, Jack. *The Irresistible Fairy Tale: The Cultural and Social History of a Genre*. Princeton UP, 2012.

———, editor. *The Oxford Companion to Fairy Tales*. 2nd ed., Oxford UP, 2015.